ORIGINAL HIGHWAYS

ROY MacGREGOR

ORIGINAL HIGHWAYS

TRAVELLING THE GREAT RIVERS OF CANADA

RANDOM HOUSE CANADA

For Bruce Westwood, who made me do it.

PUBLISHED BY RANDOM HOUSE CANADA

www.penguinrandomhouse.ca

Random House Canada and colophon are registered trademarks.

Photograph credits
Courtesy of Fred Lum/*The Globe and Mail*: page 54; CP Photo/Keith Levit:
page 88; 4nadia/Getty: page 228; Peter Bowers/Getty: page 276.
Unless otherwise indicated all photos are the property of the author.

Library and Archives Canada Cataloguing in Publication

MacGregor, Roy, 1948–, author
Original highways : travelling the great rivers of Canada / Roy MacGregor.

Issued in print and electronic formats.
ISBN 978-0-307-36138-7
eBook ISBN 978-0-307-36140-0

1. Rivers—Canada. 2. Rivers—Canada—History. 3. Canada—History—
Anecdotes. 4. Canada—History, Local. 5. Canada—Description and travel.
6. MacGregor, Roy, 1948– —Travel—Canada. I. Title.

GB1229.M33 2017   333.91'620971   C2017-902008-0

Book design by Andrew Roberts
Map created by Anthony de Ridder, based upon designs by Pomogayev and
zak00 from iStock / Getty Images
Cover photo: (Chilcotin River, British Columbia) © Chris Harris / Getty Images

Printed and bound in the United States of America

10 9 8 7 6 5 4 3 2 1

Penguin
Random House
RANDOM HOUSE CANADA

He thought his happiness was complete when, as he meandered aimlessly along, suddenly he stood by the edge of a full-fed river. Never in his life had he seen a river before—this sleek, sinuous, full-bodied animal, chasing and chuckling, gripping things with a gurgle and leaving them with a laugh, to fling itself on fresh playmates that shook themselves free, and were caught and held again. All as a-shake and a-shiver—glints and gleams and sparkles, rustle and swirl, chatter and bubble. The Mole was bewitched, entranced, fascinated. By the side of the river he trotted as one trots, when very small, by the side of a man who holds one spellbound by exciting stories; and when tired at last, he sat on the bank, while the river still chatted on to him, a babbling procession of the best stories in the world, sent from the heart of the earth to be told at last to the insatiable sea.

—Kenneth Grahame, *The Wind in the Willows*

THE GREAT RIVERS OF CANADA

Yukon

Nunavut

British
Columbia

Northwest
Territories

Mackenzie River

Fraser River

Alberta

North Saskatchewan River

Saskatchewan

Manitoba

Columbia River

Bow River

Red River

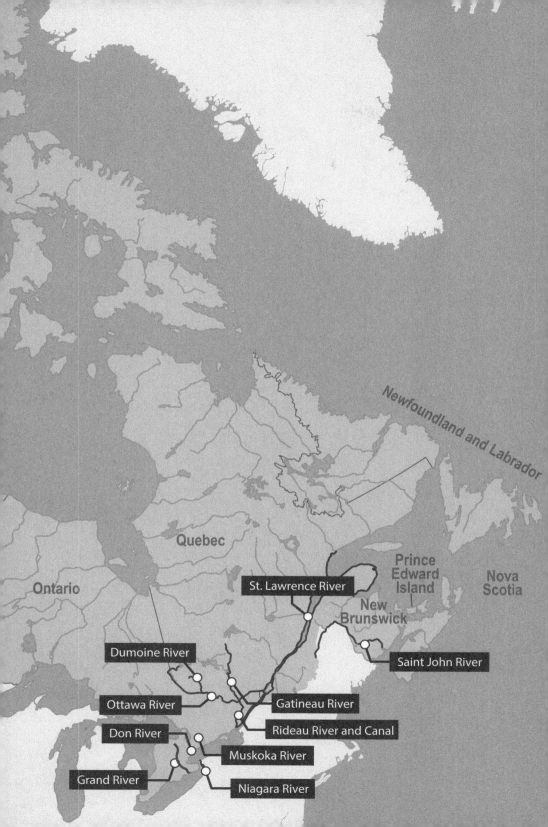

Newfoundland and Labrador

Quebec

Prince
Edward
Island

Nova
Scotia

Ontario

New
Brunswick

St. Lawrence River

Saint John River

Dumoine River

Ottawa River

Gatineau River

Don River

Rideau River and Canal

Grand River

Muskoka River

Niagara River

CONTENTS

INTRODUCTION | 1

CHAPTER ONE
CANADA'S ORIGINAL HIGHWAY: THE ST. LAWRENCE | 13

CHAPTER TWO
PRICELESS AND PRECARIOUS: THE OTTAWA | 31

CHAPTER THREE
RISING FROM THE DEAD: THE DON | 55

CHAPTER FOUR
"SYMBOL OF LIFE": THE MIGHTY FRASER | 69

CHAPTER FIVE
"WE ARE RED RIVER PEOPLE" | 89

CHAPTER SIX
WATER WONDER OF THE WORLD: THE NIAGARA | 107

CHAPTER SEVEN
"THE RHINE OF NORTH AMERICA": THE SAINT JOHN | 125

CHAPTER EIGHT
THE MACKENZIE: RIVER OF DISAPPOINTMENT OR HOPE | 139

CHAPTER NINE

RETURN TO SPLENDOUR: THE GRAND | 159

CHAPTER TEN

STRESSES ALONG THE BOW | 179

CHAPTER ELEVEN

TAX REVOLTS AND INDEPENDENCE: THE GATINEAU | 197

CHAPTER TWELVE

COLONEL BY'S AMAZING FEAT: THE RIDEAU RIVER AND CANAL | 215

CHAPTER THIRTEEN

RIVER OF POLITICS: THE COLUMBIA | 229

CHAPTER FOURTEEN

"WATER IS LIFE": THE NORTH SASKATCHEWAN | 243

CHAPTER FIFTEEN

COTTAGE COUNTRY BEAUTY AND BATTLES: THE MUSKOKA | 259

CHAPTER SIXTEEN

WHITEWATER ESCAPE ON THE DUMOINE | 277

EPILOGUE | 301

ACKNOWLEDGEMENTS | 311

ENDNOTES | 313

INDEX | 327

INTRODUCTION

A DOZEN DAYS BEFORE THE October 19, 2015, federal election, I flew from Ottawa to Vancouver for a one-on-one sit-down with then prime minister Stephen Harper. My newspaper, the *Globe and Mail*, had been approached by his staff regarding a possible interview and had been led to believe it would be substantive. When I arrived at the interview location—a rented hall in nearby Richmond—it quickly became clear that the *Globe* was merely one in a string of one-on-one meetings, various reporters from the national broadcasters and news agencies all sent to wait their turn in a suffocating room with lukewarm coffee. I was told by the prime minister's curt handlers that I would have ten minutes with him, not a moment longer.

The staff's mood was undoubtedly tied to a growing sense that the election was lost, that the Liberals under Justin Trudeau would be taking power come the first Monday following the vote. If this realization made them tense and dismissive, it made the prime minister himself relaxed and reflective. Perhaps this was partly because he and I knew each other in a different setting, a publisher having asked me two years earlier to help the prime minister refine a historical book about hockey that he had been writing for years in his spare time.

Whatever the reason, he didn't seem much interested in policy or taking shots at his opponents. He seemed relieved, actually, to be on the verge of escaping what he called "the fishbowl of politics." He talked with pride about his children, Ben and Rachel. He said he regretted that he had not worked a little harder at personal relationships and said it was "a personality trait" that was difficult for him to change. Ten minutes quickly passed and he ignored the various hand signals to cut the conversation off and move the *Globe* out of the way so a CBC crew could come in for their allotted ten minutes.

Instead, he changed the subject from what he was thinking to what I was doing. I told him that the paper had me writing a long series on Canadian rivers, and he instantly became far more engaged. He and Laureen had recently purchased property along Bragg Creek, a tributary of the Elbow and Bow rivers near Calgary, where they planned to build a home for their post-Ottawa years.

"I'm very interested in history," the prime minister said, "and it's often occurred to me that for so much of our history, rivers were the centres of everything—life, transportation, trading patterns, you name it. And it's not that they're unimportant now. It's just that they are so less central than they used to be. In fact, we often think now that a river is a pain in the ass to cross, right?

"Well, before, the river was the lifeblood of the entire region. Without a river, there's nothing."

In my previous book, *Canoe Country: The Making of Canada*, I had put forward an argument that, in essence, claimed, "No canoe, no Canada." From Indigenous survival to European exploration to a trading economy and early settlement, a case could certainly be made that the gift of First Nations had led to the nation itself. Had there been no rivers, however, what purpose would that canoe have served?

The rivers of Canada were the original highways, a complicated, thorough arterial and capillary system stretching across the country from east to west and south to north. Had there been no such east-to-west linkage—the St. Lawrence to the Ottawa, the Mattawa across to the French and the Great Lakes, the Rainy and Winnipeg rivers to the Prairies and the great prairie rivers to the mountains, rivers beyond the Great Divide then flowing on to the Pacific Ocean—there would have been no fur trade, no settlement. It may have been the promise of a railroad to the Pacific that made Canada whole, but it was the rivers that carried the people west and made that railroad necessary.

There is hardly a major settlement in Canada that cannot trace its origins to the confluence of different rivers or a particular bend in a large river. Most towns were founded on rivers, as the force of water was required for grist and saw mills, later for electricity. Today's rivers are too often taken for granted, even ignored as they travel by and through major centres. Rivers removed from such centres, on the other hand, are often revered for their beauty, their challenge, the incredible peace that busy humans seek and so often find on flowing water. Rivers previously used for getting somewhere are today so often used for getting away. Once original highways, they have become escape routes.

Rivers have been a constant in my life. I was born a million years ago in a Red Cross outpost alongside the Madawaska River, where it flows and tumbles through the small village of Whitney, on the eastern border of Ontario's vast Algonquin Park. When I was all of four days old, our mother took me, my brother Jim and sister Ann (younger brother Tom would follow six years later) to Lake of Two Rivers in the park, where her ranger father had built a log home on a rocky point along the north shore. Lake of Two Rivers is fed—and likely named— by two branches of the Madawaska entering from the west. At the eastern end of the lake, the Madawaska continues its journey toward the Ottawa River, a distance of roughly two hundred kilometres.

Our father worked in a lumber mill a short distance downstream from Lake of Two Rivers, where the Madawaska runs between Whitefish Lake and Rock Lake.

In early October 1837, David Thompson, the Great Mapmaker, then sixty-seven years old, blind in one eye, lame and impoverished, reached the Madawaska River after paddling with a crew from Georgian Bay. He had come up the Muskoka River, across Lake of Bays and up the Oxtongue River to Canoe Lake. He crossed the height of land and travelled down the Madawaska, where he recorded in his journal: "current going with us, thank God." On October 10 he reached Lake of Two Rivers after encountering "an old Indian of the name of Cha undé" who "advised us to be careful in the rapids, adding that when you are below them there is no more danger."

Today, the waters of the Madawaska still pass nearby, though they are mixed in with the other waters—the Petawawa, Mattawa, Dumoine, Noir, Coulonge, to mention only the major river sources of the upper Ottawa River that flows by our home in the Ottawa suburb of Kanata. My family and I fish it, paddle in it, have even dumped our beloved canoe in it near Combermere where the Madawaska tumbles and boils through a twisting, rock-laden slide much loved by white-water canoeists and kayakers. For fourteen years I worked on Parliament Hill, parking each morning at a hidden parking lot below the bluffs back of the parliamentary library, the Ottawa River flowing fast enough to leave the stretch of water free of ice year-round. Each evening, I drove home via the Ottawa River Parkway, rush-hour drivers annoyed by the traffic and completely unaware that they are making splendid time compared to the voyageurs who once needed poles and ropes and long portages to make their slow and difficult way up this glorious river.

"No book could possibly tell the whole story of Canada's rivers," Roderick Haig-Brown once wrote. His many treasured books on fly fishing (*A River Never Sleeps*, *The Master and His Fish*) covered many streams, particularly the Campbell River on Vancouver Island, where he lived for much of his life and served as the area magistrate. He once said, "Perhaps fishing is, for me, only an excuse to be near rivers. If so, I'm glad I thought of it."

I can list a number of rivers I have canoed all or parts of—Ottawa, Petawawa, Dumoine, Rupert, Madawaska, Kootenay, Saint John, Rideau, Muskoka, Grand, Mattawa, Amable du Fond, Columbia—and many, many more that I have travelled along by other methods, from ferries to foot. There is even a small river outside the Nunavut community of Resolute where I once put a snowmobile through the ice. Yet the number of Canadian rivers I have not seen far, far outnumber those I have. As Haig-Brown suggested, it's impossible in such a vast country to be anything but representational.

When Canadian novelist Hugh MacLennan wrote his *Rivers of Canada*, he chose seven: the Saint John, the St. Lawrence, the Ottawa, the Red, the Saskatchewan, the Fraser and the Mackenzie. It was a good representational choice. Those seven are included here and MacLennan's excellent essays on the seven are often referenced. This book adds nine more rivers to the representational list: the Columbia, the Bow, the Niagara, the Grand, the Don, the Muskoka, the Rideau, the Dumoine and the Gatineau. From the most abused, the Don River, to one of the most pristine, the Dumoine. From the farthest south, the Niagara, to the Far North, the Mackenzie. From the tame and pastoral in the East, the Saint John, to the wild and dangerous of the West, the mighty Fraser.

Hugh MacLennan actually wrote about his seven rivers twice, the first time in 1961, when Macmillan published *Seven Rivers of Canada*, and then again in 1974, when Macmillan produced a handsome coffee-table version entitled *Rivers of Canada*, which featured the lavish photography of John de Visser. I was working as a lowly assistant editor at *Maclean's* when the second book appeared. The magazine had originally published MacLennan's rivers as an ongoing series, and prior to the new book's appearance the distinguished writer and McGill professor paid a visit to the office of Peter C. Newman, the editor, where several of the staff got to meet with him. He was polite, distinguished, dapper, reserved and friendly in person.

In print, however, MacLennan was not so polite, not so friendly. Something had happened between his "first drafts" of the rivers in 1961 and the new versions he worked on for the 1974 publication. What had happened was the Sixties. Hugh MacLennan turned sixty in Centennial Year and he felt like the Canada he had been born into—at Glace Bay, Nova Scotia, in 1907—was now gone forever. He added an essay to his new collection and entitled it "Thinking Like a River." One writer called it "a powerful and anguished personal meditation." It was also angry. Very angry.

The Sixties had not been kind to this Old World soul. Student unrest, assassinations, the war in Vietnam, nuclear fear, the music, drugs, the dress and the manners of the youth coming to, and skipping, his classes at McGill upset him greatly. He couldn't tell boy from girl. One of his own students came to his office braless, "nipples at the salute," and he was convinced that had she walked down the street dressed that way only a dozen years before she would have been arrested.

"It was the fate of my generation," he wrote in what was intended as a gift book on Canada's rivers, "to have been born in the death throes of a civilization that had supported the west for two thousand years. It was our tragedy that hardly any of us understood what this had meant."

The lashing out seemed so unseemly for such a courtly, reserved man. He said the bright promise of Centennial Year and Expo 67 had not even lasted a year. He said the Beatles were now "forgotten" within a few years of claiming they were more popular than Jesus Christ. He believed the world had been turned upside down by a movement no one seemed able to stop. "In those years," he wrote, "I literally swam in the broth of students in the most harassed university in the land and I could not have dodged their anger if I had tried, which I didn't. I learned that they were rejecting, either with fury or with despair, nearly all the values and many of the methods which had produced the stupendous power of humanity in the mid-twentieth century."

One student had told him they were against "the whole God-damn phony mess." He found them to be "the weirdest-dressed young generation there ever was. It's worst members, and they were many, were so soft, spoiled, and self-degraded that when you saw them on city streets you could weep for them."

In returning to his intended subject, the seven rivers he had written of previously, he found their waters more dammed up and polluted than they had been in the 1950s, when such concerns were not even up for discussion. Now, however, they were. MacLennan was becoming, in effect, an early environmentalist, though he failed to see that out of the student rebellion that so offended him would come the environmental movement that is, today, such a formidable political force. If Canadians could only learn to "think like a river," he believed, then would they understand and appreciate "the overwhelming significance of waterways" in this vast country. The rivers needed help, but he had little faith that they were going to get any.

Six years after the publication of *Rivers of Canada*, MacLennan produced what would turn out to be his final novel, *Voices in Time*. It appeared in the fall of 1980. I was by then a staff writer for *Maclean's*, and Peter Newman sent me off to North Hatley in Quebec's Eastern Townships to profile the five-time winner of the Governor General's Literary Award. He and his second wife, Frances (his first wife,

American writer Dorothy Duncan, had died of cancer in 1957), were, as I'd expected, welcoming and gracious. We sat in the garden of their lovely country home, acorns periodically falling into the flower beds as he spoke in that soft, cultured voice that blended his Cape Breton roots with his Oxford education. He talked at length about the world he had been born into, in which he had achieved so much, and how the world seemed, in his opinion, to have lost its bearings, its grounding.

It was the darkest imaginable vision. He had slowly fallen out of critical favour in his own country. His previous novel had been slammed by the critics. His long-ago bestsellers, novels that had largely defined his country, were out of fashion, dismissed by students who thought any "Two Solitudes" interpretation was, well, quaint. He, too, was dismissive. He said his fellow writers around the world were wasting time and talent by "devoting their immense technical abilities to the dissection of cowards, drunkards, weaklings, criminals, psychotics, imbeciles, deviates and people whose sole common denominator seems to be a hatred of life and terror of living."

He had set *Voices in Time* fifty years after nuclear war had destroyed civilization in 1989. All cities, including his beloved Montreal, had been ruined and there were precious few survivors. All knowledge gained over the centuries had been wiped out.

He held out little hope for mankind's survival.

"Water is more valuable than oil," U.S. president George W. Bush said in 2001. A decade later, the mayor of Dirt in the animated feature *Rango* declared, "If you control water, you control everything." From the Oval Office to children's cartoons, the message that water matters in the twenty-first century is unmistakable.

In Canada, no one has sounded the alarm louder or more consistently than Maude Barlow, chair of the Council of Canadians and a prolific author of books on the threats facing the world's supply of fresh water. As she wrote in 2013's *Blue Future*, "The lesson we all learned as children—that we cannot run out of water because of the endless workings of the hydrologic cycle—is simply not true."

In her writings and speeches, Barlow has warned that if no action is taken on climate change, there will be drought on an unprecedented scale, involving mass starvation and the migration of millions of "water refugees." She quotes experts who argue that the Great Lakes could be dry within eight decades and that roughly 80 percent of the world's population lives where rivers are under threat. She cites a United Nations study that predicts demand for water increasing so dramatically that by the 2030s global water resources will be able to satisfy only 60 percent of demand. By 2075, she says in her most recent book, *Boiling Point*, "The water crisis could affect as many as 7 billion people," which is pretty much everybody.

As for Canada itself, we should not be so smug as to think our supply of renewable fresh water is endless. Canada does have more water than any other nation, but Canada also has multiple rivers—the Bow River and South Saskatchewan River in the Prairies being but two significant examples—under severe threat from over-extraction. Pollution remains a major concern as well, whether in waters surrounding major cities or in remote areas. In the first six months of 2016, there were more than 130 drinking-water advisories issued in First Nations communities across the country. Data collected by Environment Canada says that in 2015 alone, more than 205 *billion* litres of raw sewage and untreated waste water were dumped into Canadian oceans and waterways.

At the end of *Boiling Point*, Barlow says that "the water crisis is at our door here in Canada. All the issues we thought so far away are upon us now. A greater challenge has never faced the people of Canada. Each and every one of us has a personal responsibility to take action, to collectively confront the very power structures that have prevented the change needed to protect and honour the great water heritage of this land. Future generations have the same right to breathe clean air and drink clean water. Much rests with what we do now."

Hugh MacLennan, who passed away at the age of eighty-three in 1990—one year after the nuclear Armageddon of his *Voices in Time*—might well have been heartened to know the world he was leaving would not unfold quite so bleakly as he had feared. It might not please him that the Beatles are well remembered, but it might very much please him that so many of today's youth have indeed come to "think of themselves as organic parts in the great chain" and are very much "thinking like a river."

In this book you will meet Louis-Alexandre de Gaspé Beaubien of Montreal, who at the age of sixteen convinced his brother, Philippe, and cousins Aidan and Tatianna Mattrick to direct the considerable resources of the de Gaspé Beaubien Foundation toward finding ways to ensure safer and cleaner water for Canadians. "We come from a family that's been very privileged," says Louis-Alexandre. "They say if you've been given something in life, you need to give back—that's your duty."

You will meet Robyn Hamlyn of Kingston, who was only in her mid-teens when an international online publication dedicated to sustainable development called her "one of the most important people on the planet." Robyn has been a water activist since Grade 7 and today, at the end of her teenage years, still works tirelessly to promote "Blue Communities"—banning bottled water, building clean-water systems and declaring that access to drinking water is a fundamental human right. As she puts it, her goal in life is to "try to change the world."

The young are involved with riverkeepers and conservation authorities and wetlands advocacy groups across the country. But it is not just the young who are showing a refreshing care and respect for the rivers and fresh water of Canada. You will also meet Emil Bell, a seventy-five-year-old Cree elder from the Canoe Lake First Nation in northern Saskatchewan. To protest a pipeline spill that endangered the North Saskatchewan River during the summer of 2016, Bell set up a tepee and spent a week on a hunger strike to bring attention to the forces that threaten his beloved river.

In Emil Bell's simple words, "Water is life. No water, no life—it's that simple."

CHAPTER ONE

CANADA'S ORIGINAL HIGHWAY: THE ST. LAWRENCE

WHO WAS MARY KELLY?

She might have been a wife, a mother, a daughter, a sister. She could have been both infant and grandmother—for there are ten Mary Kellys buried here on Grosse Île, all ten lying in mass graves below the fresh-cut grass in this eerily quiet meadow. The surrounding high rocks buffet a strong nor'easter presently turning the St. Lawrence estuary into whitecaps and flying spray.

All ten Mary Kellys died during the summer and fall of 1847, when some hundred thousand desperate Irish fled the potato famine. That year, 398 ships put in at Grosse Île. They discharged the dead passengers for burial and the sick passengers for treatment, and they placed the remainder under quarantine until officials declared them free of typhus and allowed to continue to Quebec City.

The graves at Grosse Île hold 5,424 dead—most of whom escaped Ireland but not disease. "Mary Kelly" appears ten times on the memorial that sits in one corner of the peaceful meadow. The names listed here are all so very Irish—McCormick, Kennedy, Gallagher, Daly, Fitzgerald, Fitzpatrick, O'Malley, O'Reilly. They are joined by 1,500 "unknown," mostly Irish, who are also buried here. High on a rock outcropping stands a fourteen-metre-high Celtic cross, erected in 1909. Those who suffered and died on this barren island—or so a bewildering message informs the 15,000 to 18,000 visitors who come each year to this National Historic Site—did so "to prove their faith."

Grosse Île—situated where the fresh water of the St. Lawrence River begins mixing with the salt water of the gulf—served as a convenient health precaution for the residents of Quebec City, forty-eight kilometres farther upstream, who justifiably feared typhoid and cholera. Established in 1832 following fears of an outbreak of Asiatic cholera, the island quarantine station operated until 1937, during which more than four million immigrants from sixty countries entered Canada through the port of Quebec. While most names listed speak to the Irish tragedy, the memorial near the mass graves also tells the heartbreaking story of British, Scandinavians, Germans, Russians . . .

The great Canadian scholar Northrop Frye once wrote that immigrants arriving from Europe by ship would have felt "like a tiny Jonah entering an inconceivably large whale" and would have been terrified by this "alien continent" that was swallowing them. A brilliant metaphor, perhaps, but utter poppycock. While it served his rather paranoid theory that Canadian literature holds a "deep terror in regard to nature," the preposterous whale image comes from looking comfortably at a map, not the horizon.

In 1847, the average sailing time across the Atlantic was forty-five days. Those fleeing the famine were crammed into filthy quarters—some ships carrying more than four hundred passengers—and dealing daily with vomit, human waste, death, often of family members, and rolling, slamming breakers that never seemed to pause. Once they entered the Gulf and then the quieter waters of the Lower St. Lawrence, contrary to Professor Frye's theorizing, there would have been nothing but joy and celebration.

Even pioneer writer Susanna Moodie, who had arrived on the *Anne* in late summer 1832, the very year Grosse Île opened, gushed in her journal about first sight of land. "I turned to the right and to the left, I looked up and down the glorious river; never had I beheld so many striking objects blended into one mighty whole! Nature had lavished all her noblest features in producing that enchanting scene."

Moodie would be swallowed by her whale a bit later. Unable to recreate the genteel British life that she pined for now in Canada, she would become the new country's sharpest early critic and denouncer.

Surely, however, the crammed, seasick, ailing passengers on those ships fleeing famine would have felt far more that they were entering the embrace of vast green and granite arms than the mouth of a whale as they reached their destination.

No, we may not know exactly who Mary Kelly was—in any of her ten lives—but we do know that all ten Mary Kellys shared the same dream.

That somewhere up this river they would find a better world.

"You know," says first (and only) mate Gene Carson as the *General Brock II* chugs toward Boldt Castle, "you can tell how the economy is going by the St. Lawrence River.

"I don't give a damn what they say about the GDP or what you read in the newspapers, you come out here day in and day out and you see the number of boats and the people on the tour boats and the big ships going through—you'll know immediately if it's good or bad."

This particular Saturday in July is very good indeed—for the United States, as the holiday weekend is under way. The small cruise ships operating on the American side, mostly out of Alexandria Bay, are stuffed with tourists out to see the wonders of the Thousand Islands. They join the yachts, personal watercraft and gigantic ocean-going cargo ships in turning the upper St. Lawrence into a jumble of competing wakes.

On the Canadian side, the economy is maybe not quite so good. The cruise ships operating out of places like Kingston and Rockport and Gananoque have plenty of space this day, despite the attraction of a sinking Canadian dollar. Carson has sailed for almost all of his sixty years. He has worked on the Tall Ships, sailed luxury yachts in the Caribbean, seen much of the world's water, but he believes there may be no more beautiful place to be found than these Thousand Islands—actually, there are 1,864—that lie approximately half in Canada, half in the U.S.

The islands range from a national park in Canada to a full-blown castle, Boldt, that towers over an island situated in American waters. The grand home is the greatest testament on the river to a love worth remembering, a sentiment less gravely memorialized in 1948 by American singer Arthur Godfrey with his "Thousand Islands Song (Oh! Florence)" as he crooned, *"I left the one I love on one of the Thousand Islands / But unfortunately I can't remember which one / So I row, row, row, row up the river St. Lawrence / And I'm hollerin' Florence, oh! where can you be?"* The hotelier George Boldt, on the other hand, knew exactly whom he'd lost.

The 6-storey, 120-room castle was built by the owner of New York's Waldorf Astoria Hotel, as a gift to his wife, Louise. Boldt hoped it would remind her of the more regal homes back in Prussia, from which they'd emigrated before beginning a fabulously success-ful hotel career in the U.S. He had already spent $2 million on its construction when Louise died suddenly in 1904. Grief-stricken, he abandoned the project, leaving her castle unfinished. Today, restored by the Thousand Islands Bridge Authority after sitting empty for more than seventy years, it is the major tourist attraction of the area.

Many of these islands belong or belonged to families behind some of North America's most familiar brands—Macy's, Caterpillar, Zippo—and the sumptuousness of their summer homes is mind-boggling. Other islands hold tiny cottages, some none at all. There are even two very small islands that, perhaps tongue-in-cheek, boast the shortest international bridge in the world, a 9.75-metre span that joins one island in Canadian waters to another in American waters. Yet there is more than a border between two countries here. Downstream from the Thousand Islands the Mohawk Akwesasne Reserve straddles the St. Lawrence River along the region of the International Rapids. The reserve is more than 250 years old and, along with the neighbouring St. Regis Reserve that lies within the state of New York, boasts a population of around 25,000. So the St. Lawrence waterway involves not only two countries but two provinces, one state and two Native councils.

The St. Lawrence includes a major North American metropolis, Montreal, several smaller cities, multiple ports, vast First Nations holdings, more than a dozen international bridges and tributaries that include the Ottawa, Richelieu, Saguenay, St. Maurice and dozens of other rivers, not to mention commerce that includes recreational and commercial fishing, scuba diving among centuries of shipwrecks, whale-watching, cruises, major shipping. From cigarette (and even human) smuggling to lighting up much of the continent with electricity, the St. Lawrence is far more than a small part of the border.

It is a wide river that runs nearly twelve hundred kilometres. Fourteen bridges span it and numerous ferries cross from one side to the other. "Northwest of Montreal, through a valley always in sight of the low mountains of the Laurentian Shield, the Ottawa River flows out of Protestant Ontario into Catholic Quebec," Hugh MacLennan wrote as the opening words to his famous novel *Two Solitudes*. "It comes down broad and ale-coloured and joins the Saint Lawrence, the two streams embrace the pan of Montreal Island, the Ottawa merges and loses itself, and the mainstream moves northeastward a thousand miles to the sea."

When Jacques Cartier entered the estuary beyond Grosse Île in 1535, he presumed that he had come across the fabled Northwest Passage to China. The Lachine Rapids, so named because "China" surely lay just beyond them, soon convinced him otherwise. What he had found, rather, was the river that would, essentially, create the county that would be Canada.

The St. Lawrence—Cartier called it "La Grande Rivière" and "La Rivière de Hochelaga"—was already a major transportation route for Iroquois who built encampments along its shore, including the village of Hochelaga, whose inhabitants caught its fish and hunted its wildlife in the dense woods that stretched as far as the eye could see. After it became the entry point for European exploration and settlement, it would make the fur trade possible, then the timber trade. It would see wars between major nations and it would change hands, only highlighting its obvious import.

"The St. Lawrence has made nations," MacLennan claimed. "It has been the moulder of lives of millions of people, perhaps by now hundreds of millions, in a multitude of different ways."

In MacLennan's opinion, the river that flowed not far from his office at McGill University is "the greatest inland traffic avenue the world has ever known." From voyageur canoes during the fur trade to today's huge international cruise ships putting in at the Port of Quebec, the St. Lawrence has been, and remains, the inarguable passage to Canada.

The *General Brock II* has returned to its dock near Rockport. Ralph Ogilvie, who has captained the small ship for the past five years, since the former aluminum manufacturer grew bored in retirement, pauses a long moment when asked what it is about the St. Lawrence River that makes it so special.

"This river," the captain finally says, "is the lifeblood of the country—of both countries."

A short drive east of the Ontario village of Long Sault, there is a curious collection of buildings known as the Lost Villages Museum. If Grosse Île reminds us today about lost lives, then this small park is about lost ways of life.

Maps depicting this part of the St. Lawrence River used to include the villages of Mille Roches, Moulinette, Wales, Dickson's Landing, Farran's Point and Aultsville, as well as the smaller hamlets of Santa Cruz and Maple Grove. The area had been among the first settled by the United Empire Loyalists, who fled north in the 1780s. Mapmakers needn't have bothered after July 1, 1958, what remains known in these parts as Inundation Day.

That long-ago Dominion Day thirty tonnes of explosives blew out a cofferdam constructed temporarily to facilitate the building of the $460-million St. Lawrence Seaway. The river poured through the breach and then, the water held back again by the newly finished Moses-Saunders Power Dam, the communities slowly vanished under what is now known as Lake St. Lawrence. More than 6,500 people lost their land. While more than five hundred buildings were moved—including the handful that make up the Lost Villages Museum at Ault Park—many more homes, schools, small businesses and churches were washed away. Even the area's favourite teenage necking spot, Sheek Island, disappeared into the collective memory of those who had called this home.

"They took a lot away from us, the Seaway did," Harriet Donnelly of Farran's Point told a local historian in 1998. "They took away our river."

The flooding widened this stretch of the St. Lawrence River into a "lake," smoothing what had once been wild rapids. Charles Dickens had travelled over the Long Sault Rapids in 1842 on his way to Montreal from Kingston. "In the afternoon," he wrote, "we shot down some rapids where the river boiled and bubbled strangely, and where the force and headlong violence were tremendous."

The St. Lawrence watershed had long been a source of hydro-electric power, another reason to dam the river. The Beauharnois Power Station, downstream from the city of Cornwall, had been completed in 1936, its coincidentally thirty-six turbines making it then "the largest hydroelectric plant in the world." Cheap power had opened the region up to industry—paper production, mills, aluminum extraction, chemical plants, plastics—but the Seaway, with its system of locks and channels, would finally open the Great Lakes to seagoing vessels and international trade. It would turn the year-round port at Montreal into one of the world's busiest, annually handling nearly thirty million tonnes of cargo.

The damming and flooding were done at a time when there was little environmental concern. Not to tame and use such resources was considered folly. As Hugh MacLennan wrote in *Two Solitudes*, "Nowhere has nature wasted herself as she has done here. There is enough water in the St. Lawrence to irrigate half of Western Europe, but the river pours right out of the continent into the sea. No amount of water can irrigate stones and most of Quebec is solid rock. It is as though millions of years back in geologic time a sword had been plunged through the rock from the Atlantic to the Great Lakes and savagely wrenched out again, and the pure water of the continental reservoir, unmuddied and almost useless to farmers, drains untouchably away."

The idea of dredging and damming the St. Lawrence for shipping traffic dates from the 1890s, though it was not a public issue until the

1920s, when the International Joint Commission recommended the project. Prime Minister William Lyon Mackenzie King, who was believed to be cool to the idea, signed a treaty of intent with the U.S. It failed, however, to gain ratification in Congress.

In the 1930s, Prime Minister R.B. Bennett argued its case but could not win over such powerful opponents as New York, Boston and Philadelphia, which understandably feared losing business to the likes of Chicago, Detroit and Toronto. The railroads, of course, were strongly against ships carrying cargo they thought was exclusively their business. Bennett did have the support of U.S. president Franklin D. Roosevelt, but the political reality once again proved too delicate for Washington.

In January 1949 the Canadian government's Throne Speech spelled out a long list of high ambitions, including bringing Newfoundland into Confederation, joining NATO, completing the Trans-Canada Highway and, once again, constructing the Seaway. If President Harry S. Truman was not interested—and he seemed not to be—then Canada would go it alone, if necessary.

When Princess Elizabeth and Prince Philip embarked on their first royal tour of Canada, Prime Minister Louis St. Laurent seized on the swelling nationalism to announce the establishment of a St. Lawrence Seaway Commission. Further meetings took place in Washington, with newly elected president Dwight D. Eisenhower clearly warming to the idea. In November of 1953, Ike came to Ottawa on a state visit and pronounced the construction of the Seaway "inevitable and certain."

The project proved itself an enormous undertaking. "It has taken 15,000 men to perform the labor, the basic digging, dredging, hauling and building that ended with the taming of the St. Lawrence River," Lowell J. Thomas wrote in 1957, as the construction neared completion. "They have used hundreds of machines worth sixty million dollars, including in round numbers 500 heavy trucks, 250 bulldozers,

150 of the biggest shovels and draglines, and 15 dredges. They have excavated 200,000,000 cubic yards of earth and rock, and impacted 10,000,000 cubic yards in the form of dikes, around 20 miles of them, some more than 50 feet high. . . . They have cut channels, removed islands, filled in points of access, laid down roads, set up bridges, relocated everything from telegraph poles to towns." Construction began in 1954 and cost $330 million for Canada, $130 million for the U.S., all of which seems minuscule by today's measure.

Including many of those who would lose their homes to this ambitious undertaking, Canadians were wildly in favour. The Seaway struck a patriotic vein in a country coming into its own following the Second World War. Daniel Macfarlane, a professor of environmental studies at Western Michigan University, says in his 2014 book, *Negotiating a River*, "The people of the sunken communities were asked to sacrifice for the greater good"—and they did so willingly.

"In hindsight," he adds," there was a societal deference to government and a willingness to believe its grand promises, and pervasive belief that the St. Lawrence project would usher in a grand new era of prosperity, which was particularly appealing for an economically depressed area."

The acronym NIMBY had not yet been created, though some were vocally against this backyard project. In a fascinating foreword to Macfarlane's book, Graeme Wynn, a historical geographer at the University of British Columbia, quite properly links that massive 1950s North American project to today's pipeline debate. "To date," he writes, "the project remains ensnared (just as plans for a seaway once were) in US domestic politics and conflicts between the regions and interest groups."

The great difference, Wynn suggests, is that back then the debate was all formal diplomacy, whereas today it profoundly involves the public. What was once hammered out in backrooms is now hotly contested in social media. Without a venue in which to be heard, little fight was put up by those who were to be flooded out in the 1950s. Some argued for more compensation, but most obediently pulled up stakes and moved to new homes.

The Mohawks of Akwesasne claimed from the beginning that the flooding destroyed traditional lands and had negatively affected fishing in the area. In late 2008, half a century later, Ontario Power Generation (OPG) officially apologized to the Mohawks for what the Seaway had caused.

No one, however, ever got around to apologizing to the people of those drowned communities, who had moved on without much protest. What they left behind is on vivid display at the Lost Villages Museum: empty desks in the old school, faded sports photographs on the walls, formal portraits of long-forgotten town councils.

"I don't think the Seaway will make up for what it caused," Evelyn Empey of Woodlands, one of the lost villages, told local historian Rosemary Rutley years later.

"I think the less you interfere with nature the better. I'm a strong believer, if the Lord wanted it one way he'd have made it that way."

The Great Lakes fishery, once so vibrant, was severely damaged by the sea lamprey's arrival. By the late 1930s the eel had moved inland via the Welland Canal—previously, Niagara Falls had proved a natural barrier—and the Great Lakes fishery of lake trout, whitefish and cisco collapsed from 15 million pounds a year to 300,000 pounds by the 1960s, barely 2 percent of what it had once been. The opening up of the St. Lawrence Seaway brought ocean-going freighters to the Great Lakes, their ballast carrying zebra mussels, an annoying invasive species that plays havoc with shorelines, vessels and, most significantly, water-treatment plants.

Then came the goby.

Gobies constitute a vast fish family of more than two thousand species, mostly tiny, and during the past two decades they have quietly taken over much of the Great Lakes system. Research scientist Matthew Windle of the St. Lawrence River Institute of Environmental Sciences in Cornwall, Ontario, estimates the species now make up 50 percent of the fish biomass of the Great Lakes.

The tiny fish are unstoppable, though it can be argued they are both good and bad immigrants to North America. They feed on fish eggs, which is disastrous for the Great Lakes fishery. They are, on the other hand, ready feed for larger predators, producing trophy-size bass along the upper St. Lawrence. They also eat zebra mussels.

The stretch of river alongside Cornwall and including the Akwesasne Reserve and the town of Massena, New York, on the U.S. side has been identified as one of forty-three "Areas of Concern" (AOCs) by the International Joint Commission and the various governments—federal, state and provincial—dealing with the Great Lakes system. Once heavily industrialized, the AOCs are today carefully monitored for pollution and species change by the twenty-one-year-old non-profit St. Lawrence River Institute.

"Our research means nothing if we don't share it with others," says Pamela Maloney, the institute's development officer.

Windle's research included the invading goby as well as the disappearing American eel. The eels' life cycle is fascinating—born in the Sargasso Sea, moving up the St. Lawrence at ages four to seven, returning to the Sargasso to spawn in their twenties—but so, too, is the tragedy of their vanishing. The Seaway has had eel ladders in operation since the 1970s. Scientists used to count more than a million eels a year moving into the Great Lakes, but no longer.

"We have lost 98 to 99 percent of our American eels," says the aquatic biologist. "They used to be one of our most important fish."

The ladders certainly help move them up the river, and between 2006 and 2010 OPG has stocked the watershed with more than four million eels. But it is the return of the mature females to their breeding grounds in the ocean that is of particular concern. The larger ones, in particular, are doomed once they enter the turbines of the power stations.

"We know how to move them up rivers," says Windle. "It's moving them down safely that we're working on."

To help the eels, scientists are trying to "herd" them to safer passage through audio technology. There is even a program to capture them at the top of one major dam and truck them to the bottom of a large dam farther downstream in the hope that from there the eels can reach their spawning grounds safely. Scientists are making admirable progress but the sad truth is that the American eel, once a staple for First Nations living along the St. Lawrence River and the Ottawa River, is now very much an endangered species.

"It's sort of like the American bison being wiped out," muses Windle. "They were both a very important species to First Nations. But basically they've been wiped out by the European arrival."

Milwaukee journalist Dan Egan has written extensively on the threat of invasive species. In his 2017 book, *The Death and Life of the Great Lakes*, Egan argues that the importance of the Great Lakes cannot be underestimated in that, of the fresh water available for human use, one of every five litres available on the planet can be found in the five huge lakes in the heart of North America. Egan mentions an oft-quoted 1995 comment by World Bank vice-president Ismail Serageldin that "the wars of this century have been fought over oil, and the wars of the next century will be on water" but argues there is, today, a more pressing threat: "The biggest enemy facing the Great Lakes in the early twenty-first century is not would-be profiteers seeking to siphon them off to make far-away deserts bloom. The biggest threat to the lakes right now is our own ignorance."

It is Egan's belief that the St. Lawrence Seaway, which opened to such grand fanfare in 1957, has been an ecological disaster. When it opened, CBS anchor Walter Cronkite told millions of viewers that the seaway was "re-shaping a continent, completing the job nature had begun thousands of years ago—of creating an eighth sea . . . a sea of opportunity." Perhaps this is how it appeared two generations ago, argues Egan, but it is no longer a valid claim today when the Seaway sees only two ocean ships a day come to the Great Lakes during the nine-month shipping season. Instead, he says, the Seaway created "an environmental scourge whose scope and costs are spreading by the day. The St. Lawrence Seaway, you see, didn't conquer nature at all. It unleashed it in the form of an ecological catastrophe unlike any this continent has seen."

Though Egan does hold out some hope that future stringent initiatives could stop the arrival of other invasive species and that intense campaigns might rid the lakes of those already here, others are expressing grave concerns about the future health of the lakes following the results of the 2016 presidential election. When United States president Donald Trump's first budget called for the slashing of federal funds for the Great Lakes Restoration Initiative—a program directly charged with combating invasive species, algae blooms and pollution hotspots—there was outrage and calls for resistance from politicians on both sides of the border.

During the years of the Obama administration, the program had been receiving approximately $300 million a year from Washington. The Trump proposal was for zero, dismissing such "programs dealing with puddles and ditches." If the program were to survive, state, provincial and local governments would have to take up the slack. "It's like a poke in the eye with a sharp stick," said David Ullrich, executive director of the Great Lakes and St. Lawrence Cities Initiative, a coalition of 128 municipalities on both sides of the border. "Very vindictive and mean-spirited is what it is. . . . And morally, it's reprehensible because this is something we need to leave to future generations in good shape."

Pollution has long been a great concern along the St. Lawrence River. In the fall of 2015 the city of Montreal announced it would be dumping eight billion litres of raw sewage into the river over a seven-day period, leading to similar outrage. The reason was the necessary relocation of a snow chute, but no argument could calm the initial uproar this announcement caused. So upset were environmentalists and ordinary citizens that Mayor Denis Coderre ordered a temporary halt to the plan and asked his engineers to look for an alternative. When none could be found, the massive flush was on. Curiously, water-quality tests done prior to the dumping and in the month following found that there was little difference after the first couple of weeks, so effective is the huge river at flushing itself out.

In the fall of 2016, the AquaHacking 2016 Summit was held at Montreal's Palais des Congrès, bringing together water experts, technologists, politicians and interested citizens to talk about the vulnerability of the St. Lawrence River. A similar gathering—aided by funding from the de Gaspé Beaubien Foundation—had been held the year before on the Ottawa River.

The mayors of Quebec City and Montreal spoke about the dangers the rivers face and what is being done to counter such threats. Mayor Régis Labeaume of Quebec reminded the gathering of the all-too-regular threats—drought twice this century already, accidental fuel spills, the rail disaster at Lac-Mégantic, raw sewage being dumped into the river upstream from his city.

"Episodes like that give us the chills," he said, "and remind us of our vulnerability."

Mayor Coderre of Montreal said the sewage dump of the previous year actually had the benefit of raising public awareness of the import of proper water-quality management. The system was improved vastly, he said, and a new program, scheduled to be up and running in 2018, will eliminate most bacteria, viruses and pharmaceutical products from waste water.

All this, of course, involves current growth and anticipated growth. At the AquaHacking 2016 Summit, Coderre and other mayors spoke about all they were doing to ensure water safety in the coming years, only to have their entire premise challenged by William Rees, professor emeritus of the University of British Columbia and an ecological economist. As keynote speaker at the summit, Rees challenged the notion of perpetual economic growth, that the economy can and should grow indefinitely.

"We have become a parasite on the planet," Rees warned. "We are growing by consuming the host. Now any economist should recognize that growth provides benefits, but the benefits, the marginal utility of growth, declines over time. In the meantime the costs are increasing, the costs of pollution, soil erosion, depletion. . . . As those costs increase, the benefits continue to decline until you reach a futility limit. So when you are planning the St. Lawrence, keep in mind that there is an optimal scale of development, and contrary to conventional wisdom, there is an inevitable conflict between the material growth of the economy and the preservation of nature."

In April of 2016 American Rivers, an environmental group, named New York's St. Lawrence River among "America's Most Endangered Rivers." The St. Lawrence was number nine in a list of ten endangered rivers, beginning with the Apalachicola-Chattahoochee-Flint River Basin, which covers three states, Alabama, Florida and Georgia. While most of the other endangered rivers were placed on the list for reasons of pollution and outdated water management, the greatest threat to the St. Lawrence was said to be dams.

The environmental group spoke out against dam operations that take little or no account of the water levels or the flow of water, both so important to the maintenance of freshwater habitat. The St. Lawrence, they said, has suffered "significant losses" of such habitat over the decades. They pointed to two particular species that had been hit hardest: the black tern, which had declined by over 80 percent since the massive Moses-Saunders Dam was constructed, and the northern pike, a popular sports fish, that was down 70 percent in the area.

American Rivers called for Canada and the U.S. to proceed with Plan 2014, which was developed by the International Joint Commission with the input of some 180 stakeholders, from government officials to scientists and industry experts. As the river provides drinking water to some 4 million people and supports 87 species of freshwater fish, 18 species of migratory fish and 115 bird species, Plan 2014 would place the environment at the heart of any decisions regarding the river—something that was not done when the massive dam and the Seaway were built.

"The St. Lawrence River is slowly dying because dam operations haven't been updated since the 1950s," spokesperson Rupak Thapaliya said in a press release from the group. "This is the year to jumpstart the restoration of this river that is a vital lifeline for our economy, environment and communities."

Not surprisingly, 2016 passed without any such "jumpstart."

CHAPTER TWO

PRICELESS AND PRECARIOUS: THE OTTAWA

"EVERY DAY ON THIS RIVER is an adventure."

Judith Flynn-Bedard is talking from the stern of *Pier Pressure II*, the small cabin cruiser she owns with her husband, Robert, and she shakes her head at a string of memories.

There was the day a sleek boat with a menacing tiger chained to the deck pulled into the Montebello marina, where the couple rents a slip for their boat. There was the dawn she was awakened by a yacht full of drunks pulling in after a night of wild partying with hired strippers. There was the time she found a frogman checking along the hull of her boat—all in preparation for the day U.S. president George W. Bush descended from the sky in Marine One, the presidential helicopter, for a trilateral meeting with Prime Minister Stephen Harper and president of Mexico Felipe Calderón.

The Bedards, both retired from work in the nation's capital, have boated along the Ottawa River for more than thirty years. They treasure their time on the water as much as they do their time with their grandchildren, and they try to combine the two delights as often as possible. With Irish and French heritage, they connect to those who made this waterway so vital to European exploration, then the fur and timber trades. They anchor on the Quebec side, within shouting distance of Le Château Montebello, three buildings that were constructed from a total of ten thousand cedar logs during the Depression, served for decades as an exclusive private club that counted Prince Rainier and Princess Grace of Monaco among its members, and are today a luxurious Fairmont Hotels resort.

"Where else can you boat and have the world's biggest log cabin right beside you?" says Flynn-Bedard. "I can even order room service from right here if I don't feel like cooking."

In evenings they often cruise the wide waterway and enjoy a glass of wine. On the Ontario side of the river, it is a crime to have a beer or a glass of wine in even a small boat or canoe.

Not a lot makes sense along this magnificent river that, farther upstream, flows past the Houses of Parliament, which appear to have turned their backs on this historic waterway.

The Ottawa River, for thousands of years a vital transportation and trading link for First Nations, was travelled by Samuel de Champlain in 1613. (He was not, however, the first European to travel the river; that honour belongs to Étienne Brûlé, who had travelled the river and on to Georgian Bay three years earlier.) Champlain found the rapids almost impossible to traverse. He and his men managed by portaging everything, including canoes, past the most difficult runs and falls, or by "lining" the canoes up the sides of rapids with ropes whenever the water allowed and there were no rock cliffs preventing such a manoeuvre. It could be dangerous work. As Champlain recorded, "In pulling mine I almost lost my life, because the canoe turned broadside into a whirlpool, and had I not luckily fallen between two rocks, the canoe would have dragged me in, since I could not quickly enough loosen the rope which was twisted around my hand, which hurt me very much and nearly cut it off."

To celebrate the three-hundredth anniversary of Champlain's first journey up the Ottawa, the renowned explorer was honoured with a massive statue that stands overlooking the river on a majestic point not far from the Peace Tower. Samuel de Champlain is depicted making solar observations using his astrolabe, which was supposedly found in the year of Canada's Confederation, 254 years after Champlain travelled the Ottawa River, by a teenager walking through a field near Cobden. Whether the instrument was actually Champlain's is doubted by some, but not the Museum of History, which has it on display.

At least the museum knows which way an astrolabe should be held. The large statue overlooking Nepean Point has depicted Champlain holding his treasured astrolabe upside down.

There are so many things not quite right along this waterway, says Judith Flynn-Bedard, but one matter bothers more than any other. "I've seen human feces floating in the river," she says. "This river is coming right out of the nation's capital. What does that say about our politicians?

"If any river should be cleaned up, it should be this one."

The Ottawa has been described as the "unknown river of Canada." Perhaps because it is dwarfed by the St. Lawrence (of which the Ottawa is a tributary), this narrower and even more inland waterway has failed to register much with Canadians.

It is, however, a long (more than 1,200 kilometres) and massive river fed by tributaries on both the Quebec and Ontario sides. Its speed, volume and rocky descent (360 metres from the Canadian Shield to the lowlands nearing the St. Lawrence) create a recreational paradise for rafters and kayakers. The river's periodic widening into "lakes"—created by numerous hydroelectric dams—creates wide and deep pockets of river water ideal for pleasure boating and sailing. The deep waters of the Ottawa are home to ninety-six fish species and its wetlands visited by a remarkable three hundred species of birds.

There were, in the days of the fur trade, a great many difficult portages past the fast water and rapids. The fur traders travelled in both directions, their large canoes filled with supplies and trading materials on the way upstream, filled with furs on their way home. Many stretches of water had to be portaged in both directions. In the timber years, travel was all downstream, and often treacherous.

"There is scarcely a portage, a cleared point, jutting out into the river where you do not meet with wooden crosses, on which are crudely carved the initials of some poor unfortunate victim of the restless waters," Thomas C. Keefer, a civil engineer, said in a Montreal speech he gave about the river in 1854. "In a prosperous year about ten thousand men are afloat on loose timber, or in frail canoes, and as many as eighty lives have been lost in a single spring. . . . Some of the eddies in high water become whirlpools, tearing a bark canoe into shreds and engulfing every soul in it."

Today nineteen dams cross the Ottawa and often vast stretches of wide, calm water. Chats Falls, at Fitzroy Harbour fifty-six kilometres upstream from the capital, was a century and more ago a major Ontario tourist attraction, said to be second in grandeur only to Niagara Falls. The riverboat *Lady Colborne* ferried passengers in so close they were soaked by spray. There were even periodic sightings of a massive "serpent" in the area waters, one Ottawa newspaper reporting in 1880 that the number of sightings "steadily increases, and some of these fine days we hope to hear of its capture." In the late 1920s a massive dam and generating station put an end to the falls, the tourists and, apparently, the serpent.

Early tourists, who would come to marvel at such sights as the frozen "humps" of ice at the end of long rapids and come to fish and hunt along the Ottawa and its tributaries were given some valued advice in the day. Anyone thinking of coming to the area of the Ottawa River to enjoy the water and wilderness should have, it was said, "the stomach of a locomotive and the appetite of a saw-mill." Other recommendations included:

- abilities to ride without a saddle,
- to walk after as well as before dinner,
- to paddle a bark canoe, run a rapid, and swim when your canoe is swamped in a 'Cellar,' or riddled on a rock.

You must be able to eat salt pork and petrified biscuit, and drink tea which would peel the tongue of a buffalo. . . . If you would sleep on a sweltering night in June, nothing short of chloroform will render a novice insensible to the melody of those swamp serenaders, the mosquitoes, or the tactics of their bloodthirsty ally, the black fly, who noiselessly fastens upon your jugular while the mosquito is bragging in your face.

Thanks to an elaborate system of locks, boaters such as the Bedards can make their way, if they wish, to Florida, where the couple often winters. "People in Florida find out we have a boat on the Ottawa River and their attitude is, 'Oh, that must be kind of sad,'" says Flynn-Bedard. "They just don't know how huge this river is."

Today's Ottawa has been called but "a docile, domesticated descendant of the wild waterway the fur traders knew." Where fifteen kilometres of rapids once ran at Long Sault, nearing the river's mouth, early voyageurs used to doff their hats at the first sign of white water out of respect for Adam Dollard des Ormeaux, a trader who is believed to have sacrificed himself and his seventeen companions in 1660 by fending off an Iroquois war party intent on attacking the settlement at Montreal.

Once the fur traders figured out how best to travel up this difficult "highway" into the interior, development along the Ottawa was quick to follow. By the mid-1800s, the river the French had called "La Grande Rivière du Nord" was the main artery for logging the dense valley forests. The river carried huge rafts of squared timber downstream to Montreal and Quebec City. Ferries carried people and produce from one side of the river to the other, tugboats guided and served the rafts, barges brought supplies to settlers up and down the river. Steamships—one capable of carrying eleven hundred passengers, moved people up and down various portions of the river where the water was deep enough and quiet enough to be navigable, from Lachine all the way upstream to Pembroke. Smaller boats served similar roles on the upper river as far as the town of Mattawa. By 1882 the railway reached North Bay, largely killing off the barge and steamship traffic.

The extensive damming—not only along the Ottawa proper but at numerous more spots along its many tributaries—harnessed much of its wildness and changed the river dramatically, but not nearly so much as might have been the case had two rather astonishing plans to completely remake the Ottawa River watershed gone ahead.

Two years before Confederation, a British admiral stationed in Halifax and a British general in charge of the troops, along with a brigade of men, paddled the Ottawa and Mattawa rivers from Montreal to Ottawa and on to Georgian Bay. Their purpose was to determine whether more canals and locks could make the route possible for ships to travel a more northerly, and safer, route from Quebec and Montreal to Georgian Bay and beyond. The two military leaders believed it could, in fact, be done. In 1908, the Department of Public

Works even fashioned a report on the feasibility, estimating the cost at $100 million and rationalizing that cost by claiming that the route, which would be wholly through Canadian territory, would not only be safer but would cut off three hundred miles of sailing to cross Quebec and Ontario. Had Wilfrid Laurier been re-elected in 1911, it is very likely the Georgian Bay Ship Canal would have gone ahead.

In the late 1950s, yet another grandiose idea was hatched—one even more improbable than dredging a route from Mattawa to Georgian Bay. The Great Recycling and Northern Development Canal, short-ened to GRAND Canal, was the brainstorm of Newfoundland engineer Tom Kierans. Kierans's career involved an impressive history of visionary projects, from the mammoth hydro dam at Churchill Falls to serving as a key government consultant in the planning for the Confederation Bridge over Northumberland Strait. His GRAND Canal scheme was somewhat based on Holland's Zuiderzee Works and would involve damming various rivers flowing from the highlands of northern Quebec into James Bay, instead bringing their fresh water down the Ottawa River, diverting much of it across Northern Ontario to replenish the shrinking Great Lakes.

Kierans estimated there is almost twice the amount of fresh water flowing into the saltwater flats of shallow James Bay as there is flowing through the Great Lakes system into the St. Lawrence River. This water could be used for agriculture and power. It could prevent drought from threatening so much of the American Midwest. It would help control forest fires. It would also, he believed, vastly improve the commercial fishing potential of Canada's northern waters.

Kierans's theory was that, before the twenty-first century is out, fresh water will reach a crisis state in North America, and Canada will need to have reached an agreement with the United States—otherwise, "They'll just take it. We'd be crazy to fight. When you fight someone ten times bigger than you, you use your head, not your fists."

What is required, he believed, is a twenty-first-century response to what Franklin Delano Roosevelt did in the twentieth century, when the American president addressed the crisis of the Great Depression by creating huge make-work projects such as the Tennessee Valley Authority and massive dams along the Colorado and Columbia rivers.

"We need another FDR," Kierans told me in 2009. "This has got to be done, and it will be done because it has to be. But it won't be easy. People will not believe you. You have to be prepared to take criticism for it. I know, because I've been accused of selling Canada down the river—even when the truth is exactly the opposite."

A half-century ago, Kierans was able to get some major movers to agree with him, including Quebec premier Robert Bourassa and federal Liberal heavyweight John Turner, who in 1984 would briefly serve as prime minister. Some Bay Street investors thought the idea had merit, but Kierans and his supporters could never find enough financing for such a vast project, let alone to pursue the legal and environmental rulings needed before any such realigning of nature could even be considered.

Even into his nineties, Kierans was still fighting for his vision. "It's very hard to tell people you can send water to the United States and still have more water in Canada, but that's the way it would be," he said. "There is a way to get water from Canada to the United States— and at the same time increase the fresh water here."

Another nonagenarian, Jack Biddell, who once served as president of the Clarkson Gordon accounting firm, joined with Kierans to argue the project could not only be financed but "it wouldn't cost us a cent. The United States will pay for it. There will be enough fresh water for both. There are no downsides for Canada."

Tom Kierans died in 2013 at one hundred; Jack Biddell had passed away two years earlier. There is no longer talk of either the GRAND Canal plan or the Georgian Bay Ship Canal.

The Ottawa is also a storied river far beyond the exploits of the early explorers and the *coureurs de bois* of the fur trade. It was along the Ottawa that Archibald, the 13th Laird of McNab, established a short-lived feudal system in the 1820s when he brought several dozen clansmen from Scotland to settle near present-day Arnprior. When Canada experienced its first entry into world affairs in the mid-1880s, it was mostly Ottawa Valley raftsmen, loggers and First Nations who made up the nearly four hundred "voyageurs" requested by Britain to take British troops up the Nile in what would become a failed attempt to rescue General Charles "Chinese" Gordon, who was under siege in Khartoum. One Ottawa Valley logger, Joseph Montferrand, was such a legendary figure that his exploits are captured in the Stompin' Tom Connors song "Big Joe Mufferaw."

It is commonly held that the source of the river is Lake Timiskaming, which is indeed the large body of water that is found at the "top" of the Ottawa. In fact, however, the origin lies beyond Lake Timiskaming at Lac Capimitchigama, far to the northeast in Quebec's Laurentian Mountains. The flow of the full Ottawa rather circles to the west, south and east through a distance of more than twelve hundred kilometres.

The watershed of the Ottawa is said to be larger than New Brunswick, Nova Scotia and Prince Edward Island combined. Of its eleven main tributaries, some like the Petawawa River on the Ontario side and the Rivière Dumoine on the Quebec side are beloved by canoeists and kayakers for their whitewater thrills and wilderness vistas, while others like the Rideau River are settled, tamed and, thanks to a vast locks-and-canal system, a holiday delight for houseboaters. The same holds true for the Ottawa itself, a fierce and fast-moving river in the north but placid and reed-filled as it meanders through farmlands toward Lac des Deux Montagnes near Montreal.

"Look at the watershed as a leaf," suggests Chief Kirby Whiteduck of the Algonquins of Pikwàkanagàn First Nation, "and the Ottawa River as the main stem, and the veins going out as the tributaries."

The Pikwàkanagàn band is found 240 kilometres west of Ottawa, near the village of Golden Lake, and is one of ten Algonquin communities recognized as part of a massive land claim stretching from North Bay to Kingston and including much of the Ottawa River watershed.

Of particular issue to the Algonquins, says Chief Whiteduck, is the vanishing American eel, a migratory fish species that has found such difficulties in the St. Lawrence River and is now rarely found along the Ottawa. Despite a 1907 federal regulation that required fish ladders to be installed in any future dam construction, there is today not a single permanent ladder at any of the many dams.

Judith Flynn-Bedard is far from the only person in the vast watershed with a serious complaint. The Algonquins of Kitigan Zibi First Nation, upstream on the Gatineau River, which joins the Ottawa on the Quebec side across from Parliament Hill, have been under a "do-not-consume" order because of high levels of uranium in the village's water table. More than half the people of Kitigan Zibi use bottled water only.

"We hold water as sacred," Kitigan Zibi elder Peter Decontie told a 2015 gathering on the health of the watershed.

Chief Harry St. Denis of Wolf Lake First Nations near Timiskaming says that Natives lived in harmony with the river for thousands of years, while "it took government and industry a hundred and fifty years to transform it into what it is today."

The temptation among First Nations stakeholders, says Chief St. Denis, is to say, "You screwed it up, you fix it."

It's tempting, but unlikely to accomplish anything.

As Chief Whiteduck says, "You have to find the right balance."

It was June 22, 1871. Sir John A. Macdonald, first prime minister of the new Dominion of Canada, was writing to John Sandfield Macdonald, first premier of the new province of Ontario.

"The sight of immense masses of timber passing my window every morning," the prime minister wrote, "constantly suggests to my mind the absolute necessity there is for looking into the future of this great trade. We are recklessly destroying the timber of Canada and there is scarcely a possibility of replacing it."

The enormous growth of the Ottawa Valley timber trade had occurred thanks to Napoleon, whose 1806 blockade of Britain cut off wood supplies from northern Europe. The valley loggers cut the tall pines, mostly white pine, squared the logs to twenty-four inches and lashed them together to form huge rafts. They excavated canals and built multiple timber runs to avoid log jams in the faster water. Between 1826 and 1894, it was estimated more than eighty million logs had been taken from the valley. The last big raft run, organized in 1908 by lumber baron J.R. Booth to celebrate the three-hundredth anniversary of Quebec, held 150,000 feet of square timber and carried a crew of eighty men. While there were river runs held later, including a commemorative run in 2008 that is the subject of Ron Corbett's charming book *One Last River Run*, the diminishing timber trade was soon carried far more by rail and truck.

Hugh MacLennan has argued that the most important early figure along the Ottawa River was neither French, English nor Aboriginal—but a Yankee from Massachusetts. In 1799, Philemon Wright had travelled up the river to the point where the Gatineau River feeds into the Ottawa on the east side and the Rideau River plummets over a high falls on the west—the confluence not far from where Parliament Hill stands today. He was looking for a suitable place to establish a new colony for his family and followers and liked what he found where the three rivers met.

"Wright possessed the Yankee talent for complex organization which sees one activity dovetailing into a dozen others," MacLennan wrote. "He was a surveyor, a farmer, a woodsman, a lumber man, and in the end he was a shipping and financial tycoon deeply involved in international affairs. Nor was anyone in Canadian history luckier in the coincidence of his private life with a pressing public need."

Wright capitalized on the white-pine trade during and following the Napoleonic Wars. He was able to get timber rafts through to Quebec City and past the difficult Long Sault rapids by breaking the huge rafts up into smaller cribs and then forming them into rafts again once past the white water. He built farms and brought in set-tlers, and communities rose on both sides of the Ottawa. Other timber barons competed with him, and with so much timber in the valley many of them became rich, too. Workers who spent the winter in the woods felling trees and hauling the squared logs to the banks of the various rivers were paid once the river runs were on, and they flooded into Bytown and Hull, where they drank and fought, usually the Irish against the French but often just one shanty group against another. They were joined by the canal workers, mostly Irish, who were building the Rideau system under the direction of Colonel John By. Those with families settled around the growing towns, often living in poverty. The streets were muck-ridden with human and animal waste. Cholera was common. In 1847, a typhoid outbreak decimated the population. Bytown, MacLennan wrote, was "a barbarous place."

All began to change a decade later, however, when Queen Victoria—some said wearing a blindfold—chose the community on the west side of the river to be the colony's new capital. Ottawa had been a classic compromise: on the border between Upper and Lower Canada, neither too French, as Montreal was, nor too English, as York (Toronto) was, and Kingston too close to the country with which Great Britain had so recently been at war. MacLennan quotes the English writer Goldwin Smith as describing the new capital as "a sub-arctic lumber village converted by royal mandate into a political cockpit."

It is difficult today to imagine the beauty that was once the Ottawa River. Chaudière Falls is an impressive set of cascades right in the heart of the capital. Champlain noted that when Natives returned to this stunning and violent drop in the river, they would hold a special ceremony. Tobacco offerings would be placed on a wooden plate, they would dance around the plate and, following a speech or two, would toss the offering into the boiling cauldron at the bottom of the rock ledges to give thanks for safe passage.

The boiling water metaphor is deliberate. The Algonquins called the falls "Asticou," meaning "boiler," which became "Chaudière" once the French arrived and began naming significant falls and portages on maps.

In 1860, the Prince of Wales visited the colony and the highlight was a ride down the Chaudière slide on a specially built timber crib guided by expert rivermen, his heart-pounding drop through the tumbling water and spray greeted by "gaily dressed lumbermen in a hundred birch-bark canoes. Two thousand people, in six river steamers that had been assembled in Ottawa for the great day, watched the performance, and an estimated twenty thousand more spectators lined the banks to cheer."

Today, commuters moving across the Chaudière Bridge that connects Ottawa and Gatineau do not even notice what remains of the falls—long since dammed and harnessed for electricity and a variety of mills. In 2015, Hydro Ottawa announced it would construct a new twenty-nine-megawatt hydroelectric generating facility that will not further block the falls from view; the additional hydro plant will all be underground. Hydro Ottawa also promised viewing platforms and a new bridge to accommodate cyclists and pedestrians.

The Chaudière area, once noted for its dramatic scenery, has for years been an eyesore of barbed wire and abandoned buildings. Yet it was here where Philemon Wright built his first small sawmill in 1806, here where lumber baron J.R. Booth built his vast mills, here where Ezra Butler ("E.B.") Eddy made matches. The location, last owned by paper manufacturer Domtar Corporation, is a fifteen-hectare site that Windmill Development Group and Dream Unlimited—with the blessing of the National Capital Commission—intends to turn into a $1.2-billion vision that would include condos, green space and, once again, public access to the forgotten falls.

The project is called "Zibi" after the Algonquin word for river, and Windmill says the choice of name is deliberate, as they intend to honour First Nations and are committed to hiring and working with the Algonquins. Some resent the use of the word, as it seems to play off Kitigan Zibi First Nations, an Algonquin settlement along the Gatineau River and once home to the late William "Grandfather" Commanda, a revered Algonquin elder who maintained all his life that the area around the falls is a sacred Aboriginal site and should be returned to its natural state. Even the Algonquins are split on the development, with the Algonquin community of Pikwàkanagàn, near Golden Lake, Ontario, supporting Windmill's intentions while many Algonquins from Kitigan Zibi are against it. A number of Quebec First Nations leaders—as well as Canadian Museum of History architect Douglas Cardinal—have attempted, so far without success, to put a stop to the project.

Disagreement, unfortunately, is as common to the Ottawa River as it is to the House of Commons.

In 1984, the federal government established the Canadian Heritage Rivers System. CHRS status was intended to ensure that special and significant national waterways are promoted and protected and that they will be sustainably managed. There are now thirty-eight designated heritage rivers—including the Mattawa and Rideau rivers, both of which flow into the Ottawa. The Ottawa River, inexplicably, has not been counted among them.

Legendary canoeist Max Finkelstein—an Ottawa resident who once worked for CHRS—says this failure is the "gaping hole" in the national designation. Finkelstein, who has spent much of his life exploring and writing about the historic rivers of the country, has canoed virtually the entire length of the Ottawa.

"No river reverberates as strongly with the spirit of Canada," he says. "This river is priceless, and precarious. It has given us many gifts, including this country we call Canada. It's time for us to give back to the river—and we should begin by properly designating the Ottawa as a heritage river."

In 2007, approximately half the length of the Ottawa was nominated to be so designated but the nomination, absurdly, was restricted to a six-hundred-kilometre-plus strip along the Ontario side. It was almost as if there were no far shore to the river, no other side, no Quebec always within sight of the boundary line.

In the summer of 2016, with the country's sesquicentennial coming up fast, a joint federal-Ontario news release announced that the heritage designation had been granted—for the Ontario portion only. River activists, who had been working for years to get Quebec to join in on the designation, were outraged. The politicians had jumped the gun on the announcement, believing Quebec would assign its own heritage designation and include the 681 kilometres of the "Outaouais" that flows entirely within Quebec's borders.

In the opinion of Max Finkelstein, "No nomination can be considered valid unless it includes both provinces."

The point would seem inarguable. A river, by definition, needs two shores. How can one side be deemed "heritage" and the other not? This absurdity is but one of many along such an important river that runs through the nation's capital and yet has no official body to oversee its entirety, waters and both shores included. It can hardly be because the river, no longer required for exploration, the fur trade or timber runs, is today in any way insignificant. There are more than two hundred municipalities in the two provinces throughout the Ottawa River watershed. There are numerous First Nations communities, as well, making for a total population of roughly two million, with one significant city, Ottawa, a major military base at Petawawa and numerous smaller centres such as Gatineau, Hawkesbury, Pembroke, Mattawa, Arnprior, Deep River, Thurso, Rockland, Papineauville, Hudson, Montebello . . .

There are more than thirty beaches along the Ottawa River alone, and many are closed during times of heavy rain and closely monitored for water quality. Ninety wastewater-treatment plants dot the Ottawa's shores, half of them providing only the bare essential primary treatment. Raw sewage often flows into the river.

At Chalk River, 180 kilometres upstream from Parliament Hill, there is a nuclear research facility that produces much of the world's supply of medical radioisotopes and has brought much renown to Canada, including a Nobel Prize in physics (Bertram Brockhouse, honoured in 1994 for his pioneering work in neutron spectroscopy). The nearby town of Deep River was constructed in the mid-1940s when more than fifty scientists, mostly British, and their families moved to the area to work on what became known locally as "The Project."

After the two atomic bombs were dropped on Japan in 1945, staff in Chalk River and Deep River grew deeply concerned as to what use would be made of their research. Some even quit, but most stayed on after assurances that their research would be used for peaceful purposes, such as the treatment of tumours and cancers.

It is still a nuclear reactor on the Ottawa River, however, and its presence has caused concern over the years through rare but alarming leaks, including one in 1952 that prompted a two-year shutdown and one in 2009 that led to a global shortage of medical isotopes. Though the safety record has been impressive, the reactor is now considered ancient and is expected to be decommissioned in 2018.

Given all this, it is nothing less than astounding that no government agency has ever had a specific mandate to safeguard the health of this vital river.

A paper prepared by Jamie Benidickson, a professor of environmental law at the University of Ottawa, says that pollution concerns were being raised shortly after Confederation about the amount of sawdust, lost logs and raw sewage found in the river. Over a two-year period, 1911–1912, 174 deaths from typhoid were recorded.

In 1892, the famed Irish poet and essayist Oscar Wilde gave a lecture in Ottawa and began by haranguing the audience on the sorry state of their river, thanks to the constant dumping of sawdust, bark and other waste from the mills. "This is an outrage," he cried. "No one has the right to pollute the air and water, which are the common inheritances of all. We should leave them to our children as we have received them." The next day the *Ottawa Evening Citizen* chided him for going "too far."

Yet so concerned were early city dwellers about the water supply that in 1913 a consultant recommended a pipeline be built to Thirty-One-Mile Lake, Pemichangan Lake and Long Lake, deep in the Quebec highlands, and that drinking water be drawn from there rather than from the nearby Ottawa River. Ratepayers balked at the expense. A year later, the public health board declared the Ottawa River "beyond any question, a polluted source of supply at all points in the vicinity of the city."

The fight for clean water had its advocates, such as Senator Napoléon Belcourt, a prominent Franco-Ontarian who had served as Speaker of the House of Commons and was appointed by Prime Minister Sir Wilfrid Laurier to represent the city of Ottawa in the Senate. He took particular interest in the health of the river, almost entirely to do with sewage. Today there are several sophisticated advocates, including the Ottawa River Institute and Ottawa Riverkeeper/Sentinelle Outaouais. In late May 2015, Riverkeeper joined with the de Gaspé Beaubien Foundation to hold the first AquaHacking Ottawa River Summit, at Gatineau's Lac Leamy. The irony was not lost on many that politicians and environmentalists were gathering at a casino to talk about the odds of something actually being done to clean up the river.

The third generation of de Gaspé Beaubien children chose water as the cause they would promote with the foundation, which is the philanthropic arm of the wealthy Montreal family that built its considerable fortune (estimated at $740 million) with the communications giant Telemedia.

Philippe II de Gaspé Beaubien, the founder of Telemedia, and his wife, Nan-b, had gathered their grandchildren—Philippe IV and Louis-Alexandre and their cousins Aidan and Tatianna Mattrick—and suggested they begin thinking about how their generation might use the foundation for a good purpose.

"I didn't think water was a big issue in Canada, especially in Quebec," was the initial reaction of Philippe's son, Philippe III. "But they educated the family. I started waking up. I'm from Montreal. I drink my water from a tap. But all that water is coming from the Ottawa River, and every time it rains our systems on the Quebec side are not designed to handle the extra water, so we are flooding the river, our river, with raw sewage."

I was at the summit and took that opportunity to ask sixteen-year-old Louis-Alexandre if he was aware of the old saw that it often only takes three generations for a family to go from rags to riches to rags again. "I've been brought up in a family," the fourth-generation de Gaspé Beaubien told me, "where the next generation isn't allowed to piss it away."

The summit managed to bring together the two provincial environment ministers, Quebec's David Heurtel and Ontario's Glen Murray. The two ministers announced the establishment of a Joint Committee on Water Management, which will see the country's two most populous provinces—too often ships passing in the night when it comes to co-operation—work together to protect the Ottawa River, the Great Lakes and the St. Lawrence River.

Mayor Jim Watson of Ottawa and Mayor Maxime Pedneaud-Jobin of Gatineau announced the Gatineau Declaration at the summit, recognizing that "government, business and civil society all have a stewardship role to play in solving our water challenges and that raising the level of awareness and understanding of water protection issues is essential."

The Ottawa, declared Bernadette Conant, executive director of the Canadian Water Network, should become "the cleanest, most livable river in Canada."

Some would prefer to see dramatic action. Environmental analyst Daniel Brunton, a co-founder of Ottawa Riverkeeper, wants to free the rapids by tearing up the dams. The rapids, he said, "are the lungs of the river. We don't float logs down the river any more—get rid of them." That's not likely to happen soon, but water quality in the river could certainly be improved.

A year after the summit, in the fall of 2016, the city of Ottawa, province of Ontario and federal government committed $232 million toward an action plan that includes a massive storage-tunnel project that would prevent raw sewage from entering the river after major rainstorms. After one storm in 2006, a gate at the city's wastewater-treatment plant malfunctioned and remained open for two weeks, sending waste directly into the river. Three years later there were nearly four hundred "overflow events"; in 2015 that number had dwindled to eighty. The new improvements are intended to reduce overflows by another 20 percent.

"The Action Plan is a great step forward in cleaning up the river," says Finkelstein, who also attended the summit. "Reducing the raw sewage going into the river means that it is no longer the 'Big Flush' for the city of Ottawa."

But, he adds, "that's only one slice of a cleaned-up Ottawa River, and the easiest one to achieve." In his opinion, it has to be much more than the city of Ottawa buying in. Commitment from Quebec is equally essential if one day the river is going to live up to his dream:

> For me, a clean river means dipping my cup over the side of my canoe and having a cool refreshing drink of Ottawa River water like the First Nations peoples and the voyageurs and explorers and fur traders did not so long ago. It means making the Ottawa the healthiest river to run through any national capital in the world.
>
> All this is achievable. All of it once was . . . and can be again. We just have to get off our butts, and decide what our values and priorities are—and what legacy we want to leave to our children and grandkids.
>
> I hope we choose well.

Choices abound. Sewage treatment remains a major concern along the Ottawa River, as does the possibility of an oil-pipeline leak, as happened in the summer of 2016 to the North Saskatchewan River upstream from Prince Albert. The National Energy Board (NEB), an independent regulatory board that dates back to 1959, had repeatedly expressed concerns about the Trans-Northern Pipeline, jointly owned by Imperial Oil, Royal Dutch Shell and Suncor. In the fall of 2016, the aging pipeline, which can carry up to 172,900 barrels of refined fuel products a day, was ordered to reduce its operating pressure by 10 percent and improve its safety practices. Two members of the NEB—there are currently eighteen members of the NEB, ten of them designated "temporary"—protested the decision, not because the pipeline was ordered to reduce its flow, but because it was allowed to continue at all. "We are not confident that yet another similar Safety Order will guarantee that the changes necessary to make the pipeline as safe as possible will actually be made this time," they announced in a dissenting opinion.

Oil spills and pipeline breaks are serious issues that can be seen and dealt with as effectively as possible. Other serious concerns are invisible to the human eye: microplastics. These miniature (less than five millimetres in size) plastic fragments, fibres and extremely small beads do not break down. They come from the deterioration of larger plastics, but those are far from the only sources. Synthetic clothing is a major culprit, releasing hundreds of fibres into the sewers with every wash. Soaps, toothpaste and other personal care products carry these troublesome bits of plastic into the river as well. Ocean studies have found that when microbeads of plastic are ingested by, for example, oysters, production is dramatically reduced. There is relatively little data on the effect of microplastics on freshwater life, but early research has found that such bottom-feeders as catfish ingest them, as do freshwater snails, an important food source for many fish. Various plastics carry various chemicals. The microplastics may enter the food chain at the lowest levels but they quickly work their way up through the chain to human consumption.

In 2015, the United States banned the use and sale of microbeads in personal care products. The Canadian government has declared microbeads "toxic" but as of 2017 has yet to move into a full ban.

In the fall of 2016, Dr. Meaghan Murphy of Ottawa Riverkeeper and Dr. Jesse Vermaire of Carleton University compiled a report on microplastics in the Ottawa River. They and volunteers took samples from locations spanning more than 550 kilometres of the river and found that microplastic pollution levels were higher than found in some ocean studies and, surprisingly, similar to levels found in major European rivers, which are more extensively populated and industrialized. More significantly, researchers found the concentrations sixteen times higher directly downstream from the city of Ottawa's sewage treatment plant, meaning the plant is a significant source of microbead pollution in the river.

Dr. Murphy, Ottawa Riverkeeper's staff scientist, said, "It is worrying how widespread this type of pollution really is and how little we actually know of the long-term impacts on river health and human health."

For all the worrisome things finding their way into the Ottawa River, numerous small success stories are appearing up and down its watershed, too. Waste management systems have been built in communities along the Quebec side that previously lacked such facilities, and while the situation is far from perfect, it has improved.

North of Mattawa, there is a large body of water known as Lac la Cave that was created in the late 1940s by the construction of a dam and generating station. The area remains quite wild and isolated, with few camps and cottages along the shores. Those who first built there found the water murky from logging and garbage along the shores left by weekend fishermen. Today, with logging no longer a river issue, more attention paid to weekend visitors and keen riverwatchers doing regular sampling, the water is significantly cleaner. The river's own "flushing" ability has been critical to the cleansing. "Over the past fifty years," says Catherine Fortin, whose family has summered in a rustic cabin there since the early 1960s, "we've seen first-hand how this portion of the river has healed itself."

Further downstream, at Quyon, the old fuel-driven ferries have been replaced by a brand-new cable ferry that runs on fourteen large, rechargeable batteries—charged on the Quebec side, where hydro electricity is much cheaper—and can carry far more vehicles across in about half the time.

Pilot Eddie Scott, who has completed approximately a hundred thousand crossings over the three decades he has guided the seasonal ferry, says there is one huge advantage the new ferry has over all the previous ones: "No pollution."

But Judith Flynn-Bedard still won't let her grandchildren swim in the river near the Montebello marina where she keeps her boat. Not so long as she sees evidence of raw sewage in the waters.

"I'm still seeing 'floaties' when I dive," says Gord Black, whose Bristol, Quebec, company, Logs End, produces wide-plank flooring from two-hundred-year-old logs that sank to the bottom of the river during the heyday of the timber trade.

There remains a great deal of work to be done. And just perhaps, while they're fixing the river, they might consider turning Champlain's astrolabe right side up.

CHAPTER THREE

RISING FROM THE DEAD: THE DON

IT WAS CANADA'S "POTEMKIN" MOMENT.

It was the summer of 1958 and Princess Margaret was nearing the end of an extensive Royal Tour of Canada. Her well-covered travels even included British media speculation that the glamorous twenty-seven-year-old sister of the Queen had fallen for the handsome young Montreal lawyer John Turner, future prime minister of Canada, with whom she had danced and talked long into the night at a ball given at the naval base on Vancouver's Deadman's Island.

She had now come to Toronto, where a cancer treatment centre would take her name and where she would gather with schoolchildren across town from the hospital at the much more scenic Riverdale Park. Her specially outfitted railway car would be parked at the side of the Don River and she would have to cross over to the park via a footbridge.

The Don, the *Globe and Mail* editorialized on July 30, 1958, had "waters heavily polluted and laden with scum, its banks littered with all varieties of filth, and the whole sending up foul odours."

The Royal Nose must not be allowed to sniff disapprovingly while on a tour of the colony. Not with the British press recording every moment of the Royal Tour. The city of Toronto had been scrambling. City crews had been sent out to clean up the banks, painters to give the bridge a fresh coat. *What*, however, were they going to do about *the stink*?

The solution in this time long before David Suzuki or environmental impact studies was simple: mask the smell. The city poured in chlorine and, according to several reports, gallons and gallons of *perfume* upstream, perfectly timed to be carried by the slow current to the park area just as the Princess was crossing over the bridge.

The *Globe* compared the plan to Prince Gregory Alexandrovitch Potemkin's eighteenth-century deception of Catherine II of Russia, when the governor of the Crimea built fake village facades, cleaned and freshly painted existing buildings and ordered the peasants to clean up themselves and be smiling, happy and waving as the Empress travelled through the depressed region in her royal carriage.

The *Toronto Daily Star*, not to be outdone, published an editorial decrying the attempt to "sweeten the atmosphere that Her Highness may not learn how Toronto has befouled one of its beauty spots." The newspaper compared the plan to "courtiers waving handkerchiefs dipped in perfume before the nostrils of the king of France as he drove through the tenements of Paris, that his majesty's nostrils might not be offended by the odor from the open drains."

"The fact that this deception at the Don is necessary," railed the *Globe*, "is a disgrace to Toronto and to this Province. The river should be cleaned up in fact; and not just for a day, but for good."

Nothing, of course, was done. The Princess's official visit was a resounding success, the schoolchildren delighted and the air at Riverdale Park strangely sweet—for a few hours.

Jennifer Bonnell, an urban historian at York University, captures the sad fate of this river that bisects Canada's largest, busiest city in her belief that the Don River has been the "most-messed-with river" in Canada.

It is difficult to imagine today, but long before Muskoka was packed with expensive summer homes, the Don River was what Torontonians called "cottage country." The original "cottager" was Elizabeth Posthuma Gwillim Simcoe, wife of John Graves Simcoe, first lieutenant-governor of Upper Canada.

Elizabeth liked her creature comforts. She may have once been a Welsh orphan but she had inherited two family fortunes before marrying Simcoe. He was thirty-one, she only sixteen. He had fought for Britain in the American War of Independence—commanding the unit that burned down Richmond, Virginia—and had since been sent to the remaining colony to build Fort York. This new lieutenant-governor named the nearby river the Don, as he said it reminded him of the River Don in South Yorkshire, England.

The strong-willed Elizabeth grew to hate the muggy summers of muddy York. She first sought relief from the irrepressible heat by taking to the little peninsula that would later form the Toronto Islands, and here she ordered so many brush fires set to ward off the mosquitoes that other residents began to regard her as a threat to the community. The bugs, she claimed, made it impossible for her to do her small watercolours and intricate pen-and-ink drawings, and it was this passion for breezy spaces and new landscape that took her farther afield than perhaps the wife of the fort commander was expected to wander.

In the mid-1790s, Elizabeth convinced her husband to build her a summer home in the "north country." She chose a bluff overlooking a deep, wide valley and its narrow, pastoral Don River, roughly where subway riders today find the Castle Frank stop on the Bloor line. Here they built a log home, complete with gaudy Grecian columns, that the Simcoes named after their youngest son, Francis; hence, Castle Frank.

John Graves and Elizabeth Simcoe stayed only four years in what would become Toronto. Their little daughter Katherine, only fifteen months of age, was buried just outside the walls of Fort York in the spring of 1794, and by 1796 the Simcoes were once again back to England. Poor Francis, the namesake of the first regal "cottage" in Canada, was killed in action fighting for England in the Peninsular War, and John Graves himself died in 1806, just prior to taking up his new and much-longed-for appointment as governor general of India.

Elizabeth's heart, however, remained on that bluff overlooking the Don River. Her final "Canadian" entry in her diary, dated July 21, 1796, sounds very much like a Labour Day lament from "cottage country" two centuries on: "I was so much out of spirits. I could not eat, cried all the day."

What happened to the Don that so captured the affection of some-one so refined and particular as Elizabeth Simcoe? In her highly readable 2014 environmental history of the river and valley, *Reclaiming the Don*, Professor Bonnell shows how this river, once so prized for its beauty, its mouth once blessed with one of the largest marshlands in Lake Ontario, saw that lovely mouth twisted and recast, its meandering route straightened for convenience, its tributaries paved and built over and often lost, its water fouled to the point where, twice, the river caught fire.

"It's a total buried story," says Bonnell, who came across the fire reports in the city's Port Authority archives. "It's in the newspapers but it doesn't warrant any front-page mention. It was completely buried. When rivers were catching fire in the nineteen-thirties and forties it was just considered the cost of doing business. It's like, 'Oh, well.'"

The Don River eventually became the Canadian poster child for water pollution, just as Ohio's Cuyahoga River, which dramatically caught fire in 1969, became the symbol for what had gone wrong with America's waterways. No amount of perfume could mask the reality of the appalling, stinking Don.

In the fall of 1969, a couple of hundred mourners paraded a casket from the University of Toronto grounds to the banks of the Don. The cortège included a "hearse," a band playing a dirge, a weeping widow in black and a pie in the face for a top-hatted student portraying a greedy capitalist.

Monte Hummel, now president emeritus of WWF-Canada, was a key player in that parade. Earlier in the summer of 1969, Hummel had spent his honeymoon at Woodstock—he's the "hippie" organizing the famous mudslide in the 1970 movie of the musical event—and then loaded his canoe on a Volkswagen to continue the honeymoon in Northwestern Ontario. At Whitedog Falls near Kenora, he found signs advising people to "Fish for Fun." So polluted had the waters of the Winnipeg River become from mercury poisoning that the fish were inedible. It was a moment that changed his life and would, eventually, set his career.

Hummel returned to the University of Toronto, where he was finishing up a master's degree in philosophy. Along with zoology professor Don Chant, he helped found Pollution Probe at University of Toronto, soon to be known more widely as Pollution Probe. They decided to focus on the nearby Don River, which Hummel says was "pretty disgusting" at the time.

Pollution Probe then came up with the idea—"It wasn't mine," says Hummel—of holding their "funeral" for the Don River. Meredith Ware, an arts student, played the role of Elizabeth Simcoe and read excerpts from Simcoe's diary. The diary spoke of loons on the water surface, salmon below, with the waters "beautifully clear and transparent."

Another student, Tony Barrett, played the cigar-chomping, top-hatted capitalist who kept shouting things like, "That's the smell of money! What's wrong with you people?"

"People do these things all the time now," says Hummel, "but back then this was a new idea—it hadn't been done before. There was no Ministry of the Environment then. There was no Environmental Protection Act. 'Pollution' was seen as akin to 'communism.' This whole notion that you could kill a river had never been thought of before. There was a poignant message that rose above the street theatre."

It did indeed, the Sunday afternoon parade along College Street capturing the attention of the media.

"They finally had a funeral for the Don River yesterday," the *Toronto Telegram* reported the following day. "Judging from the smell of the 'deceased,' it was long overdue."

The Don River runs in two branches from its headwaters in the Oak Ridges Moraine, about forty kilometres north of the city. The branches merge about three-quarters of the way down to form the Lower Don, which travels alongside the Don Valley Parkway until it empties into Lake Ontario. There are several tributaries along its length, including German Mills Creek, Taylor-Massey Creek, Wilket Creek and Burke Brook.

The Don was obviously not always "heavily polluted and laden with scum." First Nations traders found it a perfect encampment, the waters clean and the game and fish plentiful. And the fish remained plentiful long after the arrival of the first Europeans and the early growth of the community known as York and then Toronto. There was even a time in the 1800s when the prisoners at the nearby jail protested because they were being fed too much fresh salmon from its waters.

Naturalist Charles Sauriol (1904–1995) spent more than four decades as a cottager on the Don and wrote six books on the watershed. As a youngster, he said, the Don "was a wilderness at our door, an escape from home, school, discipline . . . which held everything a red blooded nature loving boy could ask for." Sauriol titled his 1982 memoir *Remembering the Don*, perhaps because by then the "escape" was memory only.

In her research, Bonnell discovered that the Don Valley was considered a paradise to early beekeepers. In going through the records of the Ontario Beekeeping Association from the late 1800s, she found that the valley was often sown with clover to produce sweeter-tasting honey and that the beekeepers were the first group to raise concerns about the health of the watershed.

"They were interested in environmental change because it was in their economic interest to do so," she says. "They were among the first to speak out against insecticide poisoning. They spoke out against roadside spraying."

But by then, of course, the Don River was quickly becoming a lost cause.

York had become Toronto and was spreading rapidly. The river offered the perfect locations for early grist and timber mills, then tanneries, brick works, chemical factories, oil refineries and the growing city's increasingly busy port. During the First World War, a massive garbage incinerator was built on the banks of the Don, spewing smoke for more than half a century as it burned fifty thousand tonnes of trash a year. Throughout the Don Valley ravines were used for the disposal of industrial refuse, rainwater running through that landfill and into the river at the valley's bottom.

The Don watershed stands today as the most urbanized watershed in Canada, with 1.2 million people living within it and 96 percent of the catchment area "urbanized," almost entirely built up or paved over. "Over the past 200 years," writes Bonnell, "almost all of the significant wetlands within the watershed have been drained or filled to support urban development. The six tributaries of the lower river have mostly disappeared, buried by fill or encased within sewage infrastructure."

The river and valley were once considered prime locations for such structures as the colony's first government building. Simcoe had York's first Upper Canada Parliament built on what is today known as Parliament Street, the first major street west of the waterway. Gradually, however, the location became the place for necessary structures that the establishment might prefer a distance away. In a time of fears over cholera and malaria, the hospital was relocated from the city centre to the Don. An asylum followed, then a shelter and reformatory for the poor and vagrants—"idiots," as well. The Toronto Jail and Industrial Farm (better known as the Don Jail) opened near the asylum.

Bonnell believes the best way to regard the Don Valley in those days is as a "frontier of sorts," a place for the homeless, small-time crooks and other "undesirables" who enjoyed its growing reputation for lawlessness.

The valley became overrun with gangs, the most notorious being the Brooks' Bush Gang. In late 1859, John Sheridan Hogan, a highly respected citizen of Toronto, set out to cross the Don in order to visit a friend. Hogan vanished, not seen again until a decomposing body wearing his clothes was found sixteen months later by duck hunters. As there was neither money nor papers to be found in the clothes, foul play was suspected. The Brooks' Bush Gang was rounded up.

One of them told police that gang member Jane Ward had done in Hogan with a heavy stone she carried in a handkerchief and that Ward and accomplice James Brown had dumped the body over a bridge near Kingston Road after stripping Hogan of his money and topcoat.

Ward, however, was acquitted, while Brown was sentenced to

hang. His sentencing led to the first serious debate—including the presentation of a petition—on capital punishment. It was to no avail, though, as Brown was hanged on March 10, 1862.

In tracing the history of the river, what Bonnell found "most striking . . . was the Don's slippage in the eyes of Toronto's civic leaders from a place of relative importance to a place widely perceived, by the mid-nineteenth century, as polluted, dangerous, and disease-ridden."

Considered worthy only of industry, the Don River had no one speaking for it in the late 1880s when City Council agreed with a pitch by the Canadian Pacific Railway to straighten the river so the railway could have a convenient corridor into and out of the city. Ironically, that initiative was called "The Don Improvement Project." In the 1960s, more changes were made to the river's course to accommodate the construction of the Don Valley Parkway (DVP), the city's main commuter route. While it could be said that the DVP follows the course of the river, it could be equally argued that the river now follows the course of the DVP.

"The Don once curved in an interesting way down toward the lake," says Arlen Leeming, project manager of the Don and Highlands Watersheds for the Toronto and Region Conservation Authority (TRCA), "but they said, 'We know better, and what we're going to do is straighten it and have a straight shot right out into the lake and we're going to get rid of all that water and crap and not have to worry about it.'

"Basically they built a runway for water, a 'Slip'N Slide' right down the valley to the lake."

The view of the city from the Toronto Islands is nothing less than spectacular on a fine summer's day. There are no traffic sounds, no streetlights, no streetcars, subways or electric hum of a major city.

There is only the stillness that more than two centuries ago Elizabeth Simcoe found here and far up the nearby Don River.

Nearby?

The Don is nowhere to be seen. All that Arlen Leeming can do from his kayak is point with his paddle to show where it once was, where it now is—and where it will soon be.

"You see those lakers over there?" he asks, pointing to two huge tankers anchored at port, two of the roughly eighty massive ships that call each year. "And you see where the covered tennis courts are? That's going to be the 'new' mouth of the Don."

The cost, he says, is estimated at nearly $1 billion. It is all part of a massive, hugely expensive flood-protection plan that is also intended to transform 125 hectares around the mouth and Keating Channel, which connects the Don to Toronto Harbour, into parklands and mixed-use residential neighbourhoods. Flooding along the nine rivers that make their way through the Greater Toronto Area (GTA) has long been a concern, most dramatically in 1954, when eighty-one people lost their lives during Hurricane Hazel. The high waters generated by the "Frankenstorm" of 2012 (Hurricane Sandy) made it very clear there are still serious flood concerns in the GTA.

When the TRCA prepared its "report card" on the Don River watershed in 2013, stormwater management was given a resounding "F." Only 23 percent of the watershed had stormwater quality and quantity controls in place, with the best controls in the more recently developed Upper West Don and Upper East Don and the worst where they are oldest, in the city of Toronto.

The object of the Lower Don redevelopment plan, apart from the obvious flood protection, is to create "an iconic identity for the Don River"—words that date from a 2007 announcement by Waterfront Toronto that an international competition would be held to come up with a "world-class" plan for the river.

Some see it as a long-overdue "apology" to the poor Don.

As of early 2017, actual work had yet to begin. While basic design for the project had been completed and the environmental assessment had been approved, dates for start and completion had still to be determined. The finished project remains years away. Once again, the Don River is being reconfigured—though for the first time with the river itself being a prime consideration.

"The Don River is a story of resilience and a story of nature's refusal to ever give up," says Leeming. "The Don embodies that. It's a river that no matter what you throw at it, no matter what you do to it, no matter how many chemicals you put down it, no matter how many buildings you put on it, no matter whether you channelize it, it will never give up.

"It will find a way."

The notion of restoring the Don took hold in a 1989 public forum at the Ontario Science Centre, where five hundred people met and, later, created the Task Force to Bring Back the Don, a citizen advisory body to Toronto City Council. They hoped to make the river "clean, green, and accessible" and conducted riverbank cleanups and tree plantings and helped restore or create more than a half-dozen wetlands.

When Rob Ford became mayor of Toronto in 2010, he disbanded a number of advisory bodies, including the Bring Back the Don group. But it did not stop those involved from continuing to fight for its restoration.

For twenty-three years and counting, the annual Manulife Paddle the Don event has been held to raise awareness and funds—as of 2016 more than $600,000—to support education programs. A second "paddle" was part of the Canadian Water Summit held in Toronto in June 2016. "In Canada," Amarjeet Sohi, federal minister of Infrastructure and Communities, told the gathering, "we cannot begin to speak about improving the quality of life without improving the quality of water."

Canoeist Max Finkelstein's dream of one day drinking from the Ottawa River is far from anyone's wish list for the Don. The TRCA's own report card most recently listed the water quality throughout the watershed as "very poor," awarding it an "F" grade. The remaining forests in this once tree-rich valley were also deemed "poor" and given a "D" grade. Groundwater quality in the watershed, however, was said to be "good," with the best water found, not surprisingly, in the Oak Ridges Moraine, the source of the Don. If the river can be cleaned up as it flows south, good water will follow.

Of the greatest remaining problems downstream—with other rivers as well as the Don—is sewage pollution when the system overflows. While *E. coli* levels are usually under the maximum provincial accepted standards, the levels spike after heavy rains. The city has found that hundreds of home sewage systems have been incorrectly connected to storm sewers rather than sanitary sewers. In much older sections, both wastes go into a combined sewer system.

Lake Ontario Waterkeeper, an environmental advocacy group, found that out of 166 water samples collected from Toronto's harbour in the summer of 2016, one-third failed to meet federal standards for safe boating and paddling. Toronto beaches are regularly closed following storms.

Some $485 million has already been spent on stormwater management. According to the website Torontoist.com, Toronto Water's ten-year capital plan, taking the city to 2026, has budgeted $3 billion for stormwater management. And $2.8 billion will be spent over the next ten years on an implementation plan that includes downspout disconnections, construction of stormwater ponds and a basement-flooding protection program. Of specific import to the Don River and the city waterfront at the mouth of the river, Council in 2006 okayed a twenty-five-year, $1.5-billion project, which will be funded by the three levels of government and is intended to revitalize the area.

"From a funeral for the Don," says Mr. Leeming, "where they literally brought a casket down to the side of the river, to the revitalization that has occurred since then, the health of the river today is tremendously better than it was back in the sixties."

"There is a patch of green there now that is an inheritance of that day when we had the funeral," says Hummel. "We were right. We were bang on. It was an extremely effective campaign."

"The Don represents hope for me," adds Leeming. "It represents hope for the future of the Toronto region. It represents hope for re-establishing Canadians' connection to the natural environment. A lot of people that grow up and live in an urban region as populated and dense as Toronto lose touch with their connection to the environment. The Don is their ticket to re-establishing that."

Today, there are salmon in the river. Perhaps one day Atlantic salmon will again run the waters and spawn upstream. And in the spring of 2016, much to the surprise and delight of those who believe this much-abused river can come back, a family of mink was spotted playing along the banks of the Lower Don.

Forty-seven years after its "funeral," there was new birth along the Don River, new hope for the future of Canada's most urban river.

CHAPTER FOUR

"SYMBOL OF LIFE": THE MIGHTY FRASER

THEY CALL IT SEARCH AND RESCUE, but it's really Search and Retrieve—and even that doesn't happen every time the Fraser River sucks a human down into its hydraulic trap of rolling currents and undertow.

Some bodies are never found.

Barry "Icon" Gannon has been volunteering with Search and Rescue in Hope, British Columbia, for thirty-one years and, apart from a fly fisher who fell in one day right in front of where they were launching the volunteer group's jet boat, he has no recollection of their ever actually saving anyone.

Those unfortunate enough to fall or jump into the Fraser River upstream from this little mountain town that was the setting for the Sylvester Stallone movie *First Blood* don't have a chance. Not even John Rambo himself could make it through the Fraser Canyon, a stretch of water so treacherous that back in 1808 the river's namesake, explorer Simon Fraser, called it a place "where no human being should venture for surely we have encountered the gates of hell."

Gannon and two other volunteers—Troy Leech and Jim Lasser—are out for an early spring-training run in the Search and Rescue 435-horsepower jet boat. In the weeks ahead, the freshets from the surrounding mountains will raise the Fraser's water level another storey or more and make a tourist attraction of the canyon and its world-famous Hell's Gate. In this thirty-five-metre wide chasm, the river can run more than a hundred and fifty metres deep, with more than fifteen million litres pounding through per second. Visitors tend to stare down and shudder at the thought.

Even on this day, in low season, the boat is tossed about like a Poohstick in the current. During a forty-kilometre practice run the heavy steel boat grinds over newly formed shoals and bounces off a drifting log as it wrestles through rapids and strong current. At one point Lasser, the driver, completes a "gypsy turn"—all but standing the jet boat on its nose as he spins it in an instant from heading north to heading south.

Later, while moving slowly down the wider, calmer river below Hope, the three men talk at length about their deep love for the Fraser. They mark their calendars by the salmon runs, brag about the size of the sturgeon, marvel at the river's spectacular beauty that seems only to increase the higher one goes into the mountains, and they stand in awe of its power and how quickly and certainly it can take a human life.

"It's a job I wouldn't do for pay," says Leech. "I would never make that an occupation, what I do with the rescue team. But when I realized there wasn't anybody doing it, that's when I joined the group and started doing it as a volunteer."

"We lost lots of people and they were never recovered," says Albert "Sonny" McHalsie, cultural adviser at the Stó:lō Nation offices in Chilliwack, some fifty kilometres downstream from Hope.

"They're still down there."

Several times a year, the Hope volunteer group heads out in the jet boat to scout the shores and eddies for victims that drowned and later escaped the undertows to surface in the quieter waters. The rescue group's small victories come in finding the bodies. "It brings closure to the families," says Lasser. "Somebody's got to do it. We do it for the families."

On up the river the jet boat roars, past the jutting points where First Nations families set their fishing nets and wind-dry their catch on roughly fashioned racks, past the various "bars" where, in 1858, the Fraser River Gold Rush turned the shores into tent cities, past looming Lady Franklin Rock at Yale, so named for the widow of the lost Arctic explorer Sir John Franklin. Just ahead, the mouth of the treacherous Fraser Canyon stares us down.

Still bouncing off swells and twisting between whirlpools, the jet boat spins and turns back within sight of the churning rapids that, farther upstream, include Hell's Gate.

The rescue volunteers do not enter the actual canyon.

"What's the point?" says Gannon. "You're only collecting bodies, anyway."

Fin Donnelly had the craziest idea: he would *swim* the length of the Fraser River. And five years later, he would do it again.

Donnelly would be tackling what has been called "one of the world's great rivers," a river that begins more than 1,000 metres above sea level, near Fraser Pass on the Continental Divide, and runs 1,368 kilometres to Richmond, B.C., where it empties into the Strait of Georgia.

"Nobody can imagine what the river is like unless he has seen it with his own eyes," author Hugh MacLennan believed, "for there is nothing else resembling it on this continent, and I doubt if there is anything else resembling it in the world."

MacLennan thought the Fraser as significant to Canada as the St. Lawrence. Legendary B.C. journalist Bruce Hutchison claimed that the Fraser River had essentially created the province of British Columbia. Its importance to both British Columbia and Canada is undeniable. It is not by accident that it is so often referred to as "The Mighty Fraser."

From its source in the mountains beyond Prince George, the Fraser twists and tumbles down through vast tracts of wilderness and deep canyons, as well as past small communities like Quesnel, Williams Lake, Lillooet, Lytton, Boston Bar, Yale and Hope. Below Hope it flattens out and grows placid, the silt the river has carried from the B.C. interior forming broad deltas and creating some of the finest agricultural land in the world.

The river passes through much larger centres—Chilliwack, Abbotsford, Langley, Surrey, New Westminster—and forks north and south around the "island" of Richmond, by which point the Fraser is dominated by ports, cranes, ocean shipping, towering bridges, railway tracks and the industrial sprawl that spreads up the coast to Vancouver.

"The Fraser River became the economic spine of the province, linking population centres with the resources that fuelled the economy," Richard C. Bocking wrote in *Mighty River: A Portrait of the Fraser.* "The economy of the province flows in its current, and its many watersheds provide the settings within which communities are organized. Towns and cities owe their location and prosperity to the Fraser and its resources."

As Iona Campagnolo, a former federal cabinet minister who served as chair of the Fraser River Basin Council, once so eloquently put it, "Rivers have slaked our thirst, fed our hunger, fuelled our machines, cleansed our bodies, guided our travels, inspired our intellects, spirits and cultures, enriched our heritage, and from the beginning of time have generously poured their wealth into our pockets." She could have been talking about the Fraser alone.

Given that roughly two-thirds of the population of British Columbia lives along the Fraser and its tributaries, Fin Donnelly decided if he could swim the river he might draw some necessary attention to its fragility. The notion of anyone swimming down the Fraser River, however, was unthinkable to many.

According to Stephen Hume's superb biography of the river's namesake, Simon Fraser's suggestion that he and his men would descend the river was met with incredulity by the Natives Fraser's party encountered near the source. They warned that "the river below was but a succession of falls and cascades, which we should find impossible to pass, not only thro the badness of the channel, but also thro the badness of the surrounding country, which was rugged and mountainous. Their opinion, therefore, was that we should discontinue our voyage and remain with them."

Fraser and his men did descend the river, though several times they came within a heartbeat of disaster, including one of the four canoes being smashed to pieces in one of the many rapids. With the help of Nlaka'pamux guides and undertaking some of the most arduous portages imaginable—including makeshift ladders and bridges to move through the canyons—the Europeans finally did make it down to the flatter grounds and quieter waters. It was not, however, an easy paddle from there to the sea—as they were now in the country of several warring Indigenous groups.

The Musqueam, Stó:lō and Cowichans all held territory in the Fraser Delta and often fought. The Kwakwaka'wakw and Haida raided villages along the river in search of slaves. "The Indians advised us not to advance any further," Fraser wrote of the first group he encountered, "as the natives of the coast or Islanders were at war with them, being very malicious, and will destroy us."

Fraser pushed on, however, using whatever guides would agree to lead him. Aside from the guides' fear of being caught in someone else's wars, many believed Fraser and his men—some red-haired and blue-eyed like him—to be supernatural creatures from high up the river and looked on the Europeans with fear and suspicion. Fraser had trouble even procuring canoes. Finally he made it to the coast, stayed a short while, and then retreated back up the river to the relative safety of the foothills. He would report back to the North West Company that the route was unpassable.

"He had just led his expedition 800 kilometres over terrain that would challenge the abilities of the best-trained military Special Forces unit today," writes Hume. "For most of us, his accomplishments would simply be impossible. He completed his mission from present day Prince George to present day Vancouver and back in 71 days. He talked his men out of a near-disastrous mutiny when things appeared most bleak and brought every man for whom he was responsible home safely, negotiated the support of powerful Indian nations and, despite circumstances fraught with threats of violence, killed not one enemy."

Fraser continued on despite the perils and, nearly two centuries later, Donnelly found similar resolve. He was, after all, a competitive long-distance swimmer, first with a local club in New Westminster, then for the University of Victoria swim team. In the 1980s he was doing two ten-kilometre workouts a day in the university pool. He was also becoming deeply engaged in environmental concerns, first with the "War of the Woods" that was ongoing over clear-cutting timber. Inspired by Terry Fox's Marathon of Hope and convinced that humanity was "on a collision course," he was determined to wake people up to the importance of sustainability.

In 1995, when he was twenty-nine years old, Donnelly swam the river in a wetsuit from Prince George to its mouth, even tackling some of the rapids, though he wisely elected to get through Hell's

Gate with the help of one of the river-rafting companies. When he swam, he stayed about one hundred metres back of his support team moving slowly ahead by raft. It took him twenty-one days, twenty of which were spent in the water. Five years later, he began his swim farther upstream and, over four weeks, spent twenty-five days in the water.

His intent was merely to "start the conversation" about the river, about water quality and sustainability. It worked, prompting some 120 news articles about his crusade and scores of radio and television interviews as he travelled down the river.

"In the first swim," he says, "I had to deal with pulp effluent and raw sewage. I got sick just south of Quesnel at a time when part of the community was dumping raw sewage. Not only could I taste it but I could smell it—and sometimes see it. The river was a chemical soup."

Five years later he found "some real, tangible improvements." Matters had improved, though not nearly so much or so quickly as Donnelly and others were hoping. So after his second swim, friends urged him to run for local council. Donnelly never thought he would become involved in electoral politics, but he did, and he won, and won again. In 2009, he ran as the New Democratic Party candidate in a federal by-election for the riding of New Westminster–Coquitlam. He won, and was still winning as of October 19, 2016—the riding now known as Port Moody–Coquitlam—and today serves as the NDP critic for fisheries, oceans and the Canadian Coast Guard.

"I never thought I would end up here," he says of his office on Parliament Hill. "I was very pessimistic about making change."

Now fifty years old, Donnelly remains deeply committed to the cause that inspired his career. The Rivershed Society of British Columbia, which he founded in 1996, is dedicated to having people make sustainable lifestyle choices when living in sensitive areas like the Fraser River Basin.

Donnelly says he is not without hope—"If we can get it right. It will depend on decision makers and people around this community."

"The Fraser is a symbol of life," he adds. "It feeds life. It's a historical river—a heritage river—that allowed First Nations to survive and prosper along its banks and later allowed others to flourish and provide sustenance.

"It's also one of the best salmon rivers on the planet."

"It's a tough river."

So says Marvin Rosenau, a fisheries expert who teaches at the British Columbia Institute of Technology and has worked on the freshwater fisheries of B.C. for more than thirty-five years.

Dr. Rosenau was born in Chilliwack, where his grandfather settled in 1948, the year of the Fraser's Great Flood. An exceptional runoff that year flooded thousands of hectares in the Fraser Valley and carried away barns and houses and livestock. Bodies of bloated cows were found floating in the mustard-coloured smear that spread far out into the Strait of Georgia.

Every year, says the scientist, twenty million tonnes of sediment are carried out into the gulf. Canoeists ferrying across the river where its flow is strong say they can hear the silt rubbing like sandpaper along the ribs and bottom of their vessels. "Because the Fraser is such a muddy river," says Dr. Rosenau, "it frightens the daylights out of people. They don't know what's below the surface. It's scary."

But what is below the surface is one of the world's great salmon fisheries, with runs of five different species stretching from late spring through late fall. It is also home to 45,000 or 50,000 sturgeon, many of the dinosaur-era fish gigantic enough to attract sport fishers from around the world.

Dr. Rosenau witnessed first-hand the incredible powers of the

Fraser back in 1993, when he was aboard a jet boat on patrol so that he might count the number of dead sturgeon in the water and ascertain whether more or fewer were dying that year as compared to previous years. The boat flipped in the current, throwing those aboard out. All but one had life jackets on. His body was never found.

Because of work done by the likes of Dr. Rosenau and pressure applied by the likes of Fin Donnelly, the Fraser River fishery is today highly regulated. Hydro-acoustics and sonar along the river let scientists know what species are travelling in what numbers, thereby triggering commercial fishing in the lower reaches and, for the most part, ensuring that salmon reach upstream beyond Hope, where First Nations have the right to fish with gill nets and dip nets.

In the early 1900s, scientists believe, as many as sixty million sockeye salmon would enter the Fraser at spawning time. That run has diminished considerably, and some years looked as if it might not happen at all. The Stó:lō Nation has a chart of the 1997 catch, showing that Canadian commercial fishers took more than twelve million salmon, American commercial boats took more than three million and the Fraser River Aboriginal fishery caught just over one million—meaning commercial fisheries were taking more than 90 percent of the catch that once was the main source of food for the many First Nations along the waterway. Anthropologists believe that salmon was once so important here that people used to eat close to five hundred kilograms of the fish a year, a quantity now fallen to much less than half that figure.

Prior to 1913, salmon somehow powered their way upstream through Hell's Gate, but that year the salmon run came to an abrupt halt when a railroad construction crew thoughtlessly blasted tonnes of rocks into the canyon, thereby tightening the passage and increasing the flow to a point where the salmon could not get through. Millions of salmon died. More than two decades later, Canada and the

United States created the International Fishways and a "ladder" was constructed allowing the salmon to pass through a somewhat protected portion of the rapids.

As for the salmon farther downstream, a continuing concern of Dr. Rosenau and his colleagues is that many of the smaller tributaries along the lower Fraser have vanished as urbanization spreads. These streams were vital to salmon reproduction. He calculates that 20 percent of such streams have been lost forever, while 62 percent are endangered. "We need to get more [salmon] to their spawning grounds," he says.

With diminishing salmon runs, Dr. Rosenau says, public interest diminishes also. This he feels is unfortunate, as the Fraser River and Delta offer much more natural wealth than fish. The tidal flats around Richmond, he says, make this part of the river "one of the most important estuaries in the world" for birds.

"People don't really realize the treasure they have in this river," he says. "It's the pump, the battery, the juice that makes this whole eco-system go. We have to give it a chance."

In late summer of 2016, the Pacific Salmon Commission announced that the sockeye salmon run in the Fraser had fallen to its lowest level in 120 years—a situation the Watershed Watch Salmon Society feels is directly connected to climate change. Salmon like clean and cool water—between 5°C and 9°C is considered ideal. Water temperatures north of Hope were found to be between 2°C and 3°C higher than average for August.

And for all of Fin Donnelly's efforts, in the Fraser and in Parliament, the issue of pollution continues. In the fall of 2015, following provincial government permission for Taseko Mines to increase discharges at its copper mine near Williams Lake, Canadian water activist Maude Barlow took the provincial government to task: "In its Monty Python-esque explanation for allowing the increase, the B.C. government said that the Fraser River already has metals such as selenium, iron, lead, mercury, aluminum, copper, sulphates and nitrates, and these new discharges will be diluted so that, further along, the river will meet water quality guidelines. The Tsilhqot'in First Nation disagreed, saying the new effluents will further harm their fisheries and their inherent right to clean water."

A report card produced by WWF-Canada is hardly as optimistic as the provincial government. While the group rates the overall health of the river as "fair," the threats from pollution and habitat loss are deemed "high."

"The Fraser River has paid a high price for our comfort and prosperity," B.C. authors Alan Haig-Brown and Rick Blacklaws wrote in 1996. "Its health is in serious danger. We have poured into it mill effluents and other industrial waste, chemicals and super-nutrients from huge farms, and poorly treated sewage and chemical street runoff from towns and cities. We have contaminated the river's groundwater, throttled streams and tributaries with dams, choked waterways and fishways with waste from logging, and harmed the very surface of the river with air pollution.

"Fortunately, it is not too late to save the Fraser."

And yet it remains a continuing battle.

A year ago, while fishing on the river below Hope, Dr. Rosenau heard the sound of a backhoe at work. He made his way up a stream and came upon a small gold-mining operation. Once the Ministry of the Environment heard about the mine, it moved quickly to close down the operation.

"This isn't 1852," he says with a sigh of despair. "This is 2016."

The river that Simon Fraser descended and deemed impossible as a trading route eventually became a river that later "explorers" ascended in search of gold. Where they sought wealth I went looking for lunch, and found the Hope River General Store and Emory Bar RV Park at Emory Creek, about twenty kilometres upstream from Hope. Just a glance at the illustrated placemats told me what once was here: a "Map of the City of Emory."

In the late 1850s, gold was discovered at nearby Emory Bar and the rush was on. By 1858, twenty-five thousand prospectors had come to stake out their claims. That winter, five hundred men stayed over the winter in tents and a few hastily constructed shanties. When it seemed certain that Emory would become the western terminus for the Canadian Pacific Railway, plans were drawn up to build the new city. Planner envisioned thirteen streets, thirty-two blocks and four hundred lots. Emory, where the richest gold deposits along the Fraser were found, was soon on its way, with a sawmill, two hotels, nine saloons, a brewery and its share of "less reputable business."

Newcomers arrived first by packhorse, but soon enough there were paddlewheelers working the safe-passage waters of the Fraser. One steamboat, the *Skuzzy*, became the only such craft to make it through the Fraser Canyon to the upper waters. It was specially built for Andrew Onderdonk, a key contractor for the CPR, and his plan was to use it as a construction vehicle hauling freight between Lytton, one hundred kilometres north of Hope, and Boston Bar, another forty-five kilometres upstream, so it was built tough. It took several failed attempts, as well as the firing of two captains, before a third captain managed to make it through the canyon. He used a steam winch that ran between the steamboat's bow and various ring-bolts set in the rock cliffs, as well as 125 Chinese workers hauling on another line.

As an "end-of-steel" village, Emory could look forward to prosperity, but also to trouble. When a Western reporter visited one such place, Tête Jaune, in 1913, he reported that "An 'end-of-steel' village is made up of booze, billiards and belles. . . . An 'end-of-steel' village is a disgrace."

To "booze, billiards and belles" you could always add "belligerence," especially when it came to confrontations between the newcomers flooding into the region and the Indigenous tribes.

"Many of these new arrivals viewed Aboriginal people as natural impediments that had to be pushed aside like the earth and gravel hiding the river's gold," Keith Thor Carlson writes in *A Stó:lō–Coast Salish Historical Atlas*. "Cross-cultural interpersonal relationships, when they existed, were frequently disrespectful and abusive. Whisky was widely distributed, Stó:lō women were raped, and large-scale conflict erupted between Aboriginal men and organized regiments of American militia in the Fraser Canyon." In June 1858 Governor James Douglas wrote to the colonial secretary saying that skirmishes were breaking out because of "the jealousy of the savages, who naturally felt annoyed at the large quantities of gold taken from their country by the white miners." The Stó:lō placed no value on the metal but hugely valued the land and waters where they lived.

Prejudice has long found its unfortunate place along the Fraser River. In 1942, following the bombing of Pearl Harbor on December 7 of the previous year, people of Japanese origin were rounded up and sent to internment camps, often along the Fraser River watershed.

Discrimination was hardly new to the Japanese—they were called "undesirables," laws were passed to prevent them from voting and to prohibit them from holding certain jobs—but war, and press sensationalism, moved that contempt to new heights. The police impounded twelve hundred fishing boats—never to be returned to their rightful owners—and closed up schools. In February, Prime Minister William Lyon Mackenzie King issued orders-in-council to evacuate all persons of Japanese origin into "protective areas." By the time the rounding up was completed 20,881 people had been uprooted—13,309 of them Canadian citizens *by birth*.

In her lovely novel *Requiem*, author Frances Itani tells the story of Bin, an artist who spent the war years and longer at a Japanese internment camp along the Fraser and who found comfort in the calm and colours of the river. In his emotional return "home" after decades living in Ottawa, despite the incredible pain of coming again to where he was imprisoned as a child, he greets the river as if it were his friend: "And there it is. The deep canyon. The great Fraser River on my left, teeming with its own life, cutting its way through mountain, rock, soil, eroding as it flows."

That could well describe the river where Emory Creek still stands and where the City of Emory was intended to flourish but never did. By the early 1880s the CPR terminus was Yale, not Emory. By the 1890s not a trace of the "City of Emory" could be found. And Yale, which once had thirty thousand people—not to mention eighteen brothels— is now but a tiny dot on the map where tourists sometimes stop.

Kathy Hope, who runs the Hope River General Store & RV Park, would like to see more tourists stop by. "This is where the 'First Spike' was driven," she says of the area's rail history. "They always talk about the 'Last Spike'—but no one even thinks about the first."

The area boasts a museum and a national monument to Chinese railway workers and is trying to get the old church from Yale moved to new grounds. She points to a July 22, 1880, feature in the *Island Sentinel* that begins: "Emery's a 'booming'! Three steamers today— Hotel crowded—railroad tents all round—work at bridge and grading in earnest—parties after choice lots, etc."

"Boom town in gold rush—then ghost town," Hope says with a touch of resignation. "Boom town when the railroad came—then ghost town.

"I'm trying to make it a boom town again."

"We can't even spit in the river!" says an excited Sonny McHalsie.

The cultural affairs advisor and historian of Stó:lō Nation is talking about pollution and First Nations response to the delicate condition of the Fraser.

The sixty-year-old historian tells a Salish story that was handed down orally to his generation. It concerns a scourge of body sores—smallpox?—and how a boy became so despondent that he decided to kill himself. He walked into the Fraser north of Hope and slipped down through the currents to a people who lived under the water. They healed him and returned him with a message of personal hygiene that included no spitting.

"It's a cultural law," says McHalsie.

What others need to understand, he says, is that "Stó:lō" means his people and is also their name for the Fraser. "We are the river and the river is us."

That sentiment is captured in the foyer of the building where McHalsie works. A large mural by artist Stan Greene greets visitors, along with a framed statement by the artist that echoes the old story he told me himself: "We have always lived by the Stó:lō [Fraser River]. It has fed us for all time. It was our main highway. We are taught to respect the river. It has taken many lives. There is a story that came to me that when someone falls in the river and can't get out, they are taken to the bottom of the river. In a village far below lives a people and they will take care of the one who fell in. In the water they are in the human form. When they come out of the water, they are in the form of a sturgeon. There are no words that can be said to the family of the lost one. This story serves as a small medicine for them."

There are twenty-nine Stó:lō communities of various sizes along the length of the Fraser. Most First Nations have some involvement in the salmon fishery, but they, largely because of geography, stand in line waiting for the salmon to run the gauntlet of Canadian and

American commercial operations. Then they must compete for the salmon that do get through with those who come for the sport fishing, a situation that can lead to tensions.

"There are still lots of problems," says McHalsie. "The commercial industry gets to go out there first and that doesn't go down too well. Where is the conservation in the fish that go up the Fraser? It's last in line, I'm afraid. By the time First Nations gets to fish the salmon, they've already put big holes in the runs. We almost feel they time it deliberately. Where's the fish?"

McHalsie says much of the impetus for conservation has come from the Native population. "It was us who put the ban on sturgeon," he says. "It's strictly catch-and-release for the sport fishery. We only keep them if they happen to die in our nets."

Matters, however, have slowly improved. There is more consultation, more science applied to the opening and closing of the various salmon runs.

"I'd have to say that over the last few years they do have to connect with us."

The most impressive, and perhaps effective, connection has been made by the RCMP.

Back in 1997, Mountie Ed Hill and First Nations artist Roy Henry Vickers combined forces in an attempt to establish an addiction recovery centre for the province. Their "VisionQuest Canoe Journey" raised awareness, and funding, by paddling three large canoes down the Skeena River and along the coast to Victoria.

In 2001, Hill led the "Pulling Together Canoe Journey" of the big canoes from Hope, where he had long been posted, down the Fraser and into English Bay to Gibsons, where he is now retired from the RCMP and pursuing a new career as an artist. This journey was not to raise money for the addiction centre, but to ease tensions between police and First Nations, especially among the youth.

"We were talking 'reconciliation' long before it became vogue," Hill says. "You are touching a river that is more alive with culture than any river in Canada. We're all travelling together and learning together. The river is our teacher."

That first journey was so successful that a Pulling Together Canoe Society was formed and the canoe journeys have since become an annual event. The society's mission statement is "to enhance understanding between Public Service Agencies and Aboriginal Peoples by canoeing the traditional highway, strengthening our future relations."

The journeys began with five large canoes and a handful of ground crew to assist. Last year, with Hill now a participant but no longer an official with the society, there were twenty-five canoes in the trek and five hundred people involved.

RCMP constable Linda Blake serves as vice-president of the society. Of Métis heritage herself, she says the journeys have had a remarkable effect on First Nations youth: "They might find themselves quite surprised to be paddling in a canoe with a police officer—but when we began this we didn't really understand how powerful it could be. By day three you can actually feel a shift in the camp. Youth develop a sense of pride and an understanding of their culture. The police become more aware, more understanding."

Earl Moulton, another retired Mountie who, with his wife, Maureen, has helped organize Pulling Together journeys, says they have paddled into First Nations villages and seen elders openly weeping at the sight of the big canoes and the young paddlers.

Moulton was a key RCMP commander at the thirty-one-day Gustafsen Lake standoff in 1995, when four hundred Mounties were deployed to the B.C. interior after members of the Ts'Peten First Nation occupied ranchland that they declared was both sacred ground and unceded territory. The ugly confrontation ended without loss of life, but the open tensions Moulton saw between police and First Nations convinced him that something must be done to improve relations.

"When you see the distance we've travelled since," he says, "we've laid a lot of groundwork for change."

There remains much to be done, from cleaning up the river to ensuring that the sustainability Fin Donnelly swam for becomes reality. It is no small task, but then the Fraser is no small river.

"If you're on the Fraser during the freshet," says Moulton, "and if you put your ear to the top of your paddle with the blade still in the water, you can actually hear the big rocks being moved along the bottom by the force of the current. This river is always moving, always changing.

"You have to treat the Fraser with respect."

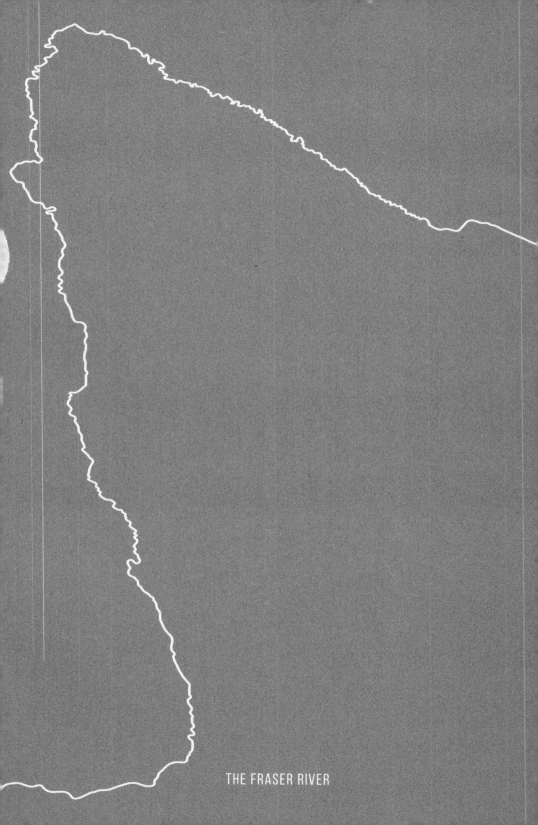

THE FRASER RIVER

CHAPTER FIVE

"WE ARE RED RIVER PEOPLE"

Come and sit by my side if you love me
Do not hasten to bid me a dieu
Just remember the Red River Valley
And the one who has loved you so true . . .

—"Red River Valley" (traditional)

JACQUES COURCELLES STANDS, HANDS ON HIPS, staring down from the top of the west bank of the Red River as it passes through the small Manitoba town of Ste. Agathe. It is April and the rust-coloured water is so low the scene would look like late August were it not for the buds on the ash and Manitoba maple trees across the river. The bank leading up to the early grass of spring looks like the thick hide of a hippopotamus, the red clay holding just enough water to glisten. Farther south, over the border into North Dakota and down Interstate 29 to Grand Forks, where so often this time of year the bad news begins, they are already talking drought.

Courcelles smiles: it's always something with the Red River.

If there is one thing a Courcelles has learned—from Jacques' own fifty-six years living on the banks; or from his parents, Jeanine and Albert, farming and raising their family here; or from his paternal grandparents, Eusèbe and Mathilde Courcelles, coming out from Quebec in the 1880s to homestead at Ste. Agathe—it is that you never know what the Red will do, so you had better be ready for anything.

Back in 1997, the muddy Red spilled onto the flat prairie like a glass of chocolate milk that a child has tipped over on the kitchen table. At one point the flood spanned forty kilometres wide by seventy-five kilometres long as it spread across southern Manitoba. Damages ran beyond $400 million as 25,000 people were forced to evacuate, leaving behind damaged and destroyed houses, barns and farm machinery. The Courcelles lost not one home but two along the west bank opposite the towering Catholic church. People called it "The Flood of the Century." (They would have called it "The Flood of the Millennium" . . . except it wasn't.)

The sign welcoming visitors to Ste. Agathe as they turn off Highway 75 says simply, "A Place to Call Home." Jacques Courcelles had to wonder about that back in 1997 as he faced the reality that his home, like his parents' home, was lost, the office where he ran his regional health-care business in ruins. But this is prairie country. As Louis L'Amour, the prolific writer from Jamestown, North Dakota, deep in the Red River Valley, once put it: "The sort of men and women it took to open the West were the kind of whom stories are told. Strongly individual, willing to risk all they possessed as well as their lives, they were also prepared to fight for what they believed was theirs."

"I live on this river," says Courcelles. "I grew up on it. Eighteen years ago, we had a choice—'Last one out turn off the lights,' or else start all over again. We chose to start over."

When Hugh MacLennan began writing about the Canadian rivers back in the 1950s, he almost passed on the Red River. "Before I became acquainted with the Red," he confessed, "I shared the general belief that it is the dullest river in Canada. It is not, of course. It is the most surprising river we have in the whole land. It is unlike any other I know."

The Red River is a major Canadian historical figure. Its vast valley, which covers so much of the mid–North American prairie, is where the buffalo truly roamed—in 1800, the North American prairies were home to an estimated fifty million bison. First Nations gathered here to meet and trade. The Crees called the river Miscousipi, meaning "river of red water." It carried voyageurs during the fur trade. The trails along and leading from the river carried the earliest settlers on Red River carts, the squeaking of the big-wheeled vehicles audible long before the travellers came into sight.

It is also a significant political figure. Métis leader Louis Riel set up his provisional government in 1869 in the Red River Colony. The Métis of the Red River Valley, aware that the newly formed Canada was considering this land as ideal for new immigrants, could get no assurances from the new government in Ottawa that they would be able to keep their own land. They met in the parish church in St. Norbert and decided to fight. With Riel at their head, some five hundred men attacked Upper Fort Garry, the Hudson's Bay Company trading post in what is today the city of Winnipeg. With the fort overrun, Riel dispatched a delegation to Ottawa to demand Manitoba be made a full province in Confederation and that the religious, property and language rights of the Métis be guaranteed. This led to the Manitoba Act of 1870, which went ahead despite Riel's having executed one of his prisoners, Thomas Scott, a staunch Orangeman from Ontario.

Under enormous pressure from Scott's fellow Orangemen, Prime Minister Sir John A. Macdonald (an Orangeman himself) dispatched Colonel Garnet Wolseley and more than a thousand men to put down what became known as the Red River Rebellion. Travelling through arduous conditions and using fur-trade voyageurs to guide him, Wolseley eventually reached the fort and quelled matters without any bloodshed. Riel, however, had already fled to the United States, where he would remain until a second uprising, this time in Saskatchewan, fifteen years later.

The significance of this moment in Canadian history cannot be overstated. Macdonald wished to make a show of strength that would dissuade possible American intentions, then very much the talk of the West. As Peter C. Newman noted in his three-volume study of the Hudson's Bay Company, "American expansionists had been mobilized by their discovery that steam was about to redraw the map of the continent." Macdonald thought that the militia could serve two purposes: quell the uprising and let the Americans know that this territory belonged to someone else. The expedition force that Wolseley led would eventually become the basis for the 1873 formation of the North-West Mounted Police, and from there the Royal Canadian Mounted Police, which still polices much of the Canadian West. And Manitoba would become the Dominion of Canada's fifth province.

It was the Red River that allowed Wolseley and his men passage to reach Upper Fort Garry, though it took them months to get there. Denied permission to travel the easier route through the United States, they had to stay on Canadian soil and water, crossing Lake Superior, paddling Lake of the Woods and then the difficult Winnipeg River to Lake Winnipeg, finally paddling upstream until they reached Upper Fort Garry in August.

That's correct, "paddling upstream" from Lake Winnipeg. Many who know of Manitoba and the Red River only from staring at the class maps in elementary school are often surprised to discover that the Red River flows north. It begins, after all, in the northern United States, on the same high ground as the source of the Mississippi.

This was once Lake Agassiz, a landlocked glacial body of water whose total area exceeded the Great Lakes combined. When the gargantuan lake gradually disappeared more than eight thousand years ago, it left behind Lakes Winnipeg, Winnipegosis, Manitoba and Lake of the Woods, as well as this usually thin ribbon of a river that runs north from Fargo and Grand Forks to Winnipeg. At Winnipeg, the Red is joined by the Assiniboine River at a confluence known as the Forks before making its way thirty-four kilometres north to the town of Selkirk and on through a wide delta to Lake Winnipeg.

As the height of land throughout this long journey is barely four metres above the river's usual water level, and the land on both banks of the river both low and flat, flooding comes easily to the Red. Oral histories among First Nations suggest that a flood in 1776 may have been the worst ever, but there are no official records. The river seriously overflows, on average, every thirty-five years or so. It has also been known to all but dry up under severe drought. At the height of the Dust Bowl, it was difficult to find water running north of Winnipeg, so minuscule was the flow coming out of North Dakota.

While each flood is unique, they all follow a general pattern: a wet autumn saturates the ground, severe temperatures before first snow cause a deep frost, lots of snow with little thawing, a late spring, a rapid melt with above-normal rain or snow—or, worst of all, a late-season blizzard. Officially, the real "Flood of the Millennium" occurred in 1826. George Simpson, the governor of the Hudson's Bay Company, reported that the Red River Settlement (now Winnipeg) was under three and a half metres of water and that five people had perished, a number he considered a miracle.

Francis Heron, a clerk in Simpson's company, was serving at Upper Fort Garry when the waters came. By the first week of May, the people were in full panic. "The forts now stand like a castle of romance in the midst of an ocean of deep contending currents," Heron recorded in his journal, "the water extending for at least a mile behind them, and they are thereby only approachable by boats and canoes."

"There has been today a peculiar noise," David Anderson, the bishop of Rupert's Land, noted of a later flood in his diary, "like the sound of many waters, such as one may imagine the distant sound of Niagara: it was the pouring of water over the plains."

People had been killed; the settlers had lost livestock and buildings. Dead cattle were seen floating by with their feet straight up. Settler David Jones wrote in his journal on May 3, "The river rose six feet last night . . . terror is strongly depicted on every countenance." Two days later he added: "On a point of the river above us, four horses and a barn were swept off by the force of the ice and the ruins floated past us today . . . the force of the ice is inconceivable; the loftiest elm trees are carried away like the most inconsiderable things."

The people fled the worst of it and yet, as the bishop and his fleeing congregation reached the northern delta, Anderson noted "violets and buttercups, raspberry and strawberry blossoms were grateful to the eye." The bishop moved about by canoe—sometimes hoisting a sail—to visit his people and thought dawn looked like "a sunrise at sea." He noted the trees still standing were in blossom, their branches filled with songbirds. With the water receding, he took quill and ink to diary and calmly noted, "When the enemy shall come in like a flood, the spirit of the Lord shall lift up a standard against him . . . now the melody of former times may be renewed."

Such optimism, even in the face of potential destruction, is the hallmark of the First Nations, Métis, Scottish and French who long ago declared the Red River Valley "A Place to Call Home."

Before the French such as the Courcelles of Ste. Agathe arrived, the European settlers mostly came from Scotland, the most resilient among them the Highlanders following their chief, Lord Selkirk. He led them to a new land where they could escape the English who, following the disastrous Battle of Culloden, had set out to destroy the Scots' ancient clan system. The Scottish lord had purchased vast shares in the Hudson's Bay Company when the fur trade was crushed during the Napoleonic Wars. His interest wasn't furs, but territory for his people.

The first group came across in 1811, using the northern route into Hudson Bay and landing where York Factory sits today. They spent the winter encamped in the freezing cold and in the summer of 1812 paddled twelve hundred kilometres upstream via the Nelson River, Lake Winnipeg and the Red River to reach the Forks. They arrived without plows to work the ground and planted using hoes and shovels.

The Highlanders came at a time of great tensions between the Hudson's Bay Company and the North West Company over the remnants of the fur trade. The "HBC" had been founded in 1670 by an English charter, while the "Nor'Westers" began in 1779, headquartered in Montreal. The two competitors would merge in 1821, but at this time they were still bitter rivals, leading to clashes between the traders and the Natives and of the traders with each other. Lord Selkirk, being the major shareholder in the Hudson's Bay Company, was considered an enemy by the North West Company. Nor'Westers attacked and killed the local HBC governor and twenty men in the Seven Oaks Massacre, only a few kilometres from the Forks. Settlers took to digging holes in their fields where they could hide and cover up their children when tensions were high. A plague destroyed their crops in 1837 and, by extension, would have destroyed the coming year's crop as well, had two men not walked sixteen hundred kilometres south to an American settlement on the Mississippi River where they were able to purchase enough seed, with $600 of Lord Selkirk's dwindling fortune, to save their settlement. As fellow Scot Hugh MacLennan wrote, "No body of settlers in Canada ever endured more prolonged or terrifying suffering than did the Selkirk people."

Perhaps they stayed because they felt they had no choice, having no home to which they might return. But this does not explain those who followed, and who chose to stay on. These people simply learned to live with a river that, every generation or so, would turn on them with a vengeance.

It was only after the great flood of 1950 that anyone tried seriously to control the Red. So severe was the flooding that 20,000 Americans were forced from their homes, followed by 100,000 Manitobans once the high waters passed the border and began moving on Winnipeg. Had the Canadian Army not been sent in to try to protect Winnipeg and help evacuate people from affected areas, it is likely that many lives would have been lost. So seriously did the authorities believe the situation was that there was a contingency plan to declare martial law and move as many as 320,000 Manitobans away from the flood plain. The cost of fighting the Canadian section of the flood reached $100 million.

Following the recommendations of a royal commission in 1958, the provincial premier of the day, Duff Roblin, managed to get then prime minister John Diefenbaker to agree to share the enormous costs of building a floodway that could protect the city of Winnipeg. Smaller communities along the Red began building dikes—Ste. Agathe, much to its regret, considered such drastic measures unnecessary—and rural residents took to rebuilding on higher ground created by bulldozers and fill. The floodway plan was to build a channel forty-eight kilometres long around the city where, when the spring runoff reached a certain level, excess water from the Red could be diverted safely around outlying neighbourhoods and rejoin the bed of the river as it headed north.

Work began in 1962. Those uprooted for the project protested but soon recognized that the channelling would go ahead regardless. The digging was extensive, more than had been excavated for the Canadian section of the St. Lawrence Seaway, nearly half what had been required to complete the Panama Canal. By 1968, when the work was done, the floodway was nearly thirty-seven kilometres long, with dikes constructed at the most strategic places. The first phase alone cost $63 million.

Derisively, people referred to it as "Duff's Ditch," a monumental folly that would never prove necessary. How wrong they were: Once the floodway was ready for use in 1969, it would be used in nine of the next eleven years. According to the provincial government, the flood-way has prevented some $40 billion in damages since it was built. After 1997, a decision was taken to expand the system further.

"Duff's Ditch was the saviour of Winnipeg," says R.S. (Bud) Oliver, a former mayor of Selkirk. "That was not a term of endearment, you know, when they first dug it. But after the first time it had to be used, well, then it was the best idea in the world."

In 2006 the Red River again flooded. It was worse south of the city but Winnipeg was also hit hard, despite Duff's Ditch and all the improve-ments since it was first built. Even so, by then the value of the spillway, while imperfect, was much appreciated. Bill Rannie of the University of Winnipeg's geography department told the *Globe and Mail* that, in his opinion, without the floodway Winnipeg "would have had to be com-pletely evacuated in 1997—it would have been a New Orleans [following Hurricane Katrina]."

I covered that 2006 flood and spent most of a week travelling along the Red River while Manitobans tried to figure out if the flood had crested or the worst was still to come. Even in the affluent neighbour-hoods of Winnipeg, homeowners were out stacking sandbags to hold back the coffee-coloured waters. A half-hour north of downtown Winnipeg, however, straight out Main Street and up Highway 9, the town of Selkirk sat high and dry, the water inching up the banks but hardly threatening. Here, the Red River is under control each spring.

I happened there only days after the ice went out and, as resident Don Phillips told me, "Once the ice goes out, we're fine. And as soon as it passes the town, the land goes down and everything just spreads out into a big, wide marsh. There's never much flooding to worry about."

That's pretty much what Sir Sandford Fleming had believed back in 1879, when the famous Western surveyor was plotting a route for the promised transcontinental railway. He recommended that the main rail crossing of the Red River for the Canadian Pacific line be at Selkirk rather than upstream in Winnipeg at the confluence of the Red and Assiniboine Rivers.

The Forks is today a meeting ground for downtown dwellers and tourists, a place for theatre, restaurants, shopping and even staying (the Inn at the Forks). The strategic spot has been called "Ellis Island," as so many came from all directions and by all means—canoe, wagon, steamboat, train, auto and air—to settle in the area. That's nothing new. The remains of Indigenous campsites here date back more than six thousand years. When adventurer and trader Pierre Gaultier de Varennes et de La Vérendrye came up the Red River in August of 1738, he noted: "I proceeded to the fork of the Assiniboine and reaching there on the 24th I found 10 cabins [lodges] of Cree, including two war chiefs, awaiting me with a large quantity of meat, having been notified of my coming. They begged me to stay with them for a while, so that they might have the pleasure of seeing and entertaining us. I agreed to do so, being glad of a chance of talking to them."

When Fleming surveyed the area nearly a century and a half later, he met people who could recall the devastation of the 1826 flood, and Fleming quickly concluded that Winnipeg was not the route a railroad should take. Instead, Selkirk, with its high banks, deeper trenches and relatively easy span of the river for railway trestles was the way to go. There was a Hudson's Bay Company post there (Lower Fort Garry), a grist mill and sawmill, a distillery, a boat-building operation and a lime kiln. After two visits to the area in 1879 he filed his recommendations. According to a 2002 paper published by University of Winnipeg geographers Scott St. George and Bill Rannie, Fleming advised the railroad go "downstream at flood-free Selkirk."

The recommendation begat a minor boom in Selkirk, but it was soon derailed by some strategic lobbying upstream. Winnipeg said it would pay $200,000 toward the construction of a bridge across the Red River. Not only that, but the railway would be forever exempted from taxes on any rail buildings or property. In 1881 the CPR accepted Winnipeg's offer. By the summer of 1881 booming Selkirk was virtually deserted. As Prairie poet W.A. MacLeod said at the time,

> When the railroad comes—it cannot come to all of us;
> Some will mourn in far-off valleys, some will curse on distant slopes.
> For the tinkling of the hammers filling many hearts with rapture
> May be spiking fast the coffin lid on other people's hopes.

The effect was immediate: Winnipeg boomed. By the 1911 census, it was the third largest city in the country after Montreal and Toronto. Winston Churchill visited Winnipeg in January of 1901, when the boom was just underway. He wrote to his mother that he had had "a most successful meeting at Winnipeg. Fancy 20 years ago there were only a few mud huts—tents; and last night a magnificent audience of men in evening dress & ladies half out of it, filled a fine opera house. . . . Winnipeg has a wonderful future before it."

There is a saying in North Dakota that "you can see Sunday company coming on Thursday afternoon." The sky is overwhelming, the horizon forever, the drive down the interstate to Grand Forks about as varied as the path of a plumb line. Cruise controls set to the seventy-five-mile-an-hour limit, cars are heavily outnumbered by the truck traffic between the American heartland and the Canadian breadbasket. The only distractions are the radio and roadkill.

The Americans usually refer to this as the "Red River of the North" to differentiate it from the Red River that flows through Texas and has been remembered in both song and film. The Red River of the North forms some of the boundary between Minnesota and South Dakota and all of the state line between Minnesota and North Dakota. At Grand Forks there stands an obelisk high on the banks of the river. This is where the Red River splits Grand Forks, North Dakota, from East Grand Forks in Minnesota and passes under the Sorlie Memorial Bridge, erected in 1929 and still standing. The brown stone obelisk reaches for the sky, ascending rings noting where the water rose to in 1996, 1882, 1979, 1897 and—two thick rings higher still—1997. Here in Grand Forks is where the Flood of the Century did its worst damage.

"The water came right up to here," says Barry Wilfahrt, tapping high on the entrance to the Chamber of Commerce building on North 3rd Street, well back of where the Red River passes on this sunny day in the spring of 2015.

Wilfahrt is the president and CEO of the Chamber, which covers both Grand Forks communities, on each side of the river. Such co-operation was not always so cozy, as North Dakota entered the Union in 1889 as a "dry" state and, somewhat consequently, East Grand Forks in Minnesota thrived as a wild frontier town with more than forty saloons and multiple bordellos. Al Capone, it is said, supplied the bootleggers on the east side of the river. According to the descriptive menu at the Blue Moose café across the river, the September 18, 1895, edition of the *East Grand Forks Courier* reported that two women, "one of them the divorced wife of a former prominent citizen here," went into G.L. Larson & Co.'s sample room, a saloon, and smashed all the glass they could find. The divorced woman's father agreed to "make good" and the matter was hushed up.

What brought the two communities together, more than anything else, was disaster, and none more so than the flood of 1997. It had been a vicious winter, with no fewer than eight blizzards striking the area and roughly three metres of snow falling. They were already dealing with flood conditions when Blizzard Hannah hit on April 4. An ice storm covered everything in a heavy slick, and then came wet, heavy snowfall followed by high winds, freezing and collapsing trees and power lines. More than a hundred thousand people were without power.

The floodwater rose so quickly and so high that much of the two small cities had been evacuated when at 4:15 p.m. fire broke out in the downtown Security Building on the North Dakota side. The battle was on. Firefighters, trying to rescue those who had refused to go, pushed through frigid waters more than a metre deep. Fire trucks heading downtown to deal with the spreading blaze flooded and stalled. Fire hydrants, now submerged, lost their pressure. They called in the army to help. Planes and helicopters dropped fire retardant. After two desperate days, the blaze was brought under control, but by then eleven buildings over two city blocks had been lost.

The *Grand Forks Herald* won a Pulitzer Prize for its coverage of the floods, despite the fact that the *Herald* offices had burned down. Mike Jacobs was editor at the time and self-deprecatingly says, "It must have been a slow news month. The prize was the gift of the river—it was just such a fantastic story."

Jacobs set up temporary quarters in nearby Grafton. They printed in yet another town. At one point, he says, a rumour spread that the river had altered its course and was now coming directly through Grand Forks and would destroy everything. When the rumour turned out to be false, he says, "Everything changed. We faced up to the loss then because we thought we had lost everything. That helped us enormously to battle back."

The recovery was long and difficult. The Red Cross arrived; volunteers poured in from all over North America. Those who had homes to return to had no power, no water. It took more than three weeks to restore drinking water. Aid poured in, from the U.S. Department of Housing and Urban Development giving $171 million in assistance to a single donation of $15 million from an anonymous woman who identified herself only as "Angel."

It would take years to rebuild, but today downtown Grand Forks and East Grand Forks on the other side of the Red are thriving. As Winnipeg did after 1950, the two Grand Forks and communities farther upstream, such as Fargo, have worked to ensure that a repeat of 1997 never happens. The Red River, however, remains a threat even when the water runs as low as it did through the spring of 2015. This was Dust Bowl country during the Great Depression. There were summers when the Red River ran dry.

"All we hear about is the flooding," Wilfahrt says, "but there is also the threat of drought."

"Drought is much more insidious than flood," adds Jacobs. "With drought, it seems there is never an end in sight. All plains people fear drought more than flood."

And yet, despite the periodic threats of flood or drought, the populations of both American communities have continued to grow. When the floodwater of '97 had receded, Jacobs penned a piece for his paper titled "Tell Me Again Why We Live Here."

Jacobs and his family had been out of their home for forty-three days. His newspaper had no building. And yet the Jacobses, like everyone else, never considered leaving. "The weather makes people more co-operative," he says. "There's a common suffering, victims in common creates a land that transcends what would be the case in more salubrious climes. There's a civility in the population that at least in the United States is quite unusual."

Won't you think of the valley you're leaving?
Oh how lonely, how sad it will be . . .

—"Red River Valley" (traditional)

Jacques and Nadine Courcelles had an idea. If the people of Ste. Agathe were determined to stay by the river that had all but destroyed their little town, the people should know more about the river and its often erratic behaviour.

With his father, Albert (who died in 2014), and a team of volunteers, Courcelles set to work building an interpretive centre on the edge of town. It would become not only a tourist attraction but also an educational tool. Nadine and other volunteers would bring in schools from all along the Red River Valley, and the children of tomorrow would grow up more aware of their unpredictable river than any generation before them.

Today, the Red River Valley Floods Interpretive Centre sits in a small park named after George-Étienne Cartier, who was once the area's member of Parliament. The volunteers planted six thousand trees, built a swimming hole, set out plots for summer campers and constructed a large building that would tell an interactive tale of the Red River Valley floods.

Throughout the building are memories and photographs from various floods. In 1950, the mayor of Emerson, Walter Forrester, and his wife, Edna, had to move up to the second floor of their home but remained with their community throughout the exceptionally high water of that spring. "It's been quite an experience," she is quoted as saying. "I'm getting sick of wearing heavy wool socks and hip waders."

A photograph of the mayor of Grand Forks, Pat Owen, shows her with President Bill Clinton and offers a quote from her during the 1997 flood: "What makes a community a place to live in is not the buildings, it's the people—the spirit and the faith that are in those people. Water cannot wash that away, and fire cannot burn that away."

The centre sits directly across from an industrial area called Riel Park, named after the first elected member for the riding of Provencher, Louis Riel. The local hero was voted in but never took his seat in Parliament—he was wanted for murder following the execution of Thomas Scott—leading to the parachuting in of Cartier. Riel was eventually captured, tried and hanged, a controversial execution that only raised his status as a hero for many French Canadians right across the country. In 1992, the province formally recognized Riel as a founding father of Manitoba.

"Louis Riel is well thought of around here," says Courcelles. "He paid for his approach. But he believed in Manitoba."

Approximately one thousand schoolchildren a year go through the centre. They study photographs and family diaries and twist through a long series of displays that tell how floods occur and what happened during the area's most severe flooding. They witness a great deal of drama but also a touch of prairie humour. A fake contest was held during the '97 flood, offering: "Third prize is a week in Bermuda. Second prize a Mercedes Benz convertible. First prize a sewer backup valve." "WATER TORTURE," screams the front page of the April 30, 1997, edition of the *Calgary Sun*.

Torture, yes, but life follows. In fact, the very reason that the Red River Valley is considered one of the world's most fertile areas is tied directly to the bed of ancient Lake Agassiz and the ebb and flow of the Red River itself. "My father farmed here for fifty years," Courcelles says. "And he believed that every time there was a flood event, he would have a great crop."

After the horrific 1997 flood and the incredible losses of Ste. Agathe, it seemed sensible to reconsider. The people had to be evacuated from the area by the Canadian Army in the middle of the night, and yet at the first opportunity they were back cleaning up. "We weren't going to give up without a fight," Courcelles says.

And that, really, is the story of the Red River Valley.

"We stay and deal with it because we are Red River people," Oliver, the former mayor of Selkirk, says. "Everybody has a choice of where they want to live. And those who stay do whatever is necessary to be able to stay."

Jacques Courcelles stops outside the door of the Ste. Agathe interpretative centre. There is still much work to be done. The swimming hole needs a liner. The kitchen has yet to be completed. The facilities for holding weddings and family reunions are unfinished.

"It enters the sphere of thunderous stupidity," Courcelles says with a smile. "Sometimes you say, 'What was I thinking?' But it's about believing in your community.

"Sometimes, you know, you have to think beyond your lifetime."

CHAPTER SIX

WATER WONDER OF THE WORLD: THE NIAGARA

OSCAR WILDE, RICHARD NIXON, PIERRE TRUDEAU, Marilyn Monroe, Winston Churchill, Shirley Temple, Abraham Lincoln, Mark Twain, Charles Blondin, "Wild Bill" Hickok, Laura Secord, H.G. Wells, Charles Dickens, the Great Farini, Helen Keller, Sir Harry Oakes, Jimmy Stewart, Princess Diana, Nik Wallenda . . .

Bit characters all—in a story where the main character has always been and will always be: The Falls.

Those famous names, with one notable exception, were all as impressed in their day by Niagara Falls as are the millions of visitors who come each year to stare in awe at one of the Seven Natural Wonders of the World. Helen Keller, who could not see and could not hear, experienced the falls through her hands. She was so moved by the vibrations she could feel on a hotel window sill that she wrote her mother to say, "I wish I could describe the cataract as it is, its beauty and awful grandeur, and the fearful and irresistible plunge of its water over the brow of the precipice. One feels helpless and overwhelmed in the presence of such a vast force."

"Endless water falling the wrong way," sniffed Oscar Wilde when he visited in late winter of 1882. The legendary Irish wit is also said to have claimed that "Every American bride is taken there, and the sight of the stupendous waterfall must be one of the earliest if not the keenest disappointment in American married life," a comment that is usually misquoted as "Niagara Falls must be a bride's second greatest disappointment."

There is no disappointment, however, on this late winter day in early 2016. With the sun painting rainbows in the mist over the Canadian-side Horseshoe Falls—Goat Island, which splits the Niagara River at the falls, separates Horseshoe Falls from its smaller American counterpart—hundreds of viewers line the walkway that runs alongside. Buses discharge tourists who have flown to Canada from China, mostly young couples with selfie sticks to capture themselves in various romantic poses with the falls as backdrop.

The white water that roars over the falls before them may be moving in excess of a hundred kilometres an hour. All the mind-boggling numbers that can be placed before cubic feet and gallons might be better illustrated by the writer who calculated that the equivalent of one million full bathtubs of water poured over the falls every single second.

Impressive as that sounds, it is still only half of what it once was. In late 1678, when Father Louis Hennepin, claimed by some to be the first European to see the falls—others say Étienne Brûlé had been there a half-century earlier—the priest declared that "the Universe does not hold its parallel." Father Hennepin also found the noise "outrageous . . . more terrible than that of thunder."

There is something about Niagara and hyperbole. According to local historian Sherman Zavitz's *It Happened at Niagara*, after a young Abraham Lincoln first visited the falls, the future president pronounced: "When Columbus first sought this continent—when Christ suffered on the cross—when Moses led Israel through the Red Sea—nay, even, when Adam first came from the hand of his maker—then, as now, Niagara was roaring here."

The "now" in "then, as now" being 1848—but not these days.

For one thing, the falls has moved, its remarkable recession charted by scientists to have shifted eleven kilometres upstream in the past twelve thousand years. Every year, more rock breaks away, sometimes chunks the size of a sixteen-wheeler. "The shape of the falls is always changing," says Environment Canada's Aaron Thompson, who also serves as chair of the International Niagara Board of Control. But as he explains, more than just erosion separates the falls that tourists photograph today from the falls First Nations knew and that so impressed Father Hennepin and Abraham Lincoln. "The rate has slowed down because so much of the flow goes to the power plants."

The power of the Niagara River and its most memorable feature was such that it created in this region North America's first great industrial centre. By diverting the water into tunnels leading to turbines, industrialists were able to create electricity, first of all direct current. Once Nikola Tesla invented alternating current—a discovery Thomas Edison campaigned against as being too dangerous—it allowed for electricity to travel distances and the great industrialization of the Niagara region spread. The first great power-generating dam to use Tesla's technology, the Adams Power Plant, was built on the Niagara River in 1895.

So, delighted with such growing possibilities, early industrialists built along the river and, consequently, more and more water was diverted into such tunnels to generate more and more power to run the plants. Lord Kelvin, the famous Irish inventor and engineer, said he believed every single drop in the river should be diverted for the purposes of creating ever more electricity: "I look forward to the time when the whole water from Lake Erie will find its way to the lower level of Lake Ontario through machinery. . . . I do not hope that our children's children will ever see the Niagara Cataract."

Fortunately, wiser heads prevailed. One early suggestion had the power companies ransacking the Niagara as much as they wished for six days a week but diverting none of its flow on Sundays so that the tourists could enjoy the falls. That idea went nowhere. In 1950, the Niagara Diversion Treaty signed by Canada and the U.S. specified how much each country could draw for power—roughly half the flow that Hennepin and Lincoln had witnessed.

"They could see that one day there would be no water going over the falls," says Thompson.

Today, the flow and diversion gates are all computer controlled and monitored so that each falls has "an unbroken crest line." More water is diverted during night hours and during winter. The International Niagara Committee, which was established by the United States and Canada in 1950, is responsible for flow and water diversions for power production. One critical flow control involved the placing of intricate steel booms at the mouth of the river each spring to help keep it clear of the heavy lake ice. "We try to keep the ice on Lake Erie as long as possible so it doesn't come in and play havoc with the flow," says Thompson.

In early 2015 a public hearing at the Niagara Falls Convention Center discussed a proposal to "de-water" the American Falls. Two 150-year-old bridges connecting to islands upstream are in dire need of repair or replacement. The idea is to divert the river so that it flows only on the Canadian side of Goat Island and over only Horseshoe Falls, theoretically restoring the Canadian falls to the size it was when Father Hennepin thought the universe held no parallel.

Goat Island is the smallest of the three islands just above the falls. Navy Island, the only Canadian island in the river, is a wildlife preserve. The largest, Grand Island, was purchased from the Iroquois in 1815 for $1,000. Years later, a man named Mordecai Manuel Noah came from New York City with plans to establish a Jewish city he would call "Ararat." He soon abandoned those plans, but other grandiose designs on the island followed. P.T. Barnum once tried to purchase it as a permanent home for his circus. Entirely on the American side of the river, Goat Island is today a state park.

The American Falls has gone dry, or fairly dry, before. On March 30, 1848, a massive ice jam briefly plugged the river at Lake Erie. It happened, by half, again in 1969 when U.S. Army engineers thought they could clean up the American side of debris that had gone over the falls over the years and perhaps even move some of the key rocks to improve the overall look of the American Falls. This new proposal, however, could see the American Falls "de-watered" for as long as it takes to complete the work on the two bridges.

Incredibly, there are those who are hoping the longer the better. They are convinced it would even be great for tourism.

There is already talk of T-shirts and bumper stickers: "I was there when Niagara Falls ran dry."

The Niagara River could be described as the most important short river in the world—except it isn't truly a river. It's a fifty-eight-kilometre-long strait, or "connecting channel," that runs north from Lake Erie and empties into Lake Ontario—as opposed to a traditional "river" draining from a large watershed and growing in size as it moves downstream. Political junkies well recall Canadian Alliance leader Stockwell Day's faux pas during the 2000 federal election campaign when, using the falls as a photo backdrop, he declared that "just as Lake Erie drains from north to south, there is an ongoing drain in terms of our young people" to the U.S.

Those of us following Day weren't at first sure that we had heard correctly. But indeed we had. Informed by a CBC reporter that he had his geography wrong, Day announced that he would have his people "check the record"—though all he really had to do was turn around and check the falls behind him.

Those who live along the river know its short course intimately—but few as well as Patrick Robson. The first hint of Robson's devotion is on his licence plate—"1812"—for it was on both sides of this river that the worst of the only war ever fought between Canada and the United States took place.

A former commissioner of planning for the Niagara Region who now works in administration at Niagara College, Robson has lived his entire life in the region. He believes the river, falls and surrounding countryside are endlessly fascinating—a story of war, peace, power, industry, tourism, pollution and, fingers crossed, solution. "It's about people and identity," he says. "Niagara Peninsula is packed with stories—and I have a passion for the stories."

Robson is driving along the Niagara Parkway, a relaxing drive along the Canadian side of the river that runs through War of 1812 battlefields, vineyards, farms, small towns and seemingly endless parkland. Winston Churchill called it "the prettiest Sunday afternoon drive in the world."

Robson points out Navy Island, a large, uninhabited Canadian island that was once home to the brief "Republic of Canada," a wild idea of Canadian revolutionary William Lyon Mackenzie. Mackenzie amassed a thousand armed men here in 1837 and wrote his "Declaration of Independence" on December 1 of that year. He would have invaded Canada had British troops not boarded his supply ship, the *Caroline*, late at night, set her afire and turned her loose to go over the falls. Mackenzie was arrested in Buffalo and charged with threatening U.S. neutrality. Found guilty, he was sentenced to eighteen months in jail. Once out, Mackenzie moved to New York City before returning to Canada in

1850, where the following year he was elected to Parliament. That, of course, is quite another story. . . .

Navy Island was once a popular choice for the United Nations headquarters. American and Canadian supporters argued that it stood as the perfect symbol for two countries that had existed peacefully for more than a century. President Harry Truman was all for it until the rich and powerful stepped in and offered free prime land in New York City. Today the island is a wildlife reserve.

Robson is among several area movers and shakers keen to turn the Niagara region on both sides of the river into an International Peace Park. The long-standing peace between the two countries is a main factor, obviously, but there are other arguments, as well. It is estimated that as many as 75,000 fugitive slaves made their way to the Canadian colonies before the American Civil War. The "Niagara Movement" was an early civil rights force founded in Niagara Falls in 1905. Across the river in Lewiston, a "Freedom Crossing" monument points over the water to sanctuary.

A few minutes down the parkway, the crowning mist of Horseshoe Falls is visible in the distance. Even though he lives nearby, a trip to the falls is a rare event for Robson. "I don't go down to the falls often," he says. "We tend to forget there are a whole host of other things going on here just off the beaten track."

He prefers the historical sites such as Lundy's Lane, Laura Secord's homestead, the Brock monument, the many battlegrounds of the war—most of the fighting, killing, burning and ransacking took place in the forts and villages along the peninsula.

The falls of today is more about duelling casinos—Fallsview and Casino Niagara on the Canadian side, Seneca on the American—tourism and such curious attractions as the "genuine two-headed lamb" at Ripley's Believe It or Not! There's even a bar on the Canadian side called "He's Not Here!"

The two Niagara Falls towns, one in New York, the other across the falls in Ontario, are renowned for their tourist tackiness. Complaints about overdevelopment, however, are hardly new. Back in 1906, the famous science-fiction writer H.G. Wells took to the pages of *Harper's Weekly* to declare "The End of Niagara," as the headline put it. "Niagara's spectacular effect," Wells wrote, "its magnificent and humbling size and splendor were long since destroyed beyond recovery by the hotels, the factories, the powerhouses, the bridges and tramways and hoardings that rose about it."

The main attraction remains the falls, of course, though there was a two-week period in June of 1952 when Marilyn Monroe gave the water a run for its money. While she was in town to film *Niagara*, with Joseph Cotten, tourists flocked to get her autograph and see her, despite temperatures that climbed to 100°F (38°C). "The falls produce a lot of electricity," the actress slyly remarked, "but the honeymooners don't use very much of it at night."

It was Niagara Falls where the great 1965 blackout had its genesis at 5:27 p.m. on November 9. When safety switches malfunctioned, more than thirty million North Americans were plunged into darkness. Pilots flying over the Eastern Seaboard saw entire cities go dark. Thousands were trapped in subways and commuter trains. The largest centre, New York City, went fourteen hours without power. Judging by birth records along the Eastern Seaboard that followed nine months later, Marilyn Monroe pretty much nailed it.

Theodosia Burr, daughter of Aaron Burr, Thomas Jefferson's vice-president, is often said to be the first honeymooner to visit the falls, when she married Joseph Alston of Charleston, South Carolina. They journeyed to Niagara with nine pack horses and several servants. Theodosia was so moved by the falls that words failed her when she wrote to her sister-in-law, saying, "To describe them is impossible; they must be seen."

Words never fail professional writers, however, and the list of renowned authors who have written about the falls, or included the falls in their stories, is lengthy. Charles Dickens visited in 1842 while on a lecture tour of North America. Dickens was profoundly impressed: "When I felt how near to my Creator I was standing, the first effect, and the enduring one—instant and lasting—of the tremendous spectacle was Peace. Peace of Mind, tranquillity, calm recollections of the Dead, great thoughts of Eternal Rest and Happiness: nothing of gloom or terror. Niagara was at once stamped upon my heart, an Image of Beauty."

When Dickens and his wife, Anne, were being rowed across, he shouted out, "Great God! How could any man be disappointed in this?" To which Anne apparently replied: "It's nothing but water and too much of that." Mark Twain, who lived in nearby Buffalo for a short period, wrote a short story about being robbed by Irish thugs who stole his clothes and money and threw him over the falls. Fortunately, "only sixteen of my wounds are fatal. I don't mind the others."

As we continue our tour, Robson explains that he is no fan of the casinos—"gamblers aren't tourists"—but he does have a soft spot for the great daredevils who once made the falls as famous for stunts as they are for size. People have been risking, and sometimes losing, their lives around the falls for centuries. Hundreds gathered on July 24, 1875, to watch Captain Matthew Webb challenge the ferocious Whirlpool Rapids below the falls. He had been the first to swim the English Channel—collecting a handsome reward for doing so—and now claimed he could make it through the wildest part of the river unharmed. They cheered when he dove in. Four days later, they found his body.

An estimated half-billion television viewers tuned in on June 15, 2012, to watch Nik Wallenda walk across a cable strung over Horseshoe Falls. The then thirty-three-year-old Wallenda—of the

Great Wallendas, three of whom died attempting similar stunts—practised for his crossing by balancing on a wire with Delilah Wallenda, his sixty-eight-year-old mother, on his shoulders while he was sprayed by a fire hose to replicate conditions he would be encountering.

Wallenda's 2012 accomplishment aside, Robson is partial to the great stuntmen of the mid-nineteenth century. In the summer of 1860, Frenchman Charles Blondin and the Great Farini (William Leonard Hunt of Port Hope, Ontario) challenged each other to the point of absurdity—and tragedy. Farini crossed the falls on a tightrope while wearing peach baskets on his feet. Blondin at one point crossed while carrying a stove on his back, stopped halfway, cooked an omelette and lowered it down to the *Maid of the Mist*, where passengers eagerly ate it. Farini matched by carrying out a washtub, lowering a bucket into the river by rope to fill it, then hauling it back up to wash handkerchiefs that had been given to him by his many female admirers. Farini took many such walks over other watery gorges, mostly in the United States. He once carried a woman across on his back but—whoops!—slipped and dropped her to her death. Such stunts were banned shortly after the Blondin-Farina high-wire duels. Special legislation had to be passed to permit Wallenda's walk in 2012. No one has been granted permission since.

The number who have died by accident or design at the falls is not known. Many bodies are never found. Going over the falls in a barrel became a popular stunt after a schoolteacher named Annie Edson Taylor survived the feat in 1901. Taylor, who decided to shoot the falls to celebrate her sixty-third birthday, used a specially built barrel and weighted it down with a large anvil for ballast. She survived with barely a scratch but confessed, "I would rather face a cannon knowing that I would be blown to pieces than go over the Falls again. I would warn anybody not to do it." Many did anyway, though few were as successful. For the remainder of Taylor's life, she was herself a tourist attraction of sorts, posing for pictures with tourists for a small fee.

More than a dozen people have survived going over the falls, some by accident. Most notable among them was seven-year-old Roger Woodward in 1960, who survived a plunge over the falls without even a barrel.

The happy endings are few and far between, though. Most deliberate events end badly. In the mid-1990s, a rather foolish young man blew over the falls on a Jet Ski—only to have his parachute fail to open.

Niagara Falls is no longer the setting for serial stunts such as Blondin versus Farini. And the heavy industry drawn here throughout the twentieth century has since vanished or moved on. "It's an economy in transition," says Robson. "It's gone from a heavy industrial economy, one of the first industrial areas of North America, to what it is today—all because of one thing, falling water."

In the wake of all that change has come a slow and difficult awareness of the damage "progress" had done to one of the Seven Natural Wonders of the World.

It is early Monday morning after reading week for the students of Brock University in St. Catharines. Geography class began at 8:00 a.m. and those students not staring at their mobile phones or laptop computers are slowly awakening to the day.

Jocelyn Baker and Deanna Lindblad of the Niagara Peninsula Conservation Authority have come to talk about water. If you could track a single drop, they tell the students, it would take 204 years for that water to travel from Thunder Bay to the mouth of the St. Lawrence River. Crossing Lake Superior alone would take 174 years, but only 2.5 years for Lake Erie and a matter of hours to run the Niagara River, over the falls and into Lake Ontario.

Steadily, the attention of the students is grabbed and held. The Great Lakes, they are told, contain 22 percent of the world's fresh water. One out of every three Canadians relies on this source for drinking water. The British newspaper the *Guardian* says that now four billion people face severe water shortages for at least one month of the year, with drought a rising concern over vast swaths of the earth. Canadians are among the very lucky.

That water, travelling so easily and quickly through the Niagara River, is what made cities like St. Catharines possible. Electricity powered industries, which built economies. So often dismissed these days, Buffalo was known as "The City of Lights" in the early 1900s. According to Kevin Woyce's illustrated history of Niagara, the Pan-American Exhibition of 1901 drew eight million visitors, most coming to stare in wonder at Electric Tower, a hundred-metre monolith lit by 44,000 bulbs.

Everything seemed possible back then. President William McKinley came and asked the crowd, "Who can tell the new thoughts that have been awakened, the ambition fired, and the high achievement that will be wrought through this exhibition?" The next day he was shot by an anarchist, Leon Czolgosz, and died eight days later.

McKinley, however, was proved right. Buffalo became a major industrial city, home to everything from General Mills to Pierce-Arrow cars. One new cereal factory was so fancy—884 windows, 200 tons of marble—that a 1914 tourism brochure boasted, "One might as well see Rome without seeing St. Peter's as to see Niagara Falls without visiting 'The Home of Shredded Wheat.'"

All that industrial development came at a cost, the most critical being waste and what to do with it. It was not something easily contained, and unfortunately not something industrialists or anyone else gave much thought to in those years. You merely dumped it into the river and, instantly, it was gone—at least as far as you were concerned. "They had easy access to dumping their waste," says Brad Hill, a scientist with Environment Canada who specializes in water quality. Their thinking was 'dilution is solution.'"

Fish were dying in the river and in the nearby Welland Canal, which had been constructed—its first version in 1829—to allow Great Lakes ships to bypass the falls. Toxic chemicals were spreading into Lake Ontario and beyond. Pollution was nothing new to the waterways. A 1918 commission declared the area below the falls "gross." And it only got worse.

"The first sewage treatment plant on the river was built only in 1936," says Lynda Schneekloth, a professor at the University at Buffalo School of Architecture and Planning. "We used the rivers as sewers for years. And we have tried, together, to take care of these waters once it became clear how badly we had treated them."

Some steps were eventually taken to address the growing issue of pollution. In 1972, Canada's prime minister Pierre Trudeau and U.S. president Richard Nixon signed the Great Lakes Water Quality Agreement. But it took a singular dramatic story to bring the health concerns to the forefront.

"The Love Canal," Jocelyn Baker tells those Brock students assembled early on Monday morning, "this was a truly important historical event."

An entrepreneur named William T. Love had long ago decided to build a canal that would allow him to divert water from the Niagara River through Buffalo. When financing dried up, he abandoned the project after digging a trench nearly two kilometres long. It filled with water and became a swimming hole for Buffalo children.

In the late 1940s, the Hooker Chemical Company purchased the canal and began filling it with barrels of toxic waste. The canal and its contents were then buried. By the 1960s, those chemicals had leached free of the landfill. Children were burning their hands on what they called "fire rocks." Investigative reporters in the 1970s uncovered staggering tales of cancers and birth defects in the area.

"It was the biggest environmental crisis in U.S. history," says Baker.

National outrage forced various levels of government to act. A school built on the property was closed and some 800 families relocated to new homes. That, however, was the only action taken. By the late 1970s more than 700 chemical plants, oil refineries, steel mills and other industries along the river were spewing some 950 million litres of dirty waste water into the Niagara every day of the year.

Even if little was done, Love Canal had the positive effect of raising the environmental issue along such heavily industrialized rivers. It seriously altered the public perception of how vulnerable a waterway can become when it is callously used as a dump site for industrial waste. Since those years matters have changed dramatically along the Niagara River. In 1987, it was among those forty-three "Areas of Concern" identified within the Great Lakes Basin. A "Remedial Action Plan" to restore the river's health has seen considerable success. Priority was given to eighteen toxic pollutants targeted for reduction, and between 1986 and 1995 the Canadian side saw such toxics reduced by up to 99 percent, while the American side had a success rate of up to 90 percent. A Brock University study on environmental restoration by engineer Annie Michaud concluded that "the past twenty-five years have seen a significant improvement in the quality of the Niagara River."

A paper co-authored by Brad Hill that studied Niagara water quality between 1986 and 2004 corroborated these findings. Most chemicals the study was investigating had significantly decreased. Its authors worried, however, that the trend was levelling off: "while considerable progress has been made in reducing the concentration of toxic contaminants in the Niagara River, much work is left to be done." It is a familiar phrase—"much work is left to be done"—around so very many of the rivers of this continent, but at least work is being done, some of it excellent, much of it promising.

Those working on the river's water quality hope to see the Niagara delisted as a "hot spot" by 2020. The hope, says Deanna Lindblad, is that the Niagara can change from "one of the most polluted, disgusting places on the face of the earth" to a river known for its biodiversity and successes. "It's important to celebrate how far we have come," she says. "And delisting by 2020 doesn't mean we walk away. There's always a concern about 'backsliding.'"

The conservation authority is spearheading a movement to have the Niagara region on both sides of the river declared a Ramsar site of international importance. ("Ramsar" refers to the Iranian city where, in 1971, an international treaty was signed to promote the conservation and wise use of valuable wetlands. Since then, 168 countries have signed on and Canada alone has 37 such designated sites.) There is some pushback in the Niagara area. Farmers have expressed concerns about more restrictive rules, developers worry about losing choice areas for housing, mayors have said they fear "jurisdiction creep." The mere word "wetlands" causes anxiety in certain quarters. If wetlands are considered of high value and worth protecting, they will not likely be available for agriculture or development. "For some," says Baker, "it's a four-letter word."

The Niagara River Ramsar Proposal meets all nine criteria for the designation, the final criterion concerning an indigenous species— the northern dusky salamander—that is found in the mist-soaked rocks under the falls. It would be North America's first binational Ramsar site, and supporters were hopeful of gaining the designation for the Canadian sesquicentennial celebrations of 2017.

The wetlands protection movement has support on the American side, and a wide consortium of interested stakeholders on both sides of the river has been "Rethinking Niagara" in recent years. The idea, says Schneekloth, who is part of the group, grew out of the profound change in cross-river exchange that came about following 9/11. The group mapped out all their shared histories, from First Nations to commerce to tourism to water quality sustainability. "We took our relationship for granted," says Schneekloth of the situation prior to the terrorist attacks. "But now, with so much attention on division, we had to reimagine ourselves as a single place with a shared border."

Her group, composed of Canadians and Americans, is trusting that either the establishment of an international peace park or the Ramsar designation, both if possible, will leave "a different kind of mark than 9/11." The idea, says Schneekloth, is to remind those who live there just "how special is our home on the Niagara neck of the Great Lakes."

Patrick Robson, pulling his car into the picturesque town of Niagara-on-the-Lake, where the Niagara River completes its short but fascinating run from Lake Erie to Lake Ontario, has known all his life just how special his home is. He's all for the peace park but isn't sure a full "re-imagining" is necessary.

"People keep saying, 'We've got to do some branding,'" he says. "*What for?* I'm pretty sure if you were to use the word 'Niagara' any-where in the world, they'd know where you meant."

They should know, as well, that Oscar Wilde had it wrong. Today it is far more "water falling the *right* way." Nor is water "endless," as he thought. It is, rather, priceless, and the Niagara River, so long abused, has become an encouraging example of that modern realization.

THE NIAGARA RIVER

CHAPTER SEVEN

"THE RHINE OF NORTH AMERICA": THE SAINT JOHN

THERE IS NOTHING PARTICULARLY EYE-CATCHING about Burpee Bar, a small, flat, brush-covered island about a dozen kilometres upstream from Fredericton. It is, however, unique—and for that reason it has been declared a reserve by the Nature Trust of New Brunswick.

Nature cannot break Burpee Bar. Ice scours it like steel wool as winter levels rise and fall and the ice pack grinds its way down the Saint John River. Spring floods drown the bar. And yet, each summer rare plants like Brunet's milk vetch and Rand's goldenrod spring up defiantly. The bar was once renowned for the Atlantic salmon that could be found in surrounding pools, the iconic sport fish large and healthy and numbering in the hundreds of thousands.

But no more. Burpee Bar might be able to handle nature, but its waters cannot survive man.

"We're basically down to counting individual fish," says Simon Mitchell, area adviser for WWF-Canada's Living Rivers Initiative. "The Saint John River historically was *the* salmon river. It wasn't the

Miramichi, it wasn't the Restigouche. It was the Saint John River."

What pollution doesn't kill, what the dams don't block, and what overfishing obviously does, is too few. Today, this stretch of the Saint John River is closed entirely to fishing.

Philip Lee would agree. Lee, a journalism professor at St. Thomas University in Fredericton, is a passionate fisher of the river—in those areas where fishing is still permitted. He is also the author of *Home Pool: The Fight to Save the Atlantic Salmon*, a passionate plea for conservation, protection and restoration.

"This may have been the largest producer of migratory fish in eastern North America," Lee says as he poles his six-metre square-stern canoe through the currents swirling past Burpee Bar. "They are here in the hundreds now instead of the hundreds of thousands."

In American author Annie Proulx's 2016 bestseller, *Barkskins*, she describes the Saint John as it was in the heyday of the logging industry— the fast current and standing waves of the river's rapids, as well as the quiet areas of "still water at the tail, where, in the old days before the rivers carried millions of bobbing, colliding logs, big salmon would lie."

Today's low numbers of salmon are verified by the Atlantic Salmon Federation, which released a report in mid-August 2016 that tallied 482 grilse (young salmon returning to the river to spawn for the first time) and 173 large salmon along the Saint John River. A year earlier it was 586 grilse and 86 large—a far cry from the mid-1990s, when the average count was more than 3,000 grilse and almost 2,000 large salmon.

"The Saint John certainly needs all the help it can get," the report concluded.

Is it the "St. John River" or the "Saint John River"? Both, apparently. The New Brunswick Ministry of Tourism, Heritage and Culture, which is responsible for toponymy—official place names—says the waterway, in both official languages, is the "Saint John River" and "Rivière Saint-Jean."

Many historians beg to differ, pointing out that the river—called Wolastoq by the Maliseet, meaning "beautiful river"—was renamed by Sieur de Monts and Samuel de Champlain in 1604 after they reached the river mouth on the Bay of Fundy on June 24, John the Baptist's feast day. Hence, "St. John." Older references to the river use "St. John," though locals and most media today use "Saint" rather than "St."— perhaps to prevent any confusion with St. John's, Newfoundland, which many confuse with Saint John, New Brunswick.

No matter what it is called, it is most assuredly beautiful. The Saint John River runs for 673 kilometres as it drains a vast ancient mountain area that lies roughly two-thirds in New Brunswick but also includes sprawling hills of northern Maine and significant water-shed in the southeastern portion of Quebec.

It is a river of vastly different personalities, raging like Niagara as it roars through Grand Falls, placid enough to be called "The Rhine of North America" as it slides through the rich farmland of the Saint John River Valley, pastoral as it passes Florenceville-Bristol ("The French Fry Capital of the World") and slips under "The World's Longest Covered Bridge" at Hartland, park-like as it moves through the city of Fredericton and twists its way past First Nations Oromocto, touching vast Grand Lake, and moving ever southward toward Saint John. It passes over falls and rapids and dams. It provides a border between the United States and Canada. And it is a major tourist attraction at Saint John, where the high tides of the Bay of Fundy and the ceaseless flow of the river create a phenomenon known as "The Reversing Falls."

"Happiness is the word which always comes to my mind when I think of the River St. John," Hugh MacLennan wrote in *Rivers of Canada*. "It is the shortest of our principal streams, being only about 420 miles long, and its system is a small one. Yet it offers so much variety of scenery that a stranger travelling along it encounters a surprise every twenty miles or so."

For centuries following the European arrival the river seemed largely taken for granted. In 1894, naturalist J.W. Bailey attempted to correct this oversight. "Of the many rivers of Northeastern America," Bailey wrote in what stands as the first serious look at the Saint John River, "it would be difficult to find one which, in the diversity of its natural features, the facilities afforded for sportsmen, and the interesting history of its colonization, is more worthy of mention than the St. John; and yet this river, viewed in its entirety, has never formed the subject of any published work."

This seems surprising, as the Saint John is a river of long history. First Nations have lived along its course for ten thousand years. The river was a critical transportation route in New France. When France and Great Britain fought during the Seven Years' War, fifteen hundred British soldiers headed up the river in early 1759, destroying Acadian settlements along the way. In one campaign known as the "Ste Anne's Massacre," New England rangers pillaged and burned the village of Sainte-Anne-des-Pays-Bas. When the captured leader of the Acadian militia refused to swear an oath of allegiance to the Crown, the soldiers killed family members in front of him, and still he would not swear.

Perhaps it was this tale that inspired Fredericton poet Alden Nowlan to describe the waters of the river he so loved as being "the colour of a bayonet."

Upstream around the mill town of Edmunston, Acadian flags are common even today, immediate reminders of the Great Expulsion that took place between 1755 and 1764. Of roughly 14,000 Acadians in the larger region, 11,500 were deported because the now-ruling British considered them disloyal. Many Acadians ended up in Louisiana, some later returning to start life again in the Upper Saint John River Valley. There is even a quirky region in this northwest corner of the province that calls itself "The Republic of Madawaska," with its own flag and "president"—really the mayor of Edmundston.

Those who feel some fealty to the "Republic" call themselves Brayons, which also refers to their unique dialect. The story links all the way back to the Treaty of Paris of 1783, which established the border between the United States and Canada. An American settler, John Baker, petitioned the state of Maine in the 1820s to annex the isolated area and its few settlers, leading to a dispute over flags and claims that at one point landed Baker in jail. The Netherlands attempted to arbitrate the dispute in the early 1830s but failed to convince Maine to drop any "manifest destiny" hopes of spreading its territory north. Ownership of the Madawaska region, part of the New Brunswick "panhandle" squeezed between Quebec to the north and Maine to the south, was disputed until 1842, when the Webster-Ashburton Treaty settled the dispute and the region was annexed to Canada East, transferring to New Brunswick in the 1850s.

A generation after the Acadian expulsion, British Loyalists fled in the other direction to escape the American Revolutionary War. An early Loyalist arrival reported back, "The Saint John is a fine river equal in magnitude to the Connecticut or Hudson . . . accessible at all seasons of the year, never frozen or obstructed by ice." It was an optimistic report and it brought fleeing Loyalists by the hundreds to settle in the growing centres of Saint John and Fredericton.

To commemorate the two-hundredth anniversary of the War of 1812 and celebrate the long and storied history of the river, Eric and Kim McCumber paddled the length of the Saint John in 2013, often wearing period costume and accompanied by other paddlers. Eric McCumber's grandfather and great-grandfather were both captains in the steamboat era of the river, and while so much of the valley has been settled and farmed, he was delighted to discover how much still appeared as his ancestors would have seen it.

"It's not a wilderness paddle," says McCumber. "But in places it can feel like it."

McCumber—a retired chemical engineer and amateur historian who has written a book on the river's first European settlement—sees the Saint John as a great "communications" system. Historians have called it "The Road to Canada" with cause. If the St. Lawrence was the first original highway, the Saint John was certainly the second.

It was the river that allowed military travel during the British-French battles over the North American colonies as well as during the expulsion of the Acadians. It was the river that led to settlement from the mouth at Saint John to eastern Quebec. Before the railways, paddle-wheelers delivered supplies along the river. The river were at the heart of the massive timber industry, carrying logs downstream from the high hills to sawmills in Fredericton and Saint John. During the U.S. Prohibition years, the upper reaches of the river were popular with bootleggers. There, where it formed the boundary between New Brunswick and Maine, the ferry between Saint Leonard, New Brunswick, and Van Buren, Maine, was said to regularly feature American travellers crossing the river quickly to return on the next ferry with "bottles of Dominion rye in hip pockets."

Today the Saint John River is a vital source of hydroelectricity. Grand Falls/Grand-Sault Dam was built in 1925 over a deep, dramatic cataract where, legend has it, a Maliseet maiden named Malabeam, who had been captured by the Mohawks, sacrificed her life by leading a Mohawk war party over the falls, thereby saving her village. The falls remain a major attraction, even though at the height of tourist season the river virtually dries up as available water is diverted for energy production.

Not so when I visited in 2016, though, as evening rains and fine daylight weather created a banner year for Zip Zag, a local zip-line operation that charges people forty dollars to fly across the spectacular gorge and back.

"It's the setting," says Christine Ouellette, who co-owns the company with her husband, Eric. "Other places have trees, but we have the falls and the gorge."

According to the local interpretive centre, on August 12, 1904, a daredevil named Van Morrell walked across the turbulent, rock-filled gorge on a 120-metre cable. He bailed the first time he tried to make it across to the 70-metre-high cliffs and returned to his starting point, but he made it on his second try. No one has tried it since.

Larger hydroelectric dams were added downstream at Beechwood and Mactaquac in 1955 and 1965, respectively. The damming dramatically changed the river's flow and created huge reservoirs. It also cut off salmon from their spawning ground, the diminishing young salmon fry often killed as they fell into the turbines while trying to make their way out to the sea.

But before any of this European settlement or development, the beautiful Wolastoq was home to the Maliseet, or Wolastoqiyik, who lived along its banks, hunting through the forested hills and catching the bountiful fish that fed and spawned in its pools. In 2011, three specific Maliseet locations along the river were designated a National Historic Site. To the Maliseet, the river was Creation itself. In the oral tradition of the people—as described by elder Gabe Paul of Pilick in 1917—a monster once stood between the Wolastoqiyik and their advancement up the waterway. When the monster was killed, it fell as a tree and, in Paul's words, "This tree became the main river . . . and the branches became the tributaries, while the leaves became the ponds at the heads of these streams."

The First Nations who lived along the Saint John River and the salmon in the river cannot be separated, says WWF-Canada's Simon Mitchell. "They are entwined," he says, "and have been since time immemorial."

———

"I've been building canoes since high school," says Steven Jones.

Now in his sixties, he carries on the trade of his father, Carl, who was one of the key builders for the world-famous Chestnut Canoe Company, the Fredericton firm whose cedar-and-canvas products were prized by such iconic Canadian paddlers as Bill Mason, Pierre Trudeau, Tom Thomson and Grey Owl. In 1920, the *Toronto Star Weekly* sent a young reporter on a fishing trip to Northern Ontario, mostly around Sault Ste. Marie. The young man, an American, reported back, "A canoe is a necessity to fish the very best waters." His name was Ernest Hemingway.

The canoes, first built by William and Harry Chestnut in 1905, became so famous that most manufacturers in North America emulated their designs, particularly for the popular "Prospector" model, which my grandfather, an Algonquin Park ranger, owned and loved. As Greg Clark, the popular outdoors writer for the *Toronto Star*, said in a letter to the Chestnuts in the early 1950s, "Your canoe is like a pair of good-fitting shoes."

The history of the Fredericton canoes—lovingly told in Roger MacGregor's 1999 book *When the Chestnut Was in Flower*—came to an end in 1979. With competition from plastics and other new materials taking over the recreational canoe market, the Chestnut factory simply closed down.

In its heyday, however, the Chestnut was lord of the Saint John River. "The Fredericton of today is preeminently a city for the cyclist and canoeist," local author Frank Risteen wrote in 1898. "Opposite the city, at the lower and the upper ends thereof, two lovely streams, the Nashwaak and the Nashwaaksis, merge their existence in the river. Who can wonder that, when the moon is high and the heart of a man is young, the birch canoe will linger there in the liquid shadows and happy souls embark to sail the river of life to unknown seas."

Years passed following the demise of the Chestnut factory in

Fredericton, but eventually First Nations Oromocto, downstream from the capital, decided the canoes could be built there. After all, many of the best canoe builders for Chestnut had come from the Maliseet community.

Steven Jones had worked for Chestnut Canoe to its bitter end. After First Nations Oromocto took over the original moulds, he was soon back at work building the same canoes he'd begun building as a teenager. "These moulds are over a hundred years old," Jones says, waving his hammer toward the back of the Great Spirit Canoes factory. "And we're still banging canoes off them."

The canoes built by Great Spirit are exact replicas of the originals but they cannot carry the Chestnut name, as it was purchased decades ago by an Ontario canoe builder.

"These are *real* Chestnuts," Jones contends defiantly.

Some aficionados of the original Chestnuts treat their vessels like works of art, but Jones has no time for such thinking. "These canoes are built to be used," he says. And used, whenever possible, on the Saint John River, which flows within sight of the Great Spirit factory.

"I've fished it," he says. "I've canoed it. I've had motorboats on it. All my life. It's a beautiful river—and these canoes were made for it."

There are issues big and small along the path of the Saint John River, but even the small ones are huge to those feeling them most directly.

The people of little Gagetown, for example, have lost their beloved ferry, which was pretty much the main tourist draw in the area. Three ferries along the river were decommissioned by the provincial government and no community is as upset as Gagetown. Farmers here, about halfway upriver from Saint John to the capital, say they now have to travel much farther to deliver produce to market. Shoppers say their trips to the larger centres take longer.

Kylia Mazariegos's complaint is far simpler: she simply wants to take her one-year-old daughter, Marleigh, on it.

"I wanted my kids to experience it," says the waitress from the Old Boot Pub by the river. "It was the most wonderful thing to go on as a kid. The whole town wants it back."

Even the most local of river issues can be big news, and the anger sizzles regularly in the *Daily Gleaner*. "The loss of the Gagetown-Jemseg ferry has directly resulted in a loss of jobs, and a downturn in tourism for the local economies," Gerald Breau argued in an August 2016 letter to the editor. "Indeed some businesses in the Gagetown area have reported a drop of 50 percent since the ferry was removed. Does this all seem to go counter to the government's goal of increasing tourism and creating jobs? Yes, of course it does.

"It is time for the government to review and reverse this decision before businesses begin to close and jobs that were supporting the local economy are permanently gone."

The sitting provincial member of Parliament, a Tory, has said the Liberal provincial government should sell the ferry to the village for one dollar. The minister of transportation says, "The decision is final—the ferry is not coming back." So enraged are the townsfolk over this cavalier attitude toward their relationship with the river that the mothballed ferry is expected to remain the top local issue in the election that is still two years away.

Another, and far greater, issue dividing the Saint John River Valley is Energy East, TransCanada Corporation's proposed 4,600-kilometre pipeline, which would convert approximately 3,000 kilometres of existing natural gas pipeline and require 1,600 kilometres of new pipeline, most of it right down the valley. If completed, it would be the largest oil pipeline in North America. Critics say it would increase national greenhouse gas emissions by thirty-two million tonnes—more than is currently generated by all the Atlantic provinces combined.

In New Brunswick, there are two fairly clear sides on the pipeline issue. One side, voiced mostly closer to the ocean, sees the creation of four thousand full-time jobs in the economically challenged province. Some $15.7 billion would be spent over nine years to build a line that would bring 1.1 million barrels of crude each day from Alberta to Saint John refineries and a new export terminal. The Conference Board of Canada says the project would pump $36 billion into the national economy over the next two decades, much of the money ending up in New Brunswick pockets.

There is, however, another side. "An oil spill anywhere in this valley would be catastrophic," says Philip Lee. "It's a river, after all."

By early 2017, the National Energy Board had still to rule on the controversial project, and the Conservation Council of New Brunswick had already moved to release a report sharply critical of the plan. "We believe the risk to the environment and existing jobs in fisheries, tourism, agriculture and forestry outweighs the potential benefits," the report concludes. Instead, the council argues, the province should concentrate on renewable power projects.

One renewable power source, however, is itself a major issue in the river valley, and that is what to do with the Mactaquac Dam, about twenty kilometres upstream from Fredericton. Expected to last a century when it was built in the mid-1960s, the facility supplies about 20 percent of the province's power, so when projections for the end of its lifespan crept to as soon as 2030, much debate ensued.

New Brunswick Power, which owns the dam, invited the public to help decide its future. There were four options: rebuild the dam and generating station, rebuild just the dam to maintain the headpond at current levels, partially rebuild the facility to expand its lifeline—or rip the dam out and let the river return to its natural flow through the area.

In late December of 2016, NB Power announced it would maintain the dam until 2068, giving the structure another four decades or so of use by committing $2.9 billion to $3.6 billion toward reinforcement, repair and equipment replacement. The chairman of the NB Power board, Ed Barrett, said, "We believe we have made a sound decision about Mactaquac that makes good business sense, meets the present and future needs of New Brunswick's changing power grid and reflects the values of New Brunswickers. As a public utility, we clearly understand that any course of action regarding Mactaquac has deep and lasting consequences."

The various options will remain open but the time frame, clearly, has been moved far into the future. Many who had hoped for full removal of the dam no longer think that likely, as one of the significant uses of the dam is flood control. Fredericton has a long history of flood problems, most recently with severe flooding in 2008. There is also the matter of outraged cottagers whose prized river shoreline would be lost. "It's not a free-flowing river anymore, and that causes me concern," says Lee, who would like nothing better than to see the salmon return to the Saint John in numbers not seen since the dams were constructed. "I do feel it needs to be released and not held back. It may or may not happen.

"It's a bit of heartbreak that way."

Simon Mitchell of WWF-Canada says that Energy East, if completed, would have around two hundred stream crossings as it made its way through the valley to Saint John. There are a great many who would prefer to avoid the risk of a spill and, instead, find future energy from solar, wind and, most promising, Bay of Fundy tidal shifts.

But, he says, the reality is that such solutions are neither instant nor certain. "This has always been a working river," says Mitchell, "and will continue to be so. So striking a balance is important."

Five years ago, the Canadian Rivers Institute published a state-of-the-environment report on the Saint John River. It estimated the population of the river basin at close to half a million residents. Forestry, the dams, hog and poultry farms, the country's third largest potato crop, mills, paper products, rayon and other industries have punished the river for two centuries. But, said the report, "The overall quality of the river has improved in the last forty years."

This improvement is mostly due to communities now treating their waste water. Agriculture sediments and, in some areas, untreated sewage remain major concerns, as does continuing pulp and paper production. In late 2015, the Twin Rivers Paper Company, based in Edmundston, was fined $320,000 by Environment Canada for a spill that occurred in the fall of 2013 and violations of the wastewater approval limit six months later.

In March of 2016, WWF-Canada released its watershed report on the river and evaluated the threats. Overuse of water was "low" and habitat loss "moderate"—but pollution was deemed a "very high" threat.

Eric McCumber, the paddler, worked in the pulp and paper industry all over Canada as well as in the Saint John River Valley. He does not mince words when he says, "The pulp mills killed the river. For generations you couldn't go near the river. People stayed away."

But no longer. On a warm summer day, there are swimmers and kayakers, canoeists and motorboats all along the river. In those areas where it is allowed, they fish for striped bass and, yes, the Atlantic salmon that once made the Saint John *the* salmon river. Sharing these waters are Atlantic and shortnose sturgeon. The shortnose sturgeon has been listed as an endangered species and, because they are now flourishing, there has been a movement to have them delisted.

"It's not perfect," says McCumber, "but it's relatively healthy. We're considered a 'have-not' province—but we have a wonderful place here."

Poling his long canoe past Burpee Bar, Philip Lee has to agree: "It's such a beautiful river. And to have something like this so close to the city—two hours upriver and you're into a completely different world."

A world where, one day, with a little luck and a lot of future thinking, they may again count the salmon by the thousands.

CHAPTER EIGHT

THE MACKENZIE: RIVER OF DISAPPOINTMENT OR HOPE

THAT BIG WAD OF BILLS . . .

Floyd Roland was ten years old when his older brother John went off to work in the oil fields as a welder. John Roland would return to the family home, well north of the Arctic Circle in Inuvik, Northwest Territories, with his pockets stuffed full of cash. He carried so many bills you could almost hear the "pop" as he pulled the money out to show his younger siblings.

To a young Inuvialuk whose large family was still mostly living off the land and the Mackenzie River—hunting caribou in winter, harvesting belugas at the mouth of the river in summer—the allure of all that money was impossible to resist: Floyd Roland was determined to fill his own pockets with the same.

Great change was coming to the Mackenzie watershed—a sprawling vastness of mountains, valleys, two vast lakes, tributaries, main river and delta making up an astonishing one-fifth of Canada—and it wasn't just the Roland brothers dreaming about what the future might bring to those living along the top of North America. As far back as 1958, then prime minister John Diefenbaker had introduced his "Northern Vision"—a "New Canada, A CANADA OF THE NORTH!"—that included millions of federal dollars for new roads that would open the North to exploration for oil and gas and minerals.

The year Floyd Roland was born, 1961, author Hugh MacLennan predicted that "in the year 2061 there will be at least three million people living in the Mackenzie Valley. There will be hospitals, schools, and at least two universities established on sites overlooking this cold, clean river." Three *million* people—and pockets filled with cash.

Floyd Roland grew up to become an auto mechanic and has vivid memories of the great Mackenzie Valley Pipeline debate of the 1970s, when the federal government commissioned Justice Thomas Berger to conduct hearings throughout the affected area. Four decades ago, it was the elders who spoke up against the pipeline, leaders like Fort Good Hope chief Frank T'Seleie, who turned on prominent Calgary oilman Bob Blair during the hearings, saying: "You are like the Pentagon, Blair, planning the slaughter of the innocent Vietnamese. Don't tell me you are not responsible. You are the twentieth-century General Custer. You are coming with your troops to slaughter us and steal land that is rightfully ours. You are coming to destroy a people that have a history of thirty thousand years. Why? For twenty years of gas? Are you really that insane?" Chief T'Seleie vowed that he would, if necessary, lay down his life so that the unborn could "know the freedom of this land."

The Indigenous people of the affected area, particularly the elders, wanted nothing to do with drilling and certainly nothing to do with a risky pipeline that could do serious damage to their land and to animal migration—let alone the costs of a major spill. Justice Berger listened to this and other emotionally charged testimony and, aware that the energy minister of the day had claimed Canada contained enough oil to last 923 years and enough gas for 329 years, decided there was no need to hurry. "If a pipeline were built now in the Mackenzie Valley," Justice Berger reported in 1977, "its economic benefits would be limited, its social impact devastating." He recommended a ten-year moratorium to give ample time for the settlement of various land claims.

So much for the anticipated boom. The town of Inuvik's population fell by 500 within a year. Today, the population of the Mackenzie Valley is about 10,000. Or, put another way, still some 2,990,000 short of Hugh MacLennan's prediction.

Floyd Roland, still believing a pipeline would one day be built, began to show interest in politics during the early-1980s settlement of the Inuvialuit Land Claim. In 1995, the auto mechanic won a seat in the Legislative Assembly of the Northwest Territories in Yellowknife. By the time a new round of hearings on the pipeline took place in 2006, he had risen to become minister of finance.

Roland was barely a teenager when Justice Berger held the first round of pipeline hearings and the elders had been so much against it. This time, however, a great many elders were in favour of development and it seemed a certainty that the Mackenzie Gas Project would meet approval.

When I attended the hearings at Fort Simpson in 2006, I ran into elder after elder who was now fully in favour of the pipeline. Alphonsine Cazon sat on a park bench outside the hearings one day and condemned the procedure. "They're crazy," she told me. "Why are they sticking their noses where it's not wanted? It's jobs. We need that. We need jobs."

The Joint Review Panel finished their hearings and recommended massive environmental conditions—with such forces as the World

Wildlife Fund Canada (WWF-Canada) onside—and in late 2010 the National Energy Board approved the $16.2-billion project that would see a 1,196-kilometre Arctic pipeline for natural gas built between the Beaufort Sea and northern Alberta.

"We applaud the leadership exhibited by the Joint Review Panel," said Dr. Robert Powell, director of WWF-Canada's Mackenzie River Basin program. "The Panel showed the way to progress from the historic pattern of exploitation to a future of environmental stewardship. It's now up to the federal and territorial governments to adopt that approach in a visionary way, in the context of the existing land claims."

The NEB put 264 conditions in place but argued that if they were met Canada's North would prosper. The pipeline, which would also tap into onshore fields, could carry enough natural gas each day to heat four million homes. The resource consortium led by Calgary's Imperial Oil included three other giant energy companies as well as the Aboriginal Pipeline Group. It would be the largest private undertaking in Canadian history.

As minister of finance Floyd Roland had said during the hearings, "We could be the next Alberta—maybe even bigger." It was a familiar refrain up and down the Mackenzie River. Something happened, though. The price of natural gas peaked, then retreated. New fields were found around the world, including the U.S. With futures running less than half what they were in 2007, the year Floyd Roland was elected premier, interest began to lag.

When I spoke with Roland in 2016, he'd left his very active public life (he served as mayor of Inuvik before running for the Conservatives in the 2015 election) to become an executive with a construction firm in Inuvik. Roland says he would go to meetings with the resource consortium and they would tell him, "This project is 'skinny'"—meaning the margin of profit had thinned to a point where they no longer thought it worthwhile. The pipeline, approved to be underway by 2015, has yet to start, and projected costs have now risen to $21 billion. In June of 2016, the NEB approved a six-year extension, giving the consortium until the end of 2022 to begin construction.

But will it ever happen?

"When I was an MLA," says Roland, "I'd come home and everyone would say, 'What's the latest on the pipeline?' Now people don't even want to talk about it. And those who do talk are saying, 'Not in my lifetime.'"

Ambitious plans that sink have a lengthy tradition along the Mackenzie River. Back on June 3, 1789, twenty-five-year-old Alexander Mackenzie set out from Fort Chipewyan, on the southern shore of Lake Athabasca, to look for the Pacific Ocean. His mentor, Peter Pond, had become convinced that the river the Dene called Deh Cho ("Mighty River") was the Northwest Passage. With a crew of four voyageurs, two bringing along their wives, as well as a German, a Native known as "English Chief" and his two wives, and a couple of young followers, Mackenzie travelled along the Slave River to Great Slave Lake, battling late ice and mosquitoes, in a small flotilla of birchbark canoes. The river that would be named for him flowed north from Great Slave.

Natives had warned the young, curly-haired Scot about the dangers of the river and the monsters to be found farther north, but he pressed on into the widening river running north from Great Slave, insisting that such a huge river could only lead to the fabled Northwest Passage to the Pacific Ocean. He was so certain of triumph that he carried along rubles to trade with the Russians.

When the river turned north at the Camsell Range, however, he knew he was wrong. The river was headed for the Arctic Ocean, not the Pacific. The paddlers reached salt water, realized this was not the ocean they had hoped for, turned around and were back in Fort

Chipewyan by September 12, having travelled more than 4,800 kilo-metres in just over three months.

Though historians quibble over whether he actually used the phrase, Alexander Mackenzie has gone down in history for calling the waterway that now bears his name the "River of Disappointment."

For people like Floyd Roland who live along the Mackenzie and love it as their home, a more appropriate tag might be "River of Frustration."

But never without hope.

> *This river belongs*
> *wholly to itself*
> *obeying its own laws . . .*
>
> *A river so Canadian*
> *it turns its back*
> *on America.*

—"Mackenzie River," F.R. Scott

Pope John Paul II came to Canada three times. In 1984 and 2002, he attracted crowds by the hundreds of thousands to empty fields and abandoned airstrips, usually within walking distance of the country's major centres. In 1987, he came, slightly unexpectedly, somewhat unnoticed, at the end of a triumphant papal tour of the United States, just to drop in for a few hours to an old fur-trading post on the banks of the Mackenzie River.

Fort Simpson was originally called "Fort of the Forks," as it sits on an island where the Mackenzie and Liard rivers meet. Founded by the North West Company, it was rebuilt and renamed after the North West Company and the Hudson's Bay Company merged in 1821. It was also known as "The Garden of the Mackenzie," as the Sacred Heart

Mission on the island produced a surprising amount of produce for being so far north.

Pope John Paul II came here to keep a promise—a promise that could so easily have been broken—to make up for a planned visit to Fort Simpson during the 1984 tour that had been cancelled by, well, an act of God: fog.

It was warm but raining, that day in 1987 when the Pope came back. Only three thousand people from the Mackenzie River Valley's sixty-eight First Nations turned out to see him—and yet they heard words that are likely to outlive anything else the popular Pope said to Canada's thirteen million Roman Catholics on his earlier visit. The Pope wore a vestment of caribou skin that had been bleached white and he stood beneath a large white umbrella. He turned to face the four directions and prayed, intriguingly, to the Great Spirit and—at a time when this country was impossibly wound up about rights and constitutional confusion—he spoke directly to the first people of this country: "I affirm your right to a just and equitable measure of self-government, along with a land base and adequate resources for developing a viable economy for present and future generations."

They were words eagerly received in 1987. Thirty years later, the people of the Mackenzie River are still awaiting that "right," still trying to come to terms with the vastness of the territory in which they live and still not sure what should be done with it.

Very close to the park where the Pope prayed and spoke that day is the Fort Simpson Visitor Information Centre, where sits the cabin of Albert Faille. The American-born trapper, who died in 1973 at the age of eighty-seven, lived in this small cabin along the nearby Nahanni River. For decades, Faille trapped and prospected throughout the Mackenzie Valley and never lost his awe of the land. As he put it, "A lifetime wouldn't be enough for a man to see all this."

The size of the Mackenzie is nothing short of intimidating. At Fort Simpson's riverside park, village elders often go to sit on a wide bench and stare out at the "Cold Amazon," as it was called by Robert Sandford, the Canadian chair for water and climate security at the United Nations University Institute for Water, Environment and Health. Some of that water sliding so calmly by Fort Simpson comes from as far away as the Columbia Icefield in the Alberta Rockies, some has come from British Columbia and the Yukon and has crashed through the wild rapids of the Liard's Grand Canyon, and much has come from Great Slave Lake, the deepest body of water in all North America.

The Mackenzie River, including its two great upstream supply lines, the Peace and Athabasca rivers, travels 4,241 kilometres before it reaches the Beaufort Sea. It is the second largest river in North America after the Mississippi. The watershed spans three western provinces and two territories, covering approximately 1.8 million square kilometres, largest by far in all of Canada and triple the size of France. The river drains a remarkable 20 percent of the country's entire land mass. Its variety is nothing short of jaw-dropping: mountains, canyons, stretching to as much as four kilometres wide at times, squeezing back into long rapids through limestone cliffs, endless black spruce—all leading to a confusing maze of delta before finally reaching the ocean.

"If rivers are the blood vessels of a country, carrying the essential stuff of life between their banks, the mighty Mackenzie is one of the main arteries," Bruce W. Hodgins and Gwyneth Hoyle wrote in *Canoeing North into the Unknown*. The river, they continued, "rises in Great Slave Lake and flows west and northwest, broad, strong and single-minded until it reaches the confused and many-channelled delta, where it empties into the Arctic Ocean. . . . Apart from one dangerous and well-publicized rapid, the Sans Sault, between Norman Wells and Fort Good Hope, the greatest hazard comes from the sudden violent squalls which can whip up huge and destructive waves on the wide body of water."

The initial attraction for the Europeans was, of course, the fur trade. Posts were established at fairly regular stops: Fort Providence, Fort Simpson, Wrigley, Fort Norman, Norman Wells, Fort Good Hope, Arctic Red River, Fort McPherson, Aklavik, Reindeer Depot and Tuktoyaktuk. But furs were far from the only commercial attraction.

Alexander Mackenzie took note of a strange yellow seepage as he paddled past where Norman Wells is today, but he had no sense then that this meant oil. It would not be long, however, before other resources would be exploited.

In the 1930s, Gilbert LaBine was prospecting near Great Bear Lake (more than halfway downstream from Great Slave Lake to the Arctic Ocean) and discovered silver, but he convinced himself that the enormous costs of transportation would not make mining it worthwhile. In 1898–99, there was a gold rush to the area around present-day Yellowknife and there are still the remains of the Giant mining operations. Pitchblende, a radioactive uranium-rich material, was also found in the Mackenzie Valley and, during the top-secret early years of the Second World War, the area held "the most important mine in the world." It was uranium from the Eldorado Mine at Great Bear Lake that supplied the Manhattan Project and led to the development of the atomic bombs that were dropped on Hiroshima and Nagasaki in 1945.

Natural resources would form the modern history of the area, from the gold rush years at the end of the nineteenth century to the discovery of oil and natural gas fields both on and off shore to the Diavik Mine 220 kilometres from the Arctic Circle, where each minute of each day a new diamond is found.

I flew in to the Diavik Diamond Mine in the summer of 2006, a three-hundred-kilometre flight north and east of Yellowknife, in an Air Tindi Dash 7 charter taking workers back for their four-days-in, three-days-out workweek. Some of the fifty workers aboard—many of them First Nations—joked that they were going "home," for they are treated very well in such isolation. "It's like staying in a hotel," Barry Sanderson, a chef, told me. "You get your own room, your own bathroom, your own phone, own television—a hundred channels."

The mining camp is on a twenty-square-kilometre island in Lac de Gras, less than an hour's flight northeast of Yellowknife. It has its own landing strip, water-treatment plant and fuel reservoirs, and enough accommodations for 750 workers. Two massive pits extend out into the lake, each protected by dikes. Yellow 210-tonne Komatsu trucks filled with earth work their way up the pits by climbing in circles along the sides. The tires alone cost $30,000 each. Two million tonnes a year are removed from the pits and dumped in the distance, creating new, ever-growing hills. Smaller, ninety-tonne trucks also make the climb, their boxes filled with black material known as kimberlite.

Kimberlite takes its name from a famous nineteenth-century diamond mine at Kimberley in South Africa. It is an unusual substance formed by small volcanoes that stirred millions of years ago and worked their way toward the surface, carrying along billion-year-old diamonds as accidental passengers. Volcanoes broke through the rocky surface around the Diavik site in the Northwest Territories about fifty-five million years ago, making them infants compared with the two-and-a-half-billion-year-old rock itself. One kimberlite vein, tagged "A154 South," is considered the richest pipe in the world by value per tonne.

The Diavik operation is about thirty kilometres from the Mackenzie Valley's first and largest discovery, the Ekati Diamond Mine, near a camp that legendary Kelowna prospector Chuck Fipke had nicknamed "Misery" before he made what may yet prove to be the greatest mineral discovery in the North. Experts have said the diamond discoveries by Diavik and other companies operating in the North today exceed the value of both the California Gold Rush of 1849 and the Klondike rush of 1897–98.

Despite a 1916 report that claimed, "The block of territory has no known natural resources of sufficient importance to attract people to the region," the potential haul for the three main mines in the Territories has been pegged at $40 billion.

Fipke found the future Diavik Mine in 1991, after years of exploration around areas previously checked by an abandoned De Beers exploration camp in the Territories. De Beers is famous both for its secrecy and for its remarkable ability to maintain the lure of diamonds over the years. "The genius of De Beers' marketers," author Matthew Hart wrote in *Diamond: A Journey to the Heart of an Obsession*, "lies in having forged a link between something people do not need, diamonds, and something they do need, love." De Beers obviously had a hunch that there were diamonds in the area but were unable to find what Fipke eventually developed into the Diavik Mine. Thanks to De Beers' famous secrecy about its explorations, even those locations the company abandons, we might never know how it missed out on one of the world's largest and most desirable mineral deposits. Because they are not "blood diamonds" mined in African regions through the forced labour of women and children, the Canadian gems are so sought after today that already Canada has become the number three diamond producer in the world.

Many in the area remain justifiably wary of development. Port Radium eventually became known as "the village of widows," so many men died after working in the mines. That same summer I visited the village of Dettah, just outside of Yellowknife, where the water had long ago been poisoned by the arsenic used in gold extraction at a nearby mine. Village elder Michel Paper, who was then ninety-three, talked to me about life before the 1930s, when the mining began. It was 1934 before he saw his first white man. He was offered a job as a labourer and handed a shovel. "I'd never seen a shovel before," he recalled. "I didn't know what it was for. I could hunt. I could snowshoe. I could run a dog team. I could fish. I could trap. But I didn't even know how to hold this shovel."

Almost instantly things began to change for the Indigenous people who lived in the valley. "Everything is here," the old man said. "A lot of gold. A lot of diamonds. A lot of oil and gas. The Creator did so many things for us. He put fish in the water and we took the fish out and He never asked us for anything. He never asked for anything. The white man asks for everything. I think the white man has more power. The white man has more power than the Creator.

"We lived so good before the white man came. Nobody ever got sick. We got our food from the land. We got our fish from the lake. We drank water from the lake. . . . There's no animals anymore. Big animals are all gone. I don't know where they've gone. We're scared to eat the fish now because we're told they're all poisoned. We're told not to drink the water."

Even today water must be trucked in from Yellowknife to this lovely First Nations village on the shores of Great Slave Lake.

There is some debate as to how the "white man" became so powerful in the Mackenzie Valley. French-born Oblate priest René Fumoleau arrived in the Territories in 1953 and served in various communities for decades. A gifted photographer and historian, he began looking into Treaties 8 and 11 in the 1970s and eventually wrote a book about his findings. According to Father Fumoleau, it was the intervention of the powerful bishop Gabriel Breynat that pushed a treaty agreement on the Natives. In the summer of 1921, some three hundred came to Fort Simpson and received $12 each and were considered then to be under treaty. Fumoleau found an elderly man, Baptiste Norwegian, who recalled the "signing" much differently from the official Ottawa version of events. Norwegian claimed no one even answered an oral

"Yes" to the commissioner—he merely started handing out the money, the Natives gathered there took what was thrust at them, and this was considered a fair treaty arrangement.

The bishop must have had a conscience. In 1938, after spending nearly four decades in the Northwest, he wrote a sort-of confessional for the *Toronto Star Weekly* magazine.

> The story of the white man's invasion of the Canadian Northwest may be named by future historians as one of the blackest blots on the pages of Canadian history. It is an ugly story. A story of greed and ruthlessness and broken promises. It is the story of the degradation of our Northwest Indians.
>
> Never before has the whole story been told. Canadians have heard only of the fortunes in furs and the gold and the silver and radium ores of this stern country. Occasionally they have seen newspaper reports of starvation and suffering among the Indians.
>
> But Canadians should know the facts of our Northwest. Because, unless they act at once they will some day bear the scorn of all peoples for having blindly allowed a noble race to be destroyed.

Jamie Bastedo, a naturalist who has lived more than thirty years in Yellowknife, says an American kayaker once complained that the Mackenzie "is too big to be called a river." Bastedo considers that a fair point, especially on a river that bulges out at one point, Mills Lake, to a twenty-kilometre-wide expanse of water.

Bastedo was commissioned by the Trans Canada Trail to produce an official guide, *Northwest Territories*, which he brought out in 2010 after travelling some three thousand kilometres along the river, including a paddle from Great Slave to the Beaufort Sea, the mouth of the Mackenzie. "Rivers are the traditional trails up here," Bastedo says, "whether liquid or frozen. The Mackenzie was the 401 of the northwest country, with all the exit lanes heading out onto the tundra."

In writing about the river "bend by bend," Bastedo discovered the rich history of the river, from the remnants of old paddle wheelers to abandoned huts at Axe Point, which served as the staging area and distribution centre for the U.S. military while constructing the Canol Pipeline between Norman Wells and Alaska during the Second World War.

At the dangerous Sans Sault Rapids, downstream from where the Mountain River joins the Mackenzie, Bastedo came across a memorial for Hugh Donald Lockhart Gordon, who drowned back in 1961 at the age of twenty. His family put up the tepee-shaped shelter to warn future paddlers to keep to the left on the dangerous run. In a logbook inside the memorial, someone has written: "To all those who travel the waters of this magical place; go with balance and safety; confidence tempered by humility. Enjoy wildlife and pleasant unexpected surprises; and find a sense of place."

"It's just a treasure trove of stories," says Bastedo. "You can't look at the Mackenzie without thinking of the people who have been here."

It is a river so large and potentially overwhelming that it has a profound influence on all who travel it. Between 1997 and 1999, legendary Canadian paddler Max Finkelstein retraced the 1793 voyage of Alexander Mackenzie. He did so during time off work—he was with the federal government in Ottawa—and with various friends, though the first long leg, Ottawa to Cumberland House, Saskatchewan, he travelled solo. The next year he and a friend paddled up the Fraser—a formidable feat—and then down the Peace River into the Mackenzie Valley. "That trip for me was a pilgrimage to being Canadian," said the Ottawa-born Finkelstein. "To see the land from a canoe, to see the landscapes changing at the speed a canoe travels, to sleep on the land—it lets the land soak into you. I really feel Canadian now."

In the early 1990s, another modern-day voyageur, John Donaldson, a Scottish-born medical researcher from Montreal, set out to replicate Alexander Mackenzie's travels. A holiday paddler before undertaking this enormous challenge, it took Donaldson, since deceased, five years to complete the 12,000-kilometre journey. He had his terrifying experiences—the rapids of the Fraser River, high winds on Lake Winnipeg, multiple bear run-ins—but he was overwhelmed with compassion for the Aboriginal people he met along the way. Best of all, though, was the letter from his six grandchildren that he received when he reached Bella Coola, British Columbia. "Your spirit and determination are an inspiration to all those you have met along the voyage and especially to us, your loving family."

It was while crossing Great Slave Lake that Donaldson began encountering fishermen who complained about deformed fish. They blamed the condition on PCBs in the water and other pollutants from mills far upstream on rivers that fed the Mackenzie.

In recent years, environmental concerns have increased. In 2006, when the pipeline hearings were being resumed, Grand Chief Herb Norwegian of the Dehcho Nation told me, "The Alberta tar sands are growing like a tumour. And now we're going to run a blood vessel to it that will just get contaminated."

A decade ago, when the National Energy Board gave the green light to go ahead after the latest inquiry into the building of a pipeline, WWF-Canada supported the initiative. Peter Ewins, a specialist in species conservation with WWF-Canada, says that it was increasingly clear that people in the communities along the Mackenzie had their "brains and hearts set on an upgraded lifestyle based on oil and gas. For them the traditional lifestyle based on harvesting wildlife and fish and berries and all that stuff is of lesser importance. So they are prepared to sacrifice the traditional beliefs of how you need to tread lightly and think seven generations at a time."

If development was inevitable, the strategy adopted by WWF-Canada was to "hitch the conservation message to" the approval and the consortium that was then determined to go ahead with the oil and natural gas exploration and removal. They did this, says Ewins, "not just because the Mackenzie was magnificent habitat, but because we thought this would be the elevation of that bar towards what would be a new standard for the natural exploitation of these regions."

The Gordon Foundation, a private philanthropic organization out of Toronto, has invested $27 million in northern community initiatives over the past quarter-century, with particular attention being paid to water quality. More than twenty communities in the Mackenzie Valley now monitor their own systems and share data on Mackenziedatastream.com, a website the foundation launched in 2015.

As well, the territories and the provinces of Alberta and British Columbia have negotiated bilateral agreements designed to protect the watershed in the future.

"It's almost like people have reframed the way they talk about sustaining their communities," says Carolyn DuBois of the foundation. "They're really positive about the future."

"I found the shelf bare."

Floyd Roland is talking from his office at Northwind Industries, where the former finance minister, former premier, former mayor is now corporate relations manager with one of the companies building the 138-kilometre highway from Inuvik to Tuktoyaktuk. The $300-million cost will be two-thirds covered by the federal government. Scheduled for completion in 2017, it will be the first and only public highway to reach the shores of the Arctic Ocean, thereby linking all three Canadian coasts, the Atlantic, the Pacific and the Arctic, by road.

He had just stopped off at Stanton's, the local grocery store in Inuvik, to pick up some milk and found none—just as he had predicted would be the case a couple of days earlier when word came that the Peel River ferry was unable to run because of high-water conditions, meaning trucks were no longer able to get through from the Dempster Highway.

The lack of service did not last long but it was a sharp reminder, in the summer of 2016, of how fickle transportation remains along the Mackenzie Valley, especially as residents were coping with the increasing effects of climate change. Water levels and ice conditions have a critical impact on transportation in the Far North year-round. In the twenty-first century it was necessary for linguists to bring together Inuktitut and Inuinnaqtun elders and interpreters to coin new words and phrases about the weather (*hila*). They now speak of *hilaupuunnakpallianinga* (global warming) and *hilaupaalannguqtirninga* (climate change). They worry about *nunguttut* (extinction).

The new highway north to Tuk will help and is expected to be completed in 2017. Nearly four years ago the $200-million Deh Cho Bridge across the Mackenzie River at Fort Providence opened. And there remains a commitment to twin the river with a highway that would serve all the communities. Until that happens, however, the people of the Mackenzie are still reliant on ferries, barges, trucks, ice roads in the winter and, for some communities, air transport during spring breakup and early fall freeze-ups.

Many believed the highway would be completed only if oil and natural gas came online. But the dream of a pipeline seems increasingly remote. When Jean-Luc Pépin was federal minister of Industry, Trade and Commerce during the early days of the Berger Inquiry, he argued against any notion of a moratorium: "It would be crazy to sit on it. In maybe 25 or 50 years we'll be heating ourselves from rays of the sun and then we'll kick ourselves for not capitalizing on what we had when gas and oil was a current commodity."

Some in the North are doing just that with alternative energy sources, convinced that with world prices, supply and shifting energy thinking, the pipeline will never come to pass. "My attitude when mayor was 'Better to have a hope than to shut it down 100 percent,'" says Roland.

Hope for the future has always been a mainstay of the North regardless of the realities. A people do not survive such harsh conditions for thousands of years without a firm belief in the future. It is no different today, even when the problems people face in the Mackenzie Valley go well beyond the fading dream of an oil pipeline. Inuvik's local natural gas well is "watered out," meaning the town is now trucking in propane from Alberta and mixing it with air to produce what Roland calls "synthetic natural gas." Liquid natural gas and diesel fuel are also being trucked in from British Columbia. The shortage began when Roland was still mayor. "It was like me phoning up a company in Alberta and saying, 'Ship me ice,'" he says. "It just made no sense."

People here are also nervous about the future of the Northern Transportation Company Limited (NTCL), an Edmonton-based company that provides shipping services, much by barges, to communities and exploration camps throughout the territory. Its operational headquarters at Hay River and terminals at Norman Wells, Inuvik and Tuktoyaktuk also make NTCL a major regional employer. The Inuvialuit Regional Corporation is a major investor in the company.

The company has been concerned for some time about its return on investment, citing low-water conditions and the drying up of oil and gas exploration. NTCL says it hasn't turned a profit in a decade and recently obtained court protection while restructuring. Higher water in the summer of 2016 was encouraging to its barge operators and a boost to those who felt NTCL could still be restructured successfully and continue serving the Mackenzie Valley's most remote areas.

As was said in the *Great Canadian Rivers* television series by Good Earth Productions, the Mackenzie "may be the only river on the continent that still plays the role that all great rivers have played."

The seemingly endless supply concerns have had the effect, Roland says, of turning the "non-talk of building a pipeline" into positive talk about alternatives, from greenhouses to solar and wind power. Inuvik has also connected with Decentralised Energy Canada, a Calgary-based company that works with communities on energy efficiencies.

"There's always going to be those who say, 'We're dying up here because of the cost of energy,' and there's some truth to that," says Roland. "But at the same time there's opportunities. With challenges come opportunities. And if we manage to pull this together, you create a true economy, not just a government economy.

"A newer, greener energy and a real economy."

And why not? Who, after all, saw oil and natural gas coming? Who saw the uranium discoveries or the diamond mines? In this far part of the continent where the river still plays its traditional role, it may well be that two other constants of the Mackenzie Valley, the sun and the wind, will carry and fire tomorrow's dreams.

CHAPTER NINE

RETURN TO SPLENDOUR: THE GRAND

IT IS MID-AUTUMN IN SOUTHWESTERN ONTARIO, the air surprisingly, perhaps even a bit alarmingly, warm, with the sun burning off an early morning fog along the Grand River. The air is so still the mist hovers rather than swirls as the river approaches the village of Glen Morris. The canoe and a couple of accompanying kayaks waltz through the random swifts and riffles, all quiet until a half-dozen mallard ducks explode into the sky from behind a large rock in the river.

The silence is notable in that this river and its many tributaries are surrounded by a million people. Industrial cities, college towns, tourist villages, First Nations, farms, freeways, backroads, wind turbines, discount tobacco shops and, by last count, 678 bridges occupy the sprawling watershed of the Grand River. The oldest bridge dates from 1837 and straddles Mill Creek in nearby Cambridge. Another, the "Kissing Bridge," is the oldest surviving covered bridge in the province. Wellesley Bridge No. 6, which spans the Nith River, plays a feature role in Jane Urquhart's celebrated First World War novel, *The Stone Carvers*.

At times, with no visible structures along great stretches of its shoreline and no roads within hearing distance, the Grand can seem— to quote Guelph songwriter James Gordon—almost "pastoral" as it gently twists through the rolling hills and farmland on its journey south to Lake Erie.

"There are lots of stretches where once you're on the river it's pretty much a natural environment," says the professional musician, who is also a Guelph city councillor. "It seems to reflect the farmland it travels through."

As a solo artist as well as a member of the folk group Tamarack, Gordon has recorded multiple songs about the Grand, tracing its First Nations history, its European settlement and its fascinating gorges. "She Is Fickle" might well be the song that best captures the Grand:

> Sometimes in the past she's been
> As wide as the mighty Nile,
> And other times she's just as thin
> As an undertaker's smile . . .

So thin, in fact, that in the summer of 1936 the river vanished, its bed completely dry for some eighty kilometres between its source near Dundalk and the town of Fergus. Drought and flood form much of the history of the Grand.

Once pristine, once navigable by sternwheelers running upstream as far as Brantford, once the subject of landscape artist Homer Watson's bucolic *The Flood Gate*, which hangs in the National Gallery, the Grand River was for decades so abused by waste and industrial pollution that in 1937 a *Maclean's* magazine article described it as "an open sewer" downstream from Kitchener and Waterloo.

Sometimes the Grand has earned her name,
Other times she's mire and muck.
And sometimes she's a swampy shame
Too shallow for a duck.

In a report presented at the first annual convention of the Canadian Institute on Sewage and Sanitation, held in Toronto on October 18, 1934, it was said that the industrial waste from two abattoirs, three tire and rubber factories, three tanneries, a glue factory and a dye-works "make the Kitchener sewage the strongest known in Canada."

And yet this late fall day in 2015, with the fog lifting, other canoe-ists have joined us on the Grand, and fly fishers are casting after the brown trout that today thrive downriver from Kitchener. There are ducks and osprey and, suddenly, an eagle swoops over the shoreline willows, down close to the water and away again with our breath. It is a bald eagle. "They're coming back," says Joe Farwell, the chief administrative officer of the Grand River Conservation Authority. "They're working their way back up the river."

The return of the bald eagle is most welcomed by the people of the Six Nations of the Grand River, some thirteen thousand of whom live on-reserve near Brantford while several thousand more dwell off-reserve. "It's an important symbol of our culture," says Paul General, who runs the Six Nations Wildlife Management Office in Ohsweken. "Our symbol is a white pine—the tree of peace—with an eagle perched on top."

It is also, of course, a symbol for the United States of America, appearing everywhere from gold coins to the presidential seal. As metaphor, then, it is impossible to say whether this eagle represents the river's return to health or, as some along the Grand River claim, a huge international food conglomerate seeing Canada's precious fresh water as easy prey.

Perhaps, of course, it is nothing more than a magnificent bird in search of a place to land now that the fog has lifted.

The Grand River runs 280 kilometres through the industrial and farming heartland of Ontario. It has worn many names—O:se Kenhionhata:tie ("Willow River") in Mohawk, called Grande-Rivière by the French traders, named Ouse River by early British settlers— and has a vast watershed that covers an area the size of Prince Edward Island. Its many tributaries include the Speed that flows through Guelph, the Conestoga that runs through St. Jacobs and the Nith River, where a young Walter Gretzky learned to skate and avoid the dangerous parts of the ice, a skill he later passed on to his son Wayne.

It is a slow-moving river, so slow at times that it seems it doesn't move at all, but this, as well as multiple easy access points, is precisely what makes it so attractive to leisure canoeists and kayakers. E. Pauline Johnson, the late-nineteenth-century Mohawk poet known as Tekahionwake, grew up on the banks of the Grand. Chiefswood, the 225-acre estate on Six Nations Reserve, where she was born, is today a historic site. When she wrote her most famous work, "The Song My Paddle Sings," she had only to look out a window to note, "The river slips through its silent bed. . . ."

The Grand River watershed's Aboriginal heritage is long and complicated. The "Neutrals," an Iroquoian-speaking tribe that refused to side with the French or the English during their multiple battles, was almost wiped out in the seventeenth century by the Seneca and Mohawk nations, who also had traditional claims to the vast territory.

A spectacular outcropping high above the Elora Gorge is called "Lover's Leap," so named because a Native maiden supposedly threw herself off in despair after hearing that her intended had died in one of those long-ago battles. Remnants of the Neutrals fled to Kahnawake, a Catholic mission south of Montreal, where they joined Mohawks who had fled north from the New York area. For decades the area of the Grand lay mostly unoccupied.

It was only after the American War of Independence (1775–1783) that Mohawk chief Joseph Thayendanegea Brant, a controversial figure in Aboriginal history, was able to convince the British to make good on their promise to aid their allies, which included the Mohawk, Onondaga, Cayuga and Seneca nations of the Iroquois Confederation. The year after the Treaty of Paris was signed in 1783, bringing an end to hostilities between Great Britain and its American colonies, the British Crown offered its Indigenous allies a chance to move from their traditional areas in New York's Mohawk Valley to Upper Canada. Brant and his people were granted the Haldimand Tract—land "six miles deep" on each side of the Grand River.

Today but a small portion of the Haldimand Tract remains under Six Nations control. Brant himself is often blamed for losing the land, selling it or giving it away. He was, Hugh MacLennan argued, "a soft touch for anyone who wanted some of his people's lands." MacLennan defends him, however, saying Brant was "a man who was as surely a father of the great province of Ontario as Simcoe or any other you can name."

Some of the original tract that does remain, such as the area around the town of Caledonia, led to a bitter land dispute and at times violent standoff over a proposed housing development in 2008. Though the river remains peaceful, such has not always been the case along its banks. Indigenous memory still stings from the formation of the Grand River Navigation Company back in 1832, a canal system largely funded by Six Nations that was intended to link Buffalo and Brantford by sternwheelers but which soon fizzled with the arrival of superior transport by rail. Six Nations historians refer to it as a great "swindle" by white investors that included a local member of Parliament.

Loyalists also came to the region following the American Revolution. They were granted land, some purchased land from Brant, and they began to clear farms and start new lives in Upper Canada. When Ontario was opened up for settlement in the decades following Confederation, Germans came by the thousands—Kitchener was originally called "Berlin"—and many Old Order Mennonites still farm here without the aid of electricity or mechanized implements.

The town of Fergus is named after lawyer Adam Ferguson, who arrived with six of his seven sons, obtained title to 2,954 hectares and set out to build a settlement for "carefully selected Scottish immigrants who possessed money and an education." It didn't quite work out that way, but the Scots presence remains in the magnificent stone farmhouses, and even barns, that dot the rolling landscape. The city of Guelph alone boasts some four hundred buildings constructed out of limestone quarried nearby.

Several of the towns—Paris, Fergus, Elora—are renowned for their beauty and are popular with tourists. But so, too, is "The Poorhouse" just outside of Fergus. This House of Industry and Refuge operated for seven decades, between 1877 and 1947, and was "home" to more than 1800 inmates. Populated by those who had become "feeble-minded," labourers and housemaids who could not afford anywhere to live and, sadly, old people considered a burden by their families, it was a place deeply and darkly dreaded.

One inmate, Beatrice Bolton, had kept house for her father before being forced to turn to the poorhouse in 1896, where she spent the next forty-nine years of her life. She lived with those described by the house registry as "crazy," "idiotic," "imbecile," "insane," "lunatics," "simple-minded," "sub-normal."

Industry was just as scarce at the poorhouse as refuge was. In the 1901 census, servant John Aiken, then sixty-seven, is described as being on call eighty-four hours a week, fifty-two weeks a year, for the grand sum of $240. Eighteen-year-old domestic Georgina Whitelaw also worked every week of the year, but her fifty-four-hour workweek paid only $180 per year.

The *Fergus News Record* of September 25, 1884, ran the headline "A Most Pitiable Case," followed by a subhead reading "Child born on the street."

"Last Saturday," reports the newspaper, "a strange woman, accompanied by two children, aged about two and a half and five respectively, was noticed wandering aimlessly about the streets of Fergus. . . . She is about 36 years of age, dark complexioned, and apparently of the tramp species."

This woman "of the tramp species" asked locals for help, saying she was about to give birth and had nowhere to turn. They ignored her pleas. She lay down on the street surrounded by what the newspaper described as "curious boys" and gave birth. Now with three children to care for, the woman was sent to the poorhouse.

The newspaper did not even bother with her name.

The land along the Grand River was remarkably fertile when settlers arrived, the watershed critical to prosperous farming. The nearly annual flooding, however, was damaging and dangerous. It was not until a horrific flood in 1929 that action was taken to control the waters. Thanks to the Shand Dam, completed in 1942, the area largely escaped the widespread Southern Ontario flooding caused by Hurricane Hazel in 1954. The brunt of the storm was felt in the Toronto area and north of the city, a weather catastrophe that dumped two hundred millimetres of rain on Southern Ontario in just twenty-four hours and left eighty-one dead and four thousand families homeless. The Grand River Valley was fortunate to have escaped so lightly, with flood-control dykes said to have prevented millions of dollars of damage along the river's course. Seven more water-management dams followed, and gradually—despite one severe flooding setback in the spring of 1974 around Cambridge—the watershed became relatively predictable. In the spring of 2017, with much of Ontario dealing with heavy rains and snowmelt, the area narrowly missed the flooding that threatened areas from the Toronto Islands to the Ottawa River.

The Grand River Conservation Authority was formed in the mid-1960s and has worked to replant trees lost over the years to deforestation. With twenty-eight million now planted, the forest cover of the watershed, which had fallen to 5 or 6 percent, now approaches 20 percent, which makes for a healthier watershed and prevents erosion along the river valley. The GRCA runs campsites and conservation areas, builds swimming pools, owns and controls twenty-nine dams, seven of which are built for flood control, but is most dedicated to bringing the river back to a healthy state. The Authority's success can be partially measured in the Grand's being designated a Canadian Heritage River in 1994, as well as being awarded the prestigious Thiess International Riverprize for outstanding achievement in watershed management.

"The river is a source of pride for people here," says Jeri-Lynn Catton, president of the one-hundred-member Waterloo Wellington Canoe and Kayak Club. "It's so readily available. Every time I go out on the water, if it's not absolutely perfect, it's at least excellent."

The damning 1937 *Maclean's* article also lamented, "Fishing in the Grand has become a memory; trout and bass have been replaced by carp, a scavenger fish." Today, thanks to the Authority and various "friends" of the river, the fishery has returned. In 2009 *The Canadian Fly Fisher* magazine listed the Grand as the top river in the province, with flycasters in search of brown and rainbow trout adding at least $1 million a year to the local economy.

"It's a great trout river," says Rob Heal, a guide and co-owner of the

Grand River Outfitting & Fly Shop in Fergus. "The water quality is good and there are great insects in this area—we figure twenty-five different hatches a season."

The river is divided into seven different fish-management zones, with four of the zones ruled catch-and-release only. Heal, who is also vice-president of the Friends of the Grand River, says the river is stocked with 24,000 trout fingerlings a year. Some twenty-two kilometres of the river are considered prime trout stream.

It is not all fly fishing, though. Below the dam at Caledonia, seventy-one-year-old Norman Emond fishes from a lawn chair, his pole on his knees and a line and bobber simply drifting in the slow current. The retired glassworker's son-in-law and granddaughter have hip waders and fly-fish closer to the dam. "I enjoy coming here," he says. "Always stop for a French fry on the way."

According to WWF-Canada, there are today eighty-two species of fish in the Grand River watershed, representing about half the fish species in all of Canada. "It's nice to see how it has come back," says Guelph councillor Gordon. "It was a garbage dump. But now you can catch a brown trout—and maybe even eat it."

Eating the fish is one thing—"I doubt I would," says Emond—but drinking the water quite another. The Grand River watershed is the source of potable water for almost one million Canadians.

There are always setbacks—several beaches along the river and tributaries were closed in the summer of 2015 after testing revealed high levels of E. coli—but the cleanup of the Grand watershed has been largely impressive. Modern waste-treatment facilities, better farming practices and changing industrial realities have all had beneficial effects.

WWF-Canada says the Grand "is now touted as one of the healthiest rivers in North America in a heavily-populated area," but cautions with the release of a study that found the water quality "fair" and the overall threat from pollution, habitat loss, invasive species and over-use of water "very high."

One invasive species, a weed known as Eurasian water milfoil, is costing residents around Wellington County's Puslinch Lake $130,000 a year. The weed and the sediment problems it causes have threatened to turn the picturesque body of water into a swamp, so the residents have turned to dredging twenty to thirty thousand tonnes of mud from the lake each summer. Puslinch is the largest kettle lake in North America, meaning it is fed entirely by runoff and springs and has no water flowing either in or out to threaten other parts of the watershed.

The privately owned lake and its milfoil problem, however, are of continuing concern to the Grand River Conservation Authority. Disposal of the gathered muck is carefully monitored, with the dredged material dried out and then offered to farmers and others to use as compost.

If they don't remove the muck from the lake bottom, residents believe, it will mean the end of fishing and swimming in the water. "I think most sane people would have walked away from this a long time ago," Art Zymerman, president of the Puslinch Lake Conservation Association, told the *Guelph Mercury* in the summer of 2015. "It's just been one thing after another." Even so, the residents remain optimistic that, with a few more years of dredging, they will ultimately retrieve their lake.

"We need to safeguard this crucial watershed," says Elizabeth Hendriks, director of WWF-Canada's freshwater program.

And that is why, suddenly, there is such concern growing over plans that Nestlé Waters, the bottled-water giant, has for Canada's most valuable resource.

Nestlé is a multinational company headquartered in Switzerland and with vast holdings and production in America. It is the largest food and beverage company in the world, with $100 billion in annual sales, and increasingly it is focused on the lucrative bottled-water market.

Nestlé Waters Canada calls itself "The Healthy Hydration Company" and maintains it is distributing safe drinking water to the world. Concerned residents of the Grand River watershed, however, say they are all for safe drinking water around the world—but not by taking away the water they need today and will need even more critically in the future. In the past decade, municipal use has increased from 35 percent to 60 percent of the available water (most of which finds its way back into the watershed), with considerably more population growth predicted in the years to come.

"We used to say we lived downstream from half a million people," says Paul General of Six Nations Wildlife Management. "Well, now it's a million people—and soon it will be much more than a million."

The people of Six Nations, says General, have a spiritual attachment to the river. "We're almost genetically attached to that river because we've been here so long," he says. "We're more than visitors. We're more than users. We're part of the river spiritually and genetically. We're taught to speak for nature, for all the creatures of the river and for the river itself when we talk about it.

"We have our concerns."

One concern for a great many living along the Grand River Valley watershed has been the increased popularity of bottled water. Nestlé Waters has made a conditional offer to buy the Middlebrook Water Company's spring-water source near Elora. In 2015, the company applied for a permit that would allow them to test the viability of the well by pumping out 1.6 million litres of water a day and then returning it to the Grand River. If the testing proves positive, large-scale retrieval of drinking water could begin if the company determines there is a market for the bottled water. And that water, of course, would be lost to the Grand River watershed.

Nestlé Waters has long operated a large bottled-water factory near Guelph, which provides valued jobs in the area. Nestlé has said that the Elora-area well would be supplementary to the main production facilities, to be used, for example, when the primary plant is offline for maintenance. The company has repeatedly said it is not looking for anything beyond the limit that has for more than a decade been imposed on the Middlebrook operation by the provincial ministry of the environment.

Further, the company says, bottled water currently uses 0.6 percent of the available water, less than half what the area golf courses take, and they harvest only what water can be replaced by nature. Critics point to the half-dozen droughts in the area since the late 1990s and argue that any further draws on the resource are a gamble. Already Kitchener has a once-a-week watering policy for summer lawns. With the area population ballooning, many feel there will not be enough water to meet future demand.

The amount that Nestlé Waters plans to take out in the initial tests is roughly equal to the 1.7 million litres per day that are drawn from the municipal wells of Elora, a town of about eight thousand. The municipality is charged $2,140 per million litres by the province. In contrast, seven industries, from cement makers to water bottlers, are charged for extraction but have long paid a mere $3.71 per million litres.

A 2015 report by Ellen Schwartzel, Ontario's acting environmental commissioner, called for a more equitable user-pay system. According to a *Toronto Star* editorial supporting her position, "the government spends $16.2 million on water quantity management programs, but recovers only 1.2 percent of that from users." Most industries get a "total free ride," notes the acting commissioner. The $3.71 they used to pay for every million litres of water was the equivalent of paying $10 for enough water to fill an Olympic-size swimming pool. In

June 2017, following considerable lobbying by water activists, the Ontario government announced that charge would rise to $503.71 per million litres of groundwater taken.

Activist groups such as Save Our Water have been lobbying hard to have the Ontario government deny the Nestlé licence. They cite reasons stretching from the United Nations confirming of the Human Right to Water and Sanitation to the fact that the well lies on traditional territory of the Haudenosaunee, the Six Nations of the Grand River. They want a three-year moratorium on such permits in the watershed, during which time scientific study might determine how much, if any, extraction the watershed can tolerate. "The Grand is one of the most vulnerable watersheds," says Donna McCaw, a retired high-school teacher who is at the forefront of Save Our Water. By charging companies like Nestlé Waters so little, McCaw says, "That's just giving away a precious natural resource. It's just wrong-headed."

In the fall of 2015 the foes of the Nestlé Waters plan held an "Our Water, Our Future" gathering where Maude Barlow, the national chair of the Council of Canadians and the author of several books on water, implored them, "Don't give up. It is always too soon to give up. It is incredibly important that you build this movement and you say no to Nestlé, that you protect the water for yourselves, for nature and future generations."

Barlow argues that new technology has made it so simple to extract groundwater that the volume is doubling every twenty years. "If the Great Lakes are being pumped as relentlessly as other parts of the world," she told the gathering, "the great lakes could be bone-dry in eighty years.

"We are basically robbing the next generation of water heritage everywhere."

A year later, in 2016, the township of Centre Wellington attempted to purchase the well from the Middlebrook Water Company, but

Nestlé, as was permitted, matched the offer and waived all conditions in order to ensure that the bottling company would have the site for "future business growth." Nestlé later said it had "no idea" that the competing bid came from a township trying to keep its water supply "safe from commercial water taking."

Widespread concern over this development led the province of Ontario to place a moratorium on new or expanded bottled-water operations, a move that prevented Nestlé from proceeding with plans to test the water quality and determine just how much water was available from the well. In December 2016 Nestlé Waters met with Centre Wellington's council and offered to "partner" with the township on the future of the well. The partnership, a Nestlé spokesperson said, would see "community needs prioritized while also identifying potential revenue streams that contribute to shared and sustainable prosperity." Centre Wellington mayor Kelly Linton found the offer "vague" and was unsure as to "what it really means."

The Ontario government has identified Centre Wellington township as a future growth area, its population estimated to increase by 40 percent by the year 2031. A water-quality stress assessment completed in 2009 identified Centre Wellington as a potential problem area because of population growth and the possibility of drought—even without losing one million litres a day to a bottling company.

Nestlé said that it was perfectly willing to pay its "fair share" so long as "all users must be treated equitably." Others, however, felt price was not even the most salient point in the debate. Maude Barlow makes the point that there is no need for a bottled-water industry in Canada in the first place, as with the exceptions of certain First Nations—including parts of Six Nations along the Grand itself—tap water is safe, regularly tested and readily available to all. As she told the media, "Allowing a transnational corporation to continue to mine this water is a travesty."

The Council of Canadians was quick to condemn the offer the company was making to the township. "Even with a 'partnership,' Nestlé still plans to use the well to bottle water in the future. Bottled water is entirely consumptive—meaning almost all the water extracted leaves the watershed and groundwater sources cannot be replenished," said Barlow. "Nestlé must sell the well entirely to the community and we need a phase-out on all bottled water takings to protect dwindling groundwater reserves."

One of Nestlé's fiercest foes turned out to be a teenaged high-schooler from Kingston named Robyn Hamlyn. A soccer nut and amateur kick-boxer, Hamlyn is also a water activist and has been since her Grade 7 teacher showed the class a documentary called *Blue Gold: World Water Wars*. The film dramatically shows how much of the world is potentially threatened by water shortages.

What, she wondered, did this have to do with Canada? Her home was on one of the Great Lakes. The Rideau River was nearby, dozens of lakes within a short afternoon drive. But something triggered Robyn Hamlyn's stubborn streak that day and she decided she would act. She would—there is no other way to put it than in her own words, "try to change the world."

On her mother Joanne's advice, she wrote to the mayor of Kingston, Mark Gerretsen, and Gerretsen, now the Liberal member of Parliament for Kingston and the Islands, agreed to see her. Slightly panicked that she, a twelve-year-old, wouldn't know what to say, she then contacted the documentary's director, Sam Bozzo, who helped connect her to the Council of Canadians. Maude Barlow advised Robyn to push Gerretsen to sign up their city as a "Blue Community."

Blue Communities is an initiative of the Council and the Canadian Union of Public Employees that advocates a three-point commitment to public access to clean water. It includes banning plastic water bottles from public facilities, promoting publicly funded and operated water systems and issuing a declaration that access to drinking water is a fundamental human right.

Shaking like a leaf, the youngster appeared before council but found her nerves just in time to make a most impressive presentation. Kingston had already banned the bottles and had its own water system—but council passed the human rights resolution.

Hamlyn continued educating herself about water. A United Nations website informed her that 700 million people in forty-three countries are short on water, with projections of 1.8 billion dealing with water scarcity by 2025. The journal *Nature Geoscience* has said that the drought experienced in western North America this past decade was the worst in eight hundred years. Canada's abundance of water will hardly go unnoticed if conditions continue to worsen. Wars of the future, many believe, could very well be fought over access to water.

By 2015 Hamlyn had made more than two dozen presentations to councils, with the Ontario communities of Kingston, Ajax, Bancroft, St. Catharines, Thorold and Welland all on board. While most councils have rejected appeals to become Blue Communities, eleven others have passed one or two of the three resolutions after hearing her out. By 2017, Canada's sesquicentennial year, she was lining up sponsors and speaking engagements with councils and service clubs across the country.

(In early 2017, now eighteen-year-old Robyn was trying to choose between heading to the University of Waterloo for Environmental Resources Studies or the University of Guelph for an honours Bachelor of Science degree in zoology. She continues making presentations to area councils and is working on a plan to speak to school groups via Skype.)

None of this has endeared her to the Canadian Beverage Association or giants like Nestlé Waters. They often make their own presentations to these councils, and it has happened that they've been there at the same time. Relations are cordial, but she can certainly be described as annoying to them.

"I'm flattered," she said of the counter-initiative of the bottlers. "Those big companies trying to stop a [teenage] girl from going and talking to councils about making changes. Whenever I think about it, I think about what Maude [Barlow] once said to me—'Serious people have serious enemies.'"

The bottled-water industry is indeed serious. It can claim, using examples such as the Walkerton, Ontario, *E. coli* tragedy of 2000, that their water is safe when tap water isn't, that the bottles are recyclable and Canadians tend to recycle well. Bottled water is also crucial in emergency situations, much of it supplied through the Red Cross by charitable donations from the bottlers.

"All Canadians should be engaged in water sustainability," says John Challinor, director of corporate affairs, Nestlé Waters Canada. While he holds nothing personal against Robyn Hamlyn, he does not believe she has the facts correct.

In a newspaper column published a few years ago by an intern at Environment Probe, a Toronto-based environmental and public policy research institute, the attack was much more personal, dismissing Hamlyn's human-rights argument outright and saying, "Maybe we shouldn't leave the destiny of our water in the hands of a thirteen-year-old." Strange, then, that *Youth-leadeR Magazine*, an online publication dedicated to the United Nations Decade of Education for Sustainable Development, would call her "one of the most important people on the planet."

Robyn Hamlyn has been called a "Trojan horse" who is being used to front a political campaign disguised as an environmental initiative. "Water is my life," she argues in reply. "To function we need water. And I want to make a difference.

"Besides," she adds, "the Trojan horse won the war, didn't he?"

The eagle has vanished over the treetops. A breeze has come up, causing the water to ripple in a northward pattern, the effect being, as Margaret Laurence wrote of another Ontario waterway in the opening lines of *The Diviners*, that "the river flowed both ways." Here, where the Grand River slips and slides over the shallows toward the town of Paris, there is no argument to be found, just the silent pleasures of a paddle and enough water to carry a canoe effortlessly downstream.

Perhaps the last word on this slow, elegant waterway—or last note—should go to Guelph councillor/musician James Gordon:

> *Listen to the river song,*
> *That's the sound of history,*
> *As it rolls its way along . . .*
> *There's a lesson that the water brings,*
> *Of survival and of hope,*
> *Listen to the song the river sings.*

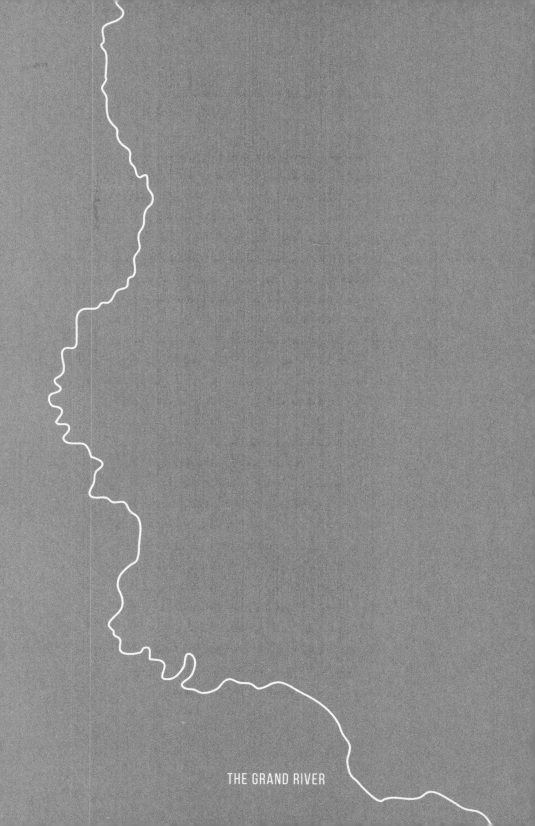

THE GRAND RIVER

CHAPTER TEN

STRESSES ALONG THE BOW

HERE, ALONG THE SHORE OF THE BOW RIVER in downtown Banff, it is possible to see for a century.

In a special room at this world-famous tourist town's Whyte Museum of the Canadian Rockies, an exhibition called *Legacy in Time* features the landscape photographs of the Vaux family— comparative photographs taken a hundred years apart.

In the years leading up to the First World War, Philadelphia siblings Mary Vaux, George Vaux IX and William S. Vaux spent their holidays photographing glaciers throughout the Canadian mountain range. A century later, George's grandson, Henry Vaux, Jr., began shooting exactly the same scenes for comparison. The black-and-white photographs, all shot from the exact location of the originals, are dramatically, even alarmingly, different. Yoho Glacier, Illecillewaet Glacier, Bow Glacier and other icefields seem vast beyond imagination in the Victorian-era photographs, little more than ice cubes in the modern pictures.

Bow Glacier, which lies nearly forty kilometres northwest of Lake Louise, can be viewed from the Icefields Parkway that runs between

Jasper and Banff. It seems particularly shrunken when the photograph from the third-generation Vaux is compared to those of the first generation. Between 1850 and 1953, regular measurements showed that the Bow had retreated 1,100 metres, with further retreat said to be accelerating today because of climate change. The Bow Glacier still contributes water to the Bow River, especially in late summer when the winter snowpack has long since melted, but the quantity is little compared to what once was. Worse, in the two years following the great floods of 2013, rains have been minimal.

Even so, the Bow is wide, green and clear as it slides past the Whyte Museum and under the bridge leading to the world-famous Banff Springs Hotel, today part of the Fairmont chain of resorts. In the 1890s, Dr. George Brett established a sanatorium at the hot springs and people came from all over to "take the waters." The claims were sometimes over-the-top: one member of Parliament rose in the House of Commons to claim he had witnessed invalids being carried into the waters only to walk out unassisted. In 1887, the federal government passed legislation to establish Banff National Park. The intention was to lease properties and rent stretches of the waterway so that the park might sustain itself, at the same time that steps would be taken to ensure the spas did not attract a "doubtful class of people"—no explanation offered, none at that time required.

It was Sir William Cornelius Van Horne, general manager of the CPR, who saw the true potential of the river valley and the soaring mountains around it. He built the Banff Springs Hotel there specifically to attract the privileged to come and take in what he advertised as its "million-dollar view." Today, a large statue of Van Horne greets travellers as they approach the hotel entrance.

A short hike downstream from the hotel, the river picks up speed and cascades over spectacular Bow Falls into a long stretch of tumbling water that is the delight of rafters, kayakers and whitewater canoeists. The river twists and falls through a breathtaking wilderness of soaring peaks, pine and larch before reaching the first of several dams. By the time the glacial waters reach the river's end some six hundred kilometres to the east, the Bow River will have been paddled in and fished in; the city of Calgary will drink its waters and flush its waters; it will flow through the First Nations reserves of the Siksika, Tsuu T'ina and Nakoda, as well as through small towns and over rolling prairie pasture and farmland; it will have created massive dams and hydroelectricity; and it will provide enough irrigation to make life in southern Alberta possible.

This river, called "Minisniwapta" in the Stoney (Nakoda) language, was a favourite subject of Group of Seven painters A.Y. Jackson and Frank H. Johnston. Johnston so loved the river that he wrote in the summer of 1924, "The pageant from Calgary right up to Banff . . . leaves one dumb. The arrangement of the whole thing is truly the work of the Supreme Craftsman. Their beauty is a silent beauty with an exhilarating joy in continually looking, looking, looking."

The Bow is the closest thing Canadian rivers have to a Hollywood celebrity, having starred with Marilyn Monroe in *River of No Return*, in *Little Big Man* with Dustin Hoffman and in *Legends of the Fall* with Brad Pitt. If times have changed since Ms. Monroe struck that famous pose with those twin Canadian icons—a Mountie and a canoe—it is nothing compared to the changes at the river source, where a once vast glacier may soon look more like a child's ice cream fallen on a summer sidewalk.

A 2015 study by the journal *Nature Geoscience* predicted that 70 percent of glacier ice in Alberta and British Columbia could disappear by 2100—perhaps as much as 90 percent in the Alberta Rockies that feed the Bow and other rivers.

Years ago, when E.J. (Ted) Hart was director of the Whyte Museum, he acquired the original Vaux pictures that were on display in 2015 alongside the more recent Vaux photographs. "Everything comes back to the river," Hart, now retired, said on a return visit to the museum. "The river was the reason for everything—the hotel, the town—even for the CPR choosing the Bow River pass—now called 'Kicking Horse'— for passage over the mountains."

Hart says people should take special note of what the century-apart photographs of the Bow Glacier are saying.

"It tells a story and it foretells a story—this river isn't going to exist forever."

Two squirrels are headed out fishing on Ghost Lake.

This is not the beginning of a long shaggy-dog—or shaggy-squirrel—joke. Brendan Palmer is an arborist, and the twenty-five-year-old Calgarian has temporarily adopted "Squirrel 1" and "Squirrel 2" until the orphans mature enough to be returned to nature. He carries them in a small backpack so he can keep up their regular feedings, even on a day off.

The Bow River is a renowned recreational fishery, in no small part because of the nutrients that are found in the waters below Calgary. Rainbow and brown trout are large and feisty, but cutthroat trout are also found here and the threatened bull trout is making a comeback thanks to stringent fishing restrictions. The native bull trout and cutthroat trout suffered most from a wrongheaded notion of the Canadian Pacific Railway back in 1903, when a carload of brook trout was taken from Lake Nipigon in Ontario out to Banff so that the tourists would have better luck. More transplants followed the next year and again in 1908. Five years later, a fish hatchery was established in Banff to ensure a steady supply of various trout. The effect on native fish was harsh. Non-native fish like brook, brown and rainbow trout are no longer released into Alberta streams where they might compete with native species, but those already there have become critical to the sport fishery.

Boldt Castle, highlight of the Thousand Islands cruise on the upper St. Lawrence River, stands six storeys high and has 120 rooms. New York hotelier George Boldt built it for his wife, Louise, who died before it was completed. Abandoned for seven decades, it was restored by the Thousand Islands Bridge Authority and is today a major tourist attraction.

The Quyon Ferry carries cars and passengers across the Ottawa River. Cables and batteries have replaced the old fuel-driven ferries. "No pollution," says pilot Eddie Scott, who figures he has made the crossing 100,000 times.

Long considered the most abused and polluted waterway in Canada, the Don River flows quietly down the middle of the country's largest city. Toronto freshwater advocates now say there is some "hope" for the Don's future. (photo, Fred Lum/ *The Globe and Mail*)

Albert "Sonny" McHalsie told me the Fraser River is sacred to the Sto:Lo First Nation: "We are the river and the river is us."

Jacques Courcelles lost his home in Ste. Agathe during 1997's "Flood of the Century" that struck the Red River. "We had a choice—'Last one out turn off the lights,' or else start all over again. We chose to start over." (photo, John Woods)

Patrick Robson is a former commissioner of planning for the Niagara Region. "Niagara Peninsula is packed with stories," he says. "And I have a passion for the stories." The Niagara River has them all: some bizarre, some daring, some tragic, some inspirational.

Christine Ouellette, co-owner of Zip Zag, a zip-line company that sends tourists across the Saint John River at Grand Falls. "Other places have trees," she says, "but we have the falls and the gorge."

Dehcho First Nations Grand Chief Herb Norwegian has long fought against the Mackenzie Valley Pipeline. The Dehcho have no interest in running "a blood vessel" through their territory that could potentially poison their traditional land.

Calgary's Peace Bridge opened in 2012 to allow pedestrians to cross the Bow River. Locals sometimes call it "Finger Trap Bridge" because of its obvious likeness to the children's game.

Robert Sandford of Canmore, Alberta, is the Canadian chair for water and climate security at the United Nations University Institute for Water, Environment and Health—and one of the country's greatest thinkers on freshwater protection.

Gilbert Whiteduck, former Chief of Kitigan Zibi Anishinabeg First Nation along Western Quebec's Gatineau River, is appalled that on any given day in Canada more than 100 Native communities are under drinking water advisories.

Max Finkelstein, who grew up on the Rideau Canal and has canoed the entire continent, dreams of one day being able to drink from the Ottawa River and this pivotal river being recognized for the treasure it is.

Curator Leah Garven of the Chapel Gallery in North Battleford and the Mann Art Gallery in Prince Albert held an art competition, "As Long as the River Flows," to draw attention to oil spills along the North Saskatchewan River. "Our river is sick," she says. "Let's talk about it."

The *Segwun* and *Wenonah II* docked on Lake Muskoka in Gravenhurst. The *Segwun* is North America's oldest operating coal-fired steamship. Tourists cruise the lakes along the Muskoka River, where private islands hold family cottages worth many millions of dollars.

Bill Purkis, who owns and runs the bait shop his father established at Bala Dam, is leading a fight against more damming along the Muskoka River. He vows never to give up: "They can scrape me off the rocks—and take me to the dump."

Wally Schaber at Big Chute on Quebec's Dumoine River. The founder of Black Feature wilderness adventures has led trips throughout Canada, but the wild, unspoiled Dumoine remains his favourite. He fights to have the watershed declared a special preserve.

The stretch from Calgary downstream to Carseland claims some fifteen hundred catchable trout per kilometre during peak season. It attracts fly fishers from around the world, including such celebrities as Steven Spielberg, Melanie Griffith and *Star Wars* creator George Lucas. Hollywood actor Sam Elliott has said he knows of no equal fly-fishing treasure in the U.S. "I know there's fishing this good somewhere in the U.S.," says the cavern-voiced actor who has played multiple Western cowboy characters. "But I haven't found it."

Fishing the deep Ghost Lake waters upstream from Calgary, Palmer prefers to troll for trout from his boat, and on a holiday weekend he and the two squirrels join hundreds of other Albertans launching their boats in the reservoirs—a few quite large—that damming has created in the Bow watershed. Ghost Dam, built in the late 1920s, created one of the river's more popular fishing spots. In total, there are thirteen dams, four weirs and eight reservoirs.

"It must be one of the most thoroughly engineered and regulated rivers on the continent," Christopher Armstrong, Matthew Evenden and H.V. Nelles wrote in *The River Returns*. "It has been developed and used in a myriad of ways for more than a century. It is not an untouched wilderness river. Quite the contrary: it has been dammed for mountain storage, hydroelectric generation, and irrigation diversion. Its flow is monitored and managed like an assembly line. Its waters have been taken in vast quantities for cities, industries, and farms and in a large measure returned in a foul state. Oil refinery residues, fuel oil, creosote, and sewage have polluted its waters. It has provided a transportation corridor for railways, pipelines, transmission towers, and highways. For sixty years, logs from the mountains were driven on its spring floods to mills in Cochrane and Calgary. Mines washed their coal and flushed their boilers with its water. Its fish have been propagated in hatcheries along its banks. It has been bridged and dredged, its channel reamed and diked. It has been mapped, measured and mathematically modelled, painted, and imagined in law and literature. Invisible lines of jurisdiction have been drawn in its water. Its banks have been industrial sites, junkyards, and parks. The Bow is about as 'human-made' as it is possible to be."

It's understandable why Alberta's favourite wilderness writer, the late Andy Russell, would call the Bow a "multiple-abuse" river. The many dams, not surprisingly, have critics. Wildly fluctuating flow and water levels below huge dams like the Ghost, the Bearspaw, the Glenmore and others play havoc with fish reproduction and survival.

Palmer, who studied environmental leadership and ecotourism at college, appreciates this but also appreciates the reality of a river that has been used for everything from buffalo hunts to timber runs, that has been twisted, rerouted, dammed, tapped and drained—yet somehow remains the Bow River as it pushes eastward and joins the Oldman River. Its used and reused waters eventually reach Lake Winnipeg via the Saskatchewan River and Hudson Bay via the Nelson River. As a metaphor for Prairie persistence, the Bow sets the standard.

"We're all opposed to change at one time or another," says Palmer. "I wouldn't like to see any more dams put up, but the ones that we do have here, we might as well make use of the recreational facilities. This is my freedom. It's where I come to relax."

"The Bow has formed the backbone of Alberta's history," says Hart. "You might not call it a great river, but it has a great history."

Had there been no Bow River, the settlement of southern Alberta and the building of the city of Calgary would never have happened. The river was, of course, known to the fur traders—seventeen-year-old David Thompson was likely among the first Europeans to travel it—but it was even called the "Bad River" on some maps, so marginal was the trade in pelts along its banks. All the same, the Europeans did travel it, perhaps not taking much fur out but most assuredly leaving something behind: new diseases. In the six decades between 1780 and 1840, nine major epidemics struck the Native tribes of the Western plains.

The settlement of Europeans meant the buffalo that drank the waters of the Bow River began disappearing, faster and faster. When Governor General the Marquess of Lorne journeyed west in 1881—his party featuring twenty-one wagons, a fifty-man police escort, journalists, artists—Lorne was approached by several of the important chiefs of the area, including Crowfoot, who begged for help with their plight. They were starving. Lorne's royal advice was that they should forget about hunting bison and instead take up farming like everyone else.

In 1847–48, when Captain John Palliser led his pre-Confederation scientific expedition to explore the Prairies, he concluded, "This was not a place where humans could live and prosper."

All that changed with the coming of the railroad that was promised to British Columbia for joining the Dominion in 1871. The original plan had been to cross the Rockies through the Yellowhead Pass, near Jasper, but the Canadian Pacific Railway chose instead the more southerly route, which reached Calgary in the summer of 1883. The company built its station on the west side of the Elbow, unfortunately on a flood plain.

As the CPR's agreement with the government was for twenty-five million acres of land "fairly fit for settlement," the selection of land became an issue. William Pearce, the federal inspector of Lands Agencies, was able to convince the railway that the open lands of the southern prairies could be made fertile through irrigation, and the Bow River watershed would supply that precious water.

"With elaborate irrigation works of weirs, channels, and ditches," he believed, "the river could make a dry land flourish with crops, trees and prosperous farms."

"It was Pearce who convinced the CPR to take up that 'useless' land as its allotment," says Hart. "He told them, 'We'll make it flower.'"

Pearce, a stubborn, often belligerent man nicknamed "The Czar of Western Canada," was prescient. His own land, Pearce Estate, south-east of Calgary, was devoted to experimental methods of irrigation. He was also a great believer in urban parks and is the reason why so much of the Bow remains accessible even as it winds and twists through the city core.

And today Calgarians clearly love their river. "We fish on the Bow, paddleboard and canoe and kayak on the Bow," says Calgary aquatic biologist Francine Forrest. "When I see the river, it just brings me happiness. It's a 'vacation' from the busy-ness of the city."

As it leaves the city, the river goes back to work, now producing more crops than power. While less than 5 percent of Alberta land is irrigated, that small fraction provides some 20 percent of the prov-ince's agriculture production. The land that Palliser thought unfit for settlement is fertile and valuable, largely thanks to the Bow River. In 1911, the *New York Times* called this the "biggest irrigation plant in America." By 1915, *Scientific American* magazine was calling Pearce's realized dream "America's Greatest Irrigation Project." It involved 2.5 million acres in three designated areas east of Calgary. Irrigation canals throughout ran four hundred kilometres. The CPR put out brochures calling the irrigated area fertile "almost beyond belief."

If it seemed too good to be true, it was. The canals were racked with problems from muskrats and beaver to leaks and weed growth. By the mid-1920s half the water was being lost to leakage. Then came the Dust Bowl, when, at the height of the watering season, the river simply dried up and vanished on the lower Bow east of Calgary. Better engineering and construction, however, and better weather patterns, soon once again made the irrigation system vital to the area, and far more reliable.

"The irrigation history of the Bow is one of the great industrial projects of Canada's history," says Hart, who has written several histories of the area of the Bow watershed. "It created an economy out of an area that was considered useless."

After the dwindling fur trade dwindled into nothing, the Bow became a venue for timber drives. The tree fellers had found themselves with an instant client in the railway slowly making its way west. For a single kilometre of track, sixteen hundred ties had to be laid down. The Eau Claire and Bow River Lumber Company was formed in 1883 by businessmen from Wisconsin and Ottawa. In the 1887 drive, six men drowned when they could not prevent their raft from getting caught in the fast-moving waters and swept over the falls near Kananaskis.

With the railway came a need for coal, the town of Canmore springing up around the mines that opened to fuel the trains. Between 1886 and 1979, Canmore Mines had extracted sixteen million tons of coal from the surrounding hills. Logging continued to be significant even after the rail line had pushed farther west, as Calgary was booming and timber was needed for home construction. Log drives to the city continued right up until 1943, when the Eau Claire mill was finally shut down.

In 1909 the Bow's Horseshoe Falls was dammed in order to generate hydroelectricity and came online in 1911. Two years later Calgary Power—backed by Montreal financier Max Aitken (later known as Lord Beaverbrook) and with future prime minister R.B. Bennett as negotiator—began to further dam most of the waterfalls on the Bow and its tributaries. Bow Falls, one of the province's top tourist attractions, was fortunately spared.

The dams went ahead in relentless numbers: Kananaskis in 1914, Ghost in 1929, a storage dam at Pocaterra in 1955, new generators at Ghost in 1954. It led to squabbles between bureaucrats and power engineers about what mattered more, beauty or power. Power usually won out, but Parks Canada gained a few concessions and, at one point, Stanley Thompson, the world-famous golf-course architect and designer of the Banff Springs Golf Club, was brought in to offer landscaping advice for areas that would be most affected by dams along the river. When the Second World War came along, the premier of the day, William Aberhart, showed little sympathy for the beauty side of the argument. Calgary needed power and Calgary would have its power.

Aberhart's thinking reflected the times. "Like wild stallions," the authors wrote in *The River Returns*, "rivers had to be broken, domesticated, made docile and useful."

In September 2015 I dropped in on a gathering of the Bow River Basin Council in Calgary. The non-profit charitable society encourages cooperative strategies for water-use management and environmental stewardship. Its membership is a widely varied bunch, including representatives from urban and rural municipalities, various levels of government, agriculture, commercial, industrial, educational and First Nations interest groups and the public. A group this varied makes for strong opinions and impassioned debate.

One such opinion came in the form of a warning for developers from lawyer Judy Stewart, a former mayor of nearby Cochrane: "Slow the hell down!"

Stewart was giving voice to a common concern. Through its various boom periods, Calgary has spread westward as wealthy homeowners build ever larger homes with, they hope, a view of the mountains. Development now nears the reservoirs that supply the area with drinking water and, each year, more ecologically valuable wetlands vanish under fill and pavement.

"The city of Calgary has destroyed 90 percent of pre-settlement wetlands," says Stewart. A struggling economy, of course, is going to halt some of the development, but a larger and longer concern is the water itself, from the melting of Bow Glacier to the irrigation of fields near Medicine Hat.

"The most important resource in the province, and the rarest, is water," says Kevin Van Tighem, former superintendent of Banff National Park. Van Tighem, author of a 2015 book on the Bow River called *Heart Waters*, worries that infrastructure changes intended to help manage the resource, such as dams and more efficient irrigation usage, are equivalent to "closing the barn door after the horses have left," and he is hardly alone. "Water comes *to* the river," he argues. "It doesn't come *from* the river."

Clear-cut forestry causes quick runoff, as does the pounding and rutting of the landscape by off-road vehicles. Scientists such as Dr. John Pomeroy, who spoke to the council gathering, say that climate change is causing snow melts to come earlier and earlier, meaning water is racing through the system before it is needed for planting, and reduced, at times sharply, when it is most needed. Though it might come at a more useful time than the snowmelt, the glacier melt, says Dr. Pomeroy, is so reduced from the retreating ice sheets that it is no longer a significant factor later in the growing season. Glacial meltwater contributes an estimated 2 percent to the Bow's annual flow. Significantly, however, that water flows through during the dead of summer, when other water sources are at their scarcest.

On June 19, 2013, a massive storm drenched the Rocky Mountain Front Range for two solid days. In sixteen hours, some two hundred millimetres of rain fell on what remained of the winter snowpack. Forty Mile Creek overflowed its dam, terrifying worried engineers that the old dam might burst. TransAlta, the power giant that controls the dam levels by computer—even to the point of posting planned water releases on its website so kayakers and rafters can know the best times to be on the rapids—were helpless to control this surge.

Lake Minnewanka, created by a massive dam inside the park, rose toward its maximum. Engineers worried again that if this dam gave, the towns of Canmore, Morley and Cochrane "would be hit by an unimaginable tidal wave of water, gravel and woody debris," writes Van Tighem. "The weight of so much water and sediment sweeping down the river would almost certainly damage or breach Ghost and Bearspaw dams. Most of downtown Calgary and its inner-city neighbourhoods—always swamped by flood waters and mud—would have been destroyed."

The big dams held, but the flooding was still extensive, as was the damage. Five people died and a hundred thousand Albertans were displaced. More than two thousand troops were deployed to help, often with evacuations. The province set up twenty-eight emergency operation centres and declared thirty-two states of local emergency. Most severely affected were low-lying river communities like High River and Canmore. The Calgary Zoo was devastated, sustaining $50 million in damage, but workers managed their panicked evacuation without a single lost mammal. Four flamingos and many fish did perish, however. The waters flooded the famous Stampede grounds and rose as high as the tenth row in the Saddledome, iconic home of the NHL's Calgary Flames.

In late 2016, I hiked in to some of the tributaries, both large and small, of the Bow River. The damage to Calgary, the surrounding towns and the Trans-Canada Highway had received most of the attention. I wanted to see what damage had been done off the beaten path. There were still, on some trails, yellow warning signs—"Trail Closed: Flooding Damage"—where the erosion had made foot travel dangerous. I was able to see the wreckage along the Kananaskis River, which had swollen to a point where it destroyed the golf course at Kananaskis Lodge. There was also still evidence of the severe flooding and damage that occurred near Bragg Creek, where the Elbow River heads toward Calgary and its confluence with the Bow.

On the Heart Creek Trail near Canmore, the province has established a guided tour with periodic signs explaining and illustrating what happened when the big storm dumped some 250 millimetres of water into this narrow canyon that runs between Heart Mountain and Mount McGillivray. "The once clear and peaceful creek is a brown torrent filled with tumbling rocks and floating logs," reads one sign with photographic proof of the devastation. "As the debris lodges against the canyon's walls, the raging flood changes course, scouring new paths of destruction."

Another sign along the popular trail says: "The canyon is choked with piles of fallen trees, stripped of their bark by the abrasive, sediment-laden water. All seven original trail bridges are gone, most half-buried and upside down in the debris piles. The bridge previously located deepest in the canyon travelled the longest distance, coming to rest only 200 metres from the Trans-Canada Highway." To save the highway, emergency crews diverted the stream before the onrush became impossible to hold. The trail is back, the bridges restored, but the creek no longer follows the course it held for decades.

Despite the obvious havoc of the 2013 floods, Dr. Pomeroy and other scientists fear that the West of Canada, like California, has entered a period of higher temperatures, little rain and drought conditions. Dr. Pomeroy, who is himself a Canmore resident and holds the Canada Research Chair on Water Resources and Climate Change at the University of Saskatchewan, believes the Bow "is an example of a river leaving the Ice Age.

"It's sort of like the opera—the fat lady has already sung."

———

There have been vast improvements on the Bow. Irrigation is far, far more efficient today than it was when huge concrete viaducts—now standing like forgotten dinosaurs near the town of Brooks—diverted river water that was then much lost to evaporation, leakage and debris plugging.

Also, the city of Calgary has profoundly improved its water-treatment facilities following years of complaints from communities downstream. Interestingly, it was a crusading journalist named Ralph Klein who first drew public attention to the troublesome water conditions. He later became mayor of the city, provincial minister of the environment and premier.

Klein was "fish crazy" and often canoed and fished the Bow. "The only thing I've learned is that this river's got more moves than a stepped-on snake," Klein once told the *Calgary Herald*.

While he was mayor during the 1980s, his office oversaw a $124-million upgrade of the Bonnybrook sewage treatment plant. Klein was environment minister when routine water samples from the Bow as it flowed into Calgary were found to contain large globules of pentachlorophenol and creosote. Tabbed "The Blob," the discovery sent shudders throughout the Bow watershed.

In the fall of 1989 "dinner plate–sized globules" appeared on the river bottom and toxic traces of these carcinogens were discovered as far as 265 kilometres downstream. Action taken by Alberta Environment was appreciated by those who had raised the alarm, but pollution concerns remain.

Sewage has been a concern since the Banff Springs Hotel had the novel idea of building its own sewage removal system, which simply carried the hotel's waste out into the middle of the river. Modifications to that system during the first half of the twentieth century included releasing hotel waste directly above the falls. "This placement led to surely one of the greatest ironies in Canadian parks history. The most photographed waterfall in Canada, Bow Falls, had in effect been turned into a sewage aerator."

Klein established the Bow River Quality Council, ensuring that municipalities, First Nations, farmers and recreational users all had a voice in the care of the waterway. That, of course, hardly means they sing from the same page. The Bow remains a subject of much controversy in the province.

Recent work completed by WWF-Canada found that the Bow scored "poor" in terms of overall health of the watershed, "fair" for water quality and "good" for fish health. As far as threats to the watershed, the conclusion was "very high," given the overuse of its waters, the continuing pollution from agriculture practices and the potential for pipeline incidents.

"The Bow River is beautiful, and important culturally, historically and economically," said David Miller, the former mayor of Toronto who is now head of WWF-Canada. "While it is the most regulated river in Alberta, the risks facing it were not well known. After our assessment we found that overall, the Bow River is at a high risk.

"We need to start raising awareness about these issues."

The risk is connected to the fact that the vast majority, virtually all, of the river's water is "allocated" to some specific use, from drinking water to power to irrigation. Dr. Pomeroy notes that the peak flow of the river occurs in mid-June, which just happens to be when water is most needed by farmers. However, in 2014–15 temperatures were roughly 4°C above normal, causing the melt to come four to six weeks earlier than normal. By June there was zero runoff and rain came too late. Dr. Pomeroy fears this could be "a harbinger of things to come."

He also believes the Bow has to be managed more efficiently. They called the 2013 devastation "The Flood of the Century," but he says this is a "deception"—as at least twice in the previous century there were greater floods.

"Downtown Calgary," he says, "should never have been put where it is. But since downtown Calgary will remain where the Bow and Elbow rivers converge, better planning, monitoring and preparation will be required in the years to come. We must be better at managing water, and avoiding another event like the 2013 flood."

It is not only infrastructure that is required, in Dr. Pomeroy's opinion, but thinking. Climate change is bringing vast changes, potentially in every direction from drought to flood, and yet so many people and politicians seem in denial.

"We built Canada on water," he says. "The fur trade, industry, agriculture—and yet we take it all for granted. We're going to struggle if we don't pay attention to it. In part, we need to stop describing our water as 'bountiful.'

"I'm not so sure it is anymore."

"The river's health," adds Michael P. Robinson, president and CEO of the Glenbow Museum, "is a metaphor for our own."

A metaphor, indeed, for an entire country so inextricably tied—historically, economically and psychologically—to its rivers.

THE BOW RIVER

CHAPTER ELEVEN

TAX REVOLTS AND INDEPENDENCE: THE GATINEAU

Come all you young fellows
Come listen to my song . . .
About the famous battle that was fought at Brennan's Hill . . .

—"The Battle of Brennan's Hill," Thomas Hayden (1866–1933)

SNEEZE GOING UP THIS SHARP RISE on Highway 105, running along Western Quebec's picturesque Gatineau River, and you would miss Brennan's Hill entirely. No historical plaque, nothing but a handful of houses, an ancient hotel, an overused sofa sitting on the side of the road and—*gesundheit!*—you're down the other side and away.

Yet it was here, during a snowy autumn late in the nineteenth century, where the only armed tax revolt in Canadian history took place—our own Boston Tea Party, but with a decidedly different outcome.

"Armed to the teeth," warned a subhead in the November 14, 1895, *Ottawa Evening Journal*—the towering headline above shouting, "PAY OR SEIZURE."

The Battle of Brennan's Hill, also known as the Low Rebellion, involved some two hundred mostly Irish settlers in Low Township, some sixty kilometres northeast of Parliament Hill up the Gatineau River. For fifteen years they had adamantly refused to pay their taxes, many of them having fled Ireland to escape what they deemed unreasonable and unfair authority.

The rebels—or "kickers," as they were called—had their defenders. In a long letter to the *Journal*, Dr. C. Mason Gordon, a long-time physician in the area, said "all the world and his wife are jumping on the defiant citizens"—and he thought unfairly. The Irish settlers, he argued, were "more Irish than those who live on the hill sides in Ireland," and these were the heirs of those Irish who had fled the island to escape "the ancient oppressor."

"Ruffianism and crime never had a foothold in the township," the good doctor continued. "During twelve years past I cannot recall to mind an important crime committed by a resident of Lowe, nor do I know of a single illegitimate birth among the Roman Catholic Irish during that time. Their honesty is proverbial; their word better than the bond between most men; their hospitality to the stranger and kindness to the distressed is unequalled; and yet sensational quill-drivers with [next to no] experience . . . who happen to run across a few of the more ardent members of the community, possibly seasoned with Mick's lime juice, could refer to the township as a hot-bed of sedition, rebels, Gatineau savages."

Local clergy were asked to advise their parishioners to pay up, did so, and were ignored. Police would now be sent in to serve notice on the 185 delinquent taxpayers and give them fifteen days to settle their back taxes or have their property seized.

"'The bailiffs and provincial police,' said County Solicitor Major tonight, 'will remain here until every cent of the taxes are paid. We are not going to do this thing by halves now. The ratepayers of Lowe have given us too much trouble already, and now they must pay and pay promptly. Their day of grace is past.'"

The law officers were chased off the land and forced to retreat to Brook's Hotel in Low, where they waited for the train to take them back down the river. When bailiff Joseph T. Flatters of nearby Aylmer arrived with notices, they tore them up and locked him in Jim Brennan's root cellar for two days without food or water before sending him packing. A Miss O'Rourke, who was $2.35 in arrears, told the policeman who came to her farm that she'd pour boiling water on anyone who tried to serve her, then grabbed a stick of firewood and chased him down the lane.

The provincial solicitor general eventually decided there was no alternative but to call in the army, some 120 soldiers from the 4th Princess Louise Dragoon Guards, the 2nd Ottawa Field Battery and the 43rd Battalion, Ottawa and Carleton Rifles, each man armed with up to seventy rounds of ammunition. They set out by rail at noon, November 17: "The train consisted of three passenger coaches containing the officers and men, four stock cars containing 47 horses for the mounted party and two box cars filled with camping outfits, ammunition and oats for the horses."

It was a nerve-wracking trip, the soldiers aware of racing rumours about the valley that the kickers were planning to blow up the trestles. But the army arrived without incident and pitched tents in Low and the show of force alone was enough: the kickers capitulated and paid up. Two days later, the soldiers returned to Ottawa, not a single shot fired, the only armed tax revolt in Canadian history now . . . history. One of the leaders of the rebellion, Edward McSheffrey, would become mayor of the first municipal council of Low, a law-abiding pillar of society.

The gallant 43rd came up and pitched their tents in Low
The people of our township to visit they did go
They used us very friendly, they seemed to be nice men
But that was their best policy with the town of Brennan's Hill

They started them for Willis's they duty for to do
To see them marching down the road they were a splendid crew
The winding paths around the hills that led them to their den
But they could not find Willis, he was out at Brennan's Hill

The place it was deserted and nothing could be found
So Bailiff Groulx he got to work and seized the ground
They returned back to Ottawa to practice up their drill
And thanked the Lord they were safe from the boys of Brennan's Hill.

—"The Battle of Brennan's Hill"

"There's a bit of a frontier mentality here," says Marc Cockburn, who lives in the quaint riverside village of Wakefield. An archivist with the federal government and volunteer with the Gatineau Valley Historical Society, Cockburn adds: "The farther you go up the Gatineau from Ottawa, the more independent people get, the more rebellious."

"The attitude is sort of 'I don't care who you are, just don't tell me what to do,'" adds Michael Francis, long-time mayor of Low until he retired from municipal politics in 2009.

In 1993, renowned Canadian photographer Malak published a coffee-table book on the Gatineau River, with words by Ottawa journalist Ron Corbett. "If there were threads of commonality among the settlers," Corbett wrote, "these were ambition, stubborn independence and eccentric individualism."

Eccentric for sure, none more so than former prime minister William Lyon Mackenzie King. High in the Gatineau Hills, King built his beloved Kingsmere where, as he recorded in his journals, he could get "away from the world of humans" and commune with the spirits of his dead mother and various dogs, all named Pat. The Mackenzie King Estate, which includes ruins from the Parliament Buildings following the 1916 fire and stone arches from the British Parliament obtained following a renovation, is today a major area tourist attraction.

King was very much responsible for the assemblage of Gatineau Park, a 35,600-hectare tract of lakes, woods, steep hills and sweeping meadows to the north of the river that is much beloved by area hikers and cross-country skiers. The idea of such a park so close to the capital was first suggested by Montreal architect Frederick Todd in 1903, and in 1937, King's government began purchasing land. Today, the park is part of vast tracts and properties controlled by the National Capital Commission. The NCC leases some land within the park to home-owners and some properties within the park are privately held. The prime minister's summer residence is at Harrington Lake in the park, as is the farmhouse at Kingsmere that is the official residence of the Speaker of the House of Commons.

On a nearby hill overlooking Wakefield, former prime minister Lester Pearson is buried with his wife, Maryon, beneath a simple grey tombstone. Decades before Pearson won the Nobel Peace Prize or became prime minister, he had formed a pact with two civil service friends, Norman Robertson and Hume Wrong, that their final resting place would be by the Gatineau River and not far from the Five Lakes Fishing Club, of which Pearson was a charter member. The elite retreat was the inspiration of senior civil servant Clifford Clark, who, seeing the storm clouds gathering over the world in the late 1930s, decided that "the problems of ministers and senior officials were going to become crushing for many years." They'd need a retreat for themselves and their families, a place where they "could find some escape."

In Ottawa, "escape" and "The Gatineau" tend to go hand in hand. Founding leader of the NDP Tommy Douglas owned a little cottage just upstream from Wakefield. Pearson had his own cottage just across the Gatineau River from Mont Cascades, a popular downhill ski area. Group of Seven painters J.E.H. MacDonald and A.Y. Jackson were fond of the Low dam and rapids area of the river.

Among the many smaller rivers and creeks that feed the Gatineau is the Picanoc River close by the village of Kazabazua, where yet another former prime minister, Pierre Trudeau—in the company of current prime minister Justin Trudeau, then but a boy—once got into a rather heated discussion with canoeing legend Bill Mason over what should have been on the Canadian flag. Not the maple leaf, which Trudeau defended, but the canoe, championed by Mason as much superior in that the canoe, unlike the maple tree, is found throughout the country.

Arguments are easy to come by along the Gatineau River Valley.

A century after residents chased away the bailiffs, they were chasing away the Quebec language police. Still strongly Irish, but with a significant francophone element, there was little sympathy to be found here for the sovereignty movement and none whatsoever for changing signs that had stood in one language for decades.

The most notorious incident involved *The Low Down to Hull and Back News*, a charming little local weekly run by Art Mantell when he wasn't working next door in his junk and antiques shop. In 1998, an official from La commission de protection de la langue française showed up and Mantell (who died in 2013) began snapping pictures of the agent as she worked her way through his workplace. She demanded he hand over the photographs, insisting that it was against the law in Quebec to publish someone's image without their permission.

Mantell's response was to slap her image on the front page of the next edition, with a huge headline declaring, "We Can't Show You This Photo."

You just never know what you'll find along the Gatineau River. On the day that my wife, Ellen, and I travelled along the river with Michael Francis and his pontoon boat, we passed a small island north of the Paugan Dam near Low and noted a single tent pitched by the shore, with no one about. This was where Senator Patrick Brazeau had come in an attempt to come to terms with his shattered life. In 2008, only twenty-seven years old and serving as national chief of the little-known Congress of Aboriginal Peoples, he found himself appointed to the Senate—"the taskless thanks," as it is known around Ottawa—by then prime minister Stephen Harper. He had shown up for work in a Porsche. Eight years later, he was dealing with charges of impaired driving, was suspended from the Senate while prosecutors investigated him for fraud, had a sexual assault charge dropped, had been drinking heavily and had slit his own throat with a meat cleaver, thinking he would just sink down and die on the kitchen floor.

After the failed suicide attempt he had to confront the mess of his personal life. "Everything just came to a tipping point," he told the *Ottawa Citizen*'s Gary Dimmock. "I'm not proud of that moment because I let a lot of people down. I'm just glad to be alive . . . and I'm a damn lucky guy I still have my family with me."

So Brazeau, from Maniwaki and Kitigan Zibi farther north on the Gatineau River, came to the waters that the Kitigan Zibi people say are "the way home." He had texted his girlfriend after cutting himself; she had called a neighbour and the neighbour had raced over and called 911. Paramedics had broken through the locked door, struggled with the suspended senator and saved his life.

"It's time to get back to the basics and start appreciating life," he said. And shortly after, with the Senate fraud charges dropped, he returned to the Red Chamber, hopefully a much changed person.

There is drama along the Gatineau but also great humour, and not just Miss O'Rourke chasing the cop down her laneway while brandishing a stick of firewood. In the mid-1970s, a political movement emerged briefly to change the name of West Hull Municipality to the Algonquin name for the river. West Hull councillor Peter Schnobb led the campaign. From respected Algonquin elder William Commanda he learned that the Algonquins had called it "Tenagadin" before it was named on maps after a fur trader from the 1600s, Nicolas Gatineau du Plessis. Schnobb believed he had the support of the Quebec Toponymy Commission and suggested that perhaps "Tenaga"—clearly a derivative but also the name of a small hamlet in the area—might be the way to go. No sooner did word get out, though, than other villages felt insulted and wanted to be included. These included Kirk's Ferry, Cascades, Old Chelsea, Kingsmere, Farm Point, Larrimac, Hollow Glen, Burnet, Gleneagle and others. A mover-and-shaker in Burnet suggested a compromise: string together the opening letters of several of the hamlets to create a new name that all could embrace.

The suggestion was "Farking Blarkirgall." The name was indeed changed—but to "Chelsea."

Nothing, obviously, quite compares with the armed tax revolt of 1895. It reverberates still, if rather less dramatically. On May 7, 2016, eighty testy voters packed the old Brennan's Hill Hotel and called for the resignation of their mayor, Morris O'Connor. The testy group—modern "kickers," so to speak—griped about everything from fiscal mismanagement to differences today between French and English media coverage.

True to local habit, the mayor swung back, gleefully announcing that not only would he not resign but "I'm even thinking of re-running."

The Gatineau River runs 386 kilometres in a relatively straight line from north of Quebec's massive Baskatong Reservoir south to the city of Gatineau, once known as Hull, where it empties into the larger Ottawa River. Its surprisingly clean water reflects black, largely because of the tall pines that shade its banks; the deciduous trees—many of them oak—higher up on the slopes make the Gatineau a photographer's delight come the fall colours. In any season, it is one of the loveliest rivers in the country.

When Samuel de Champlain travelled up the Ottawa River in 1613, he passed by the mouth of the Gatineau in early June, noting in his journal that the Aboriginals he encountered ("Algoumequins," he called them, known as Algonquin today) used the river as a way to avoid enemies who might lie in wait farther down the Ottawa, "knowing that they will not seek them in such difficult . . . places."

The Gatineau then was a wild river of many rapids. In the 1920s three hydroelectric dams were constructed—two close to each other at Chelsea and Rapides-Farmer, and the large Paugan Dam at Low—and the dams helped the lower Gatineau grow fat and complacent. When they finished the Paugan in early 1928, the *Ottawa Evening Journal* ran a headline saying "Gatineau River Changing Face of Country." The waters behind the dam were up more than thirteen metres the first day following the closing of the Paugan gates. "Man's plastic surgery is filling up the valleys," the newspaper reported.

While there are still challenging rapids upstream toward the Algonquin First Nations at Kitigan Zibi and the town of Maniwaki, the water below the dams is wide and calm, the mild currents and eddies swirling in a slow, almost hypnotic surface waltz. "It's easy rowing upriver now because there's almost no current," says the heroine of Low author Brian Doyle's juvenile novel *Mary Ann Alice*. "Floating along this way feels like flying. I still feel the real river way down underneath me."

Centuries before the dams slowed up the Gatineau, the wildness of the river kept the loggers at bay, so long as there was plenty of white pine to be harvested along the Ottawa. By the 1820s, however, the timber barons, led by Philemon Wright, began to eye the rich stands of the upper Gatineau. Wright used his influence as a member of the legislature to create the "Gatineau Privilege," a restrictive law that put the river and its watershed under exclusive control of a handful of families, all of whom grew rich on Gatineau timber. The "Gatineau Privilege" existed from 1832 to 1843. Ruggles Wright, Tiberius Wright, Christopher Columbus Wright, Peter Aylen and Thomas McGoey were each allowed to take two thousand red and white pine logs a year from the Gatineau Valley. The arrangement was nothing short of a mostly family monopoly, engineered by an elected politician from that same family. "Conflict of interest" was a term virtually unknown then in the region that would one day form the capital of Canada.

With no dams the drivers could run the logs, a simple task in the quieter waters of the Gatineau, a risky business in its faster waters. There are still small white crosses along the banks to mark where lives were lost in the river runs. After the dams went up, the logs came down the river in booms and passed over the dams by chutes. The last log drive on the Gatineau River took place in 1992.

Rail access, logging and dam construction had led to farming, where possible, and the growth of communities, some of which were then lost to flooding from the dams. On a small island offshore from the village of Lac-Ste-Marie stands a tall, sad cross, lighted at night, where the centre of the village was once located.

Low, eight thousand strong during the construction of the Paugan Dam, is home today to fewer than one thousand. The string of small towns retain their charm, however, with small shops, covered bridges, ski hills, hiking trails and, most of all, the lure of a picturesque river that is largely undeveloped along its banks, in no small part because so much of the shore belongs to Quebec Hydro.

For many years, an old-fashioned steam train, the Hull-Chelsea-Wakefield Railway, drew more than its share of visitors to the National Capital Region, taking tourists along the river all the way to Wakefield, where they would disembark, visit the charming shops, galleries and restaurants of the village, and then make the thirty-three-kilometre return to the city. Some fifty thousand tourists a summer would take the journey, pumping tens of millions of dollars into the area economy. Unfortunately, a fierce rainstorm in June 2011 washed out stretches of the old Canadian Pacific Railway line. With cleanup costs estimated at $5–$7 million and millions more required to stabilize the tracks and trestles into the future, it was decided in 2017 that the Wakefield steam train will never run again.

For a river that passes through multiple small communities all the way north to the Baskatong Reservoir, and which ends in the very heart of the city that shares its name—Quebec's fourth largest city, in fact, home to a quarter-million people—the Gatineau is surprisingly clean.

"The river gets grade A marks for swimming," says Cockburn, the Wakefield archivist. Indeed, it is "one of the cleanest major rivers in Southern Quebec," according to Friends of the Gatineau River, a volunteer group founded in 1991 that keeps a keen eye on regular monitoring of the water quality.

The Gatineau River is little known compared to the Ottawa River into which it flows. There is no Champlain exploring the Gatineau; it is much smaller and far less peopled. Yet area canoeists and kayakers make their way eagerly to this waterway, where they find the Gatineau's countless islands created by the flooding—some of them so small a person can barely stand on them—fascinating to explore. The solitude of the river, the scent of pine and the slow, calming currents have made recreation and escape the modern economic engine of the Gatineau Valley, if rather a smaller engine than in the heyday of logging.

Paddlers also appreciate the rarity of speedboats or racing personal watercraft. Along with the hazard of so many small islands, the river hides many more deadheads—pulpwood-length logs that get tangled along the shoreline or caught in the mud, only to be periodically loosened by the flow of the river.

"They slow the boats down a lot," says Michael Francis, the retired mayor of Low, who, with his wife, Edie Van Alstine, keeps a cottage on the river. "They're great speed bumps."

> *Last log on the river*
> *Slow the motorboat down*
> *Take some time to consider*
> *Once was a time now look beyond. . . .*

—"Last Log on the River,"
song from musician Ian Tamblyn's play
A River Runs Through Us

In order to become one of the most prominent timber barons in the history of the Ottawa Valley, New Englander Philemon Wright had first to lead several families from his home near Boston north to the mouth of the Gatineau River, believing they could establish a new community. They arrived in 1800, began clearing the land and were soon visited by First Nations chiefs, Algonquins and Mohawks from the Gatineau Valley and as far away as Oka, near the mouth of the Ottawa River. They informed Wright that the land belonged, and had always belonged, to them.

"Wright settled the claim," local historians John W. Hughson and Courtney C.J. Bond wrote, "with fair words and the trivial sum of thirty dollars."

It would, of course, turn out to be not quite so simple.

The first Indigenous settlements along the Gatineau River belonged to the Anishinabeg, which means "the real people." By the time the Europeans arrived, there were Algonquin encampments all along the Gatineau River, and they were increasingly being pushed upstream by the lords of the "Gatineau Privilege" and their insatiable appetite for timber.

Chief Antoine Pakinawatik led a movement to push back and establish a reserve. At one point in 1845, he and several Algonquin companions paddled six hundred kilometres to Toronto—down the dangerous Gatineau River, across the Ottawa River, through the Rideau Canal and River to Kingston and along the shores of Lake Ontario—to petition the governor general, Lord Elgin, to grant them lands around the HBC's River Desert trading post, near the present-day village of Maniwaki. If Lord Elgin ever responded to the Algonquin chief, the details have been lost to history. Pakinawatik and his fellows then petitioned the Department of Indian Affairs in 1847, only to be told that if they wanted their own lands they would have to move to Manitoulin Island. The Gilmour Lumber Company, which had purchased most of the Wright family's timber rights, was adamantly against the petition. It opposed the founding of reserves that might prevent the downing of pine along the Gatineau River.

Chief Pakinawatik, recognizing that he was up against the forces of privilege and patronage, capitulated by then arguing that his people should be given a fifteen-square-kilometre tract of land at the confluence of the Desert and Gatineau rivers. With their land secured, the Algonquin could turn from hunting and fishing to farming, and with the assistance of the Oblate missionaries they could continue to practise their adopted Catholic religion. Powerful bishop Joseph-Bruno Guigues threw his support behind this proposal, on condition that the Oblates be given six hundred acres with which they could attract settlers. As well, the bishop insisted that the title and rights to the Algonquin lands be under the authority of the Catholic Church. Bishop Guigues then petitioned Lord Elgin again. Chief Pakinawatik and sixty Algonquin men signed or marked their names on a birchbark scroll, the various orders-in-council were signed and, on August 30, 1851, the British Parliament signed an act that authorized the setting aside of 230,000 acres of land in Lower Canada for the use of certain "Indian tribes."

In the official history of the Kitigan Zibi, this tale is prominent. "It had taken the Eurocanadians only 80 years to appropriate the Ottawa River Valley Watershed, save for the 45,750 acres which they reluctantly gave to its first inhabitants, the Algonquin nation."

The River Desert Reserve was now approved and established just south of Maniwaki. In 1994, the band council voted to change the name to Kitigan Zibi Anishinabeg, meaning "the People of the Garden River," a tribute to how important the Gatineau River watershed is to the Algonquins.

The population of Kitigan Zibi is today roughly 2,300 and the vast reserve covers more than 180 square kilometres, making it the country's largest Algonquin First Nation community. The reserve boasts its own school, police force and impressive health and cultural centres. It looks, and is, prosperous.

The notion that Philemon Wright somehow settled matters forever with "fair words" and a "trivial sum" now seems preposterous, as Kitigan Zibi is involved in modern land-claims negotiations and has become a key player in First Nations attempts to bring a halt to massive redevelopment projects in Ottawa that they and other Algonquin First Nations along the Ottawa River watershed claim infringe on sacred territory.

Gilbert Whiteduck, who stepped down last year as chief of Kitigan Zibi, is currently fighting for the return of artifacts from the Smithsonian's National Museum of the American Indian. Previous negotiations with the Canadian Museum of Civilization (now the Canadian Museum of History) saw seventy-five boxes of human remains, some as old as six thousand years, repatriated and buried anew on the reserve. Whiteduck says that the Algonquins will "never, ever" extinguish their claims, even if a financial settlement is reached on the vast tracts of Quebec and Ontario lands the Algonquins feel were unfairly taken from them.

No longer serving as chief, he continues to fight, not only for the return of the artifacts but for better services for the reserve. For the past dozen years, Kitigan Zibi has been under a "do-not-consume order" because of high levels of uranium that have been found in the area water table. More than half the people are still using bottled water only.

"People get complacent," says Whiteduck. "They kind of get used to it. But I'm still pissed off about it."

(Water is a major First Nations concern. Back in 2011, a National Assessment of First Nations Water and Wastewater, conducted by the federal government, found that 73 percent of water systems in First Nations communities were at high or medium risk. Five years later, in 2016, these matters were still a grave concern. A tally conducted in May, and excluding British Columbia, found that there were 130 drinking water advisories [DWAs] that month. "On any given day, there are roughly 100 First Nations under DWAs and that number is sometimes upwards of 130. Nearly 30 reserves have been under water advisories for five-plus years, 14 for over 10 years, and three for more than 15 years.")

The Whiteduck family has long been involved in band politics. Older brother Jean-Guy was a long-time chief. Gilbert, the youngest of seven, followed suit. He agrees with Marc Cockburn's observation that there remains along the Gatineau River a bit of a frontier mentality. "There's something to that," laughs Whiteduck. "Our chiefs stood up for their people."

Whiteduck's toughest test as leader came only three months after his election in 2008, when, in the first week of September, two teenage girls, Maisy Odjick and Shannon Alexander, disappeared and have never been found. Nine years later, the community still has large billboards of the smiling young women, begging for any information that anyone may have.

"It hangs like a dark cloud over me," he says.

Maisy and Shannon now number among the many missing and murdered Aboriginal women. Between 1980 and 2012, the RCMP have stated, there were 1,181 recorded incidents of women murdered or who disappeared without a trace from Aboriginal communities across the country. It has become a major national issue. Back in 2008, it was a story briefly told and quickly forgotten for most Canadians, if they heard of the missing teens at all.

Whiteduck's stepping down was in part due to health concerns, in part because of frustration from dealing with the authorities, and he is helping organize a Quebec-specific investigation into missing or murdered Aboriginal women. "We weren't ready," he says of the crisis that struck when the girls vanished. "Who do you turn to? Who does searches? How do you arrange to get a helicopter?" As chief, Whiteduck turned to the Sûreté du Québec, the provincial police force, asking them to launch an aerial search. He got nowhere.

A year later, a small lion called Boomer, which was in the care of a rather eccentric resident of Kitigan Zibi, managed to escape from a backyard and was seen wandering the woods and streets of the community before he was lured into a police cruiser by several of Police Chief Gordon McGregor's best steaks. "Almost immediately we had a parking lot full of media," Whiteduck says. "The SQ had their helicopter up almost immediately. When the girls went missing, there was no media, no helicopter."

The frustration is as obvious in his eyes as in his voice. He may no longer be chief, but that does not mean you lie back and accept things as they are in the Gatineau Valley. "There's something to that," he says. "Our chiefs have always stood up for their people, and I stood up for mine.

"I was never afraid. Sometimes you had to pay for it, but I believe in what I'm saying and I speak my mind."

As has always been the case along the swirling waters of the Gatineau River.

CHAPTER TWELVE

COLONEL BY'S AMAZING FEAT: THE RIDEAU RIVER AND CANAL

"SO THEY GREASED UP THIS *RAT*, set it on fire and threw it up onto the roof."

The young tourist guide in Ottawa's Major's Hill Park, which sits directly across the Rideau Canal from Parliament Hill, is well into her astonishing story about the final days in the construction of what would eventually become a UNESCO World Heritage Site.

She is standing in wincingly bright sunlight just in front of the statue commemorating Colonel John By, builder of the Rideau Canal. If the colonel, posed so proudly in full military regalia, might be surprised by her wild tale, it is nothing compared to the shock he would feel knowing that in Canada he is today held in high honour. His final days back home in England were spent heartbroken and disgraced, before he died of a stroke at age fifty-six.

The young guide's story continues: "The men who had worked on the canal were all now out of work, see, and they'd become accustomed to their daily rum and now they had none. So they thought if the burning rat found its way into the blockhouse where the rum was stored, the flames would set off powder that was also stored there, and the explosion would blow open the doors and then they'd have their rum."

Welcome to the River of Tall Tales, some of them true.

Not far from where the guide spins her flaming rat story—she swears one of the museum staff told her, and that the "rat tale" is in a book . . . somewhere—once sat the Russell House hotel, where back in 1905 the Stanley Cup champion Ottawa Silver Seven celebrated their victory. The players got so drunk that star forward Harry Smith, on a dare from a teammate, drop-kicked the Cup into the canal and, horrifically hungover, had to return the next day to retrieve it from the relatively dry bed of Colonel By's waterway.

Farther upstream along the Rideau Canal and River sits the charming village of Manotick, where, the story goes, the Ghost of Watson's Mill still haunts. Ann Crosby Currier, a beautiful teenager from Lake George, New York, was newly married to one of the mill owners, Joseph Merrill Currier, who was more than twice her age. While on a tour of her husband's workplace on March 11, 1861, Anne's crinoline dress caught in a spinning shaft and she was flung so hard against a nearby pillar that the blow killed her instantly. Locals still claim there are times when her sad figure appears at a high window in the mill, which long ago was converted into a museum.

(Joseph Currier, just to finish the story, was so heartbroken he sold his shares in the mill and moved to Ottawa, where he became the area's first member of Parliament. He married again—this time to Hannah Wright, granddaughter of Philemon Wright, the founder of nearby Hull—and he built his new love a spectacular new home: 24 Sussex Drive.)

So many stories . . . Near Jones Falls, some 130 kilometres along the Rideau system southwest of Ottawa, you might hear the yarn about the lost barrel of silver coins. The barrel is said to contain U.S. fifty-cent pieces used to pay the canal workers nearly two centuries ago. The hundreds, maybe thousands, of silver coins would now be priceless. Some still search for the lost treasure to this day.

At Sheldon's Corners, not far from the town of Smiths Falls on the Rideau River, legend has it that an unmarked grave holds the remains of Elizabeth Jane Barnes, "The Witch of Plum Hollow." Better known locally as "Mother Barnes," the Irish-born Elizabeth was said to have been the seventh daughter of a seventh daughter. Visitors came from all over North America to pay her twenty-five cents to solve mysteries, including at least one murder, with her gift of "second sight." The coins she earned were enough to raise her own children—yes, all seven of them.

Then there is the pitiful tale of Patrick Sweeney, a canal construction worker who drowned in 1831 while attempting to swim across the Rideau River to retrieve some whiskey he had stashed in a bush on the other side. "When last seen alive," the coroner reported, "he was going down with a bottle or flask in his mouth . . ."

Ken Watson is the resident historian for the Friends of the Rideau and the author of four books on the waterway. The retired geologist has heard most of the stories and knows some of them are true—Mother Barnes, Patrick Sweeney's drowning, Ann Currier's dress—and some might have a bit of truth to them: the men who built the canal were indeed paid by coin.

He has never, however, heard the tale of the greased and flaming rat. "There are lots of stories out there," he says. "This is a land of clearly tall tales. I'd rather have the truth behind the story."

And the one great true story behind the Rideau waterway is the sad tale of the man who today stands bronzed rather than tarnished in Major's Hill Park: Colonel John By. "It's just an absolutely heartbreaking story," says Watson. "By had to have been an absolutely remarkable man. He seemed to have it all—military leader, engineer, surveyor—and he basically got plunked in here and told to make this thing navigable. And he did exactly that. The Rideau Canal is a wonderful example of nineteenth-century engineering that still exists essentially in its original form.

"But they hung him out to dry. He was so poorly done by."

The Rideau waterway is unique in that it flows both ways from its source and high point at Upper Rideau Lake in eastern Ontario, the canal system running some 202 kilometres between the Ottawa River and Lake Ontario. It includes the Rideau River, several lakes and the Cataraqui River and passes through the national capital as well as a number of small communities—Merrickville and Smiths Falls being two of the better known—before reaching its second city, Kingston.

When UNESCO named the waterway a World Heritage Site in 2007, the designation included the canal and its forty-seven locks, Fort Henry and the Kingston fortifications—appropriate in that the canal system was built entirely for military reasons, though never used as such.

At the beginning of the War of 1812, former U.S. president Thomas Jefferson claimed that taking the British colony to the north would be "a mere matter of marching." It didn't turn out that way—we won the war, as all Canadians know—but the British Empire was struck by a case of anxiety following its battles with Napoleon on the Continent and the Americans in North America. Preservation of the Empire, it believed, would depend on strengthened fortifications and secure transport routes for militia and supplies. The Duke of Richmond, then governor-in-chief of British North America, had a previous survey showing the potential of a Rideau route—well away from the U.S. border, able to connect Montreal with Fort Henry at Kingston—and pitched the idea to the Duke of Wellington, the man who a few years earlier had defeated Napoleon at Waterloo and who now served as master-general of ordnance, in charge of forts and canals.

Richmond set off from Quebec City to see the area for himself but did not return. Somewhere along the way the pet fox of one of his soldiers bit him and he died of rabies in a log cabin near the Jock River, a tributary of the Rideau.

On March 1, 1819, Wellington wrote a memorandum advocating the construction of the canal, though it took five years before a civil engineer named Samuel Clowes was asked to do a cost analysis of the project. Clowes estimated it could be done for the ludicrously low estimate of £62,258. In some ways, Colonel John By's political fate was sealed before he even arrived in Canada: crushed by numbers.

In April 1826 By, an officer of the Corps of Royal Engineers, left for Canada with his wife and two daughters. He arrived to a new, higher cost estimate and soon reported back that he felt the canal system could be built in four years, but "I have great doubts whether it can be performed for £169,000."

Right from the start, By was making decisions that would add to the costs. As the first engineer to examine the waterway, Clowes had recommended that the first locks up from the Ottawa River be located more to the east, downstream from present-day Parliament Hill and closer to where the Rideau River joins the Ottawa in a dramatic falls. By wanted the first set of locks, eight of them, to be near the high cliffs upstream from Clowes's suggested spot. The cliffs, By reasoned, would provide a far more defensible position should there be future attacks from the south. He was considering matters from a military point of view rather than engineering. The location would be more costly, but also more strategic. By also changed the proposed size of the locks. He wanted them half as long again and more than twice as wide as the original proposal. A compromise was reached but By largely got his way. His argued the need to move large military vessels between Ottawa and Kingston. (Military vessels of any size never would be needed, but the larger locks turned out to be a blessing for today's holiday watercraft traffic.) All this was certain to cost. In the summer of 1827 he had revised the estimate to £474,000. Once he received permission to build the larger locks, he increased that estimate to £576,578.

Digging the canal was gruelling, slow work. The men worked with shovels and pickaxes, transporting the earth and rocks by wheelbarrow, often with the aid of oxen or workhorses. In those days before dynamite, they blasted through rock by hand-drilling holes in the stone so they could fill the holes with black powder or the more dangerous and unstable merchant powder and set off the blasts with long fuses. They built cranes to move and set in place large stones fashioned by Scottish stonemasons. The unskilled labour was mostly poor Irish immigrants, the remainder French Canadians. Each year By had more than two thousand men working full-time on the canal system he estimated would take six years to complete.

Only a year into the project, however, Wellington was already worried about the growing expense. "It appears to me that Lieut. Colonel By has lost sight of the Plan and Estimates."

The late 1820s were a time of political turmoil in Britain—reform was in the air—and wild budget overruns in the colonies were easy targets. "He was working from a budget plucked out of the air," says Hunter McGill, the chair of the Friends of the Rideau. "No one had a clue what it would cost."

There was another, more terrible, cost: human life. Far below the statue to Colonel By in Major's Hill Park, along a narrow walkway surrounded by grass and seasonal flowers, a Celtic cross stands by the first locks in the system, "In Memory of 1000 workers & their families who died building this canal 1826–1832." No one knows the exact number. (Construction deaths were common then, but also during later projects. On August 10, 1966, the Heron Road Bridge over the Rideau River near Ottawa's Riverside Hospital collapsed during construction, killing nine men.) By's many labourers died from ill-timed explosives; they died when dams collapsed; and they died, by the hundreds, from "lake air," the name then in vogue for malaria.

The swamps of eastern Ontario were so impenetrable and mosquito-infested that work often came to a halt in August, known as the "sickly month," when the heat was crippling and the disease-carrying bugs swarmed anything with a beating heart. The type of malaria was *P. vivax*, carried by a mosquito type identified as *Anopheles quadrimaculatus*. An estimated 60 percent of the workers contracted malaria and about 2 percent died of it. The only medicine that proved effective then was quinine, and it was too expensive for most workers and their families to afford. Today, in the small communities of Merrickville, Burritts Rapids and Smiths Falls, fieldstones mark the graves of those who died from disease.

John MacTaggart, who had been sent over from England to survey the land that By and his men would have to dig through, wrote in his memoirs: "I dare say there is not any more to be said against sickness in this climate, than in England; but if we have to wander in the wilderness, amongst swamps, as many have—to sleep among them, and be obliged to drink bad water—the Dysentery, Fever and Ague, and all matter of bilious fevers, are sure to succeed one another." At Jones Falls in the summer of 1828, MacTaggart noted: "the sickness in Upper Canada raged like a plague . . . no one was able to carry a draught of water to a friend; doctors and all were laid down together."

By came down with malaria himself, not once but twice, yet refused any opportunity to return to England before the canal was done. Through these miserable conditions, he eventually persevered. Back home, he had been the subject of two inquiries, though neither would condemn him as completely as some in government wished. Even so, on May 25, 1832, the Treasury declared that "Immediate steps [must be taken] for removing Colonel By . . . and for placing some competent person in charge of those works."

He was being censured in Britain, it turned out, at almost precisely the same time as he was being feted in Kingston for the completion of his remarkable canal. On March 13, 1832, Kingston paid tribute to By with a testimonial dinner held at Carmino's Hotel. There was champagne and Madeira to drink. And speeches, though they may not have been heard. One of the "speakers" had his remarks published later that week in the *Kingston Chronicle*, which noted that there had been so much champagne drunk at the event that no one could say for sure if the speech had been delivered.

Colonel John By sailed for England not even aware of the Treasury's censure. The canal system had cost £777,146. That figure was massively higher than the early estimates, but hardly out of line with other canals being constructed. In 2012 Parks Canada said the replacement value of the "assets" of the Rideau Canal system would be more than $929 million; but no matter, when By reached home there was no one to defend him.

Stunned and heartbroken by his condemnation, By wrote to one friend saying he felt "dreadfully ill-used." Sick and increasingly desperate, By petitioned the government in the hopes that "I may be honoured with some public distinction as will show that my character as a soldier is without stain, and that I have not lost the confidence or good opinion of my Government."

It never happened. His wife, Esther, wrote asking that some "public mark" be awarded to her husband "to prove to the world" that he had served King and country well. In the video that plays at the various visitor centres along the waterway, Esther is weeping as she pens the letter. A few months later, her husband was dead, her wish unfulfilled.

Today, more than a million visitors a year come to marvel at what

Colonel John By constructed. The little community that sprang up on the shores of the Ottawa River, known as Bytown, would decades later become Ottawa and, in 1857, twenty-one years after his death, be chosen by Queen Victoria to become the nation's capital.

The canal stands as one of the major engineering feats of the nineteenth century, a marvel that, to this day, operates much as Colonel John By left it, the locks and swing bridges largely operated by hand. In 2007, when UNESCO declared the Rideau Canal system a World Heritage Site, the organization said it met the initial criteria of representing "a masterpiece of human creative genius."

The "public mark" was finally delivered 171 years after a tearful Esther By begged for it.

"I've spent more of my life on the water than I have on the land," laughs Don Mackay, who was born and raised on the Rideau and has spent the past thirty-three years working for Parks Canada.

He once operated the Davis Lock, also known as a "solitude lock," a remote station on the waterway that connects Sand Lake to Opinicon Lake. Today he is a public safety coordinator, teaching this summer's batch of students how to canoe before they head out along the waterway. "There's something for everyone here," says Mackay. "There are lakes if you want lakes; there's the river, of course; there's urban and country. It doesn't matter what you come for, it's there—two hundred and two kilometres of *everything!*"

According to the Rideau Valley Conservation Authority (RVCA), some 620,000 people live in the watershed. Hundreds of thousands more cottage, camp, canoe and boat on the waterways each year. With approximately two hundred inns and bed-and-breakfasts along the system, twenty golf courses and numerous marinas, water traffic can be intense. The little Narrows Lock that joins the Upper Rideau to Big Rideau Lake, for example, sees some five thousand vessels pass through in a season, from groups of canoe paddlers to the forty-five-passenger, twelve-crew *Kawartha Voyageur* cruise ship.

Proponents of the entire Rideau waterway bemoan the fact that most visitors are aware only of its dramatic rise of locks between Parliament Hill and the Château Laurier hotel or the "world's longest skating rink" that each winter begins at the top of those locks and runs all the way to Dow's Lake. "When we met with Parks Canada," says Watson of the Friends group, "we told them, 'All your ads show the "ditch." Show people the lakes, show them the wide-open water.'"

True enough. There are riches throughout the Rideau Valley. This was first noted by surveyor John Burrows in 1827. Once he made it past the rapids and through the swampland, he came to a chain of lakes that delighted him. "It is a beautiful sheet of water," he wrote under a pen drawing in his journal. "The extent of view after passing the islands shown above is indeed beautiful. I think there can be but one idea formed after viewing these lakes, and that must be a wish that nothing less than a steam boat canal be formed from Kingston to the Ottawa."

It took a few generations, but eventually there were steamboats plying the canal system as it first became a transportation route for settlers and supplies. Moss Kent Dickinson, whose parents took him to the 1832 opening of the canal as a birthday present for turning ten, would eventually be known as the "King of the Rideau." By the 1850s he had sixteen steamers and sixty barges working the canal. By 1864, he was the mayor of Ottawa.

The coming of the railway put an end to such transportation of people and supplies, but the canal, river and lakes of the Rideau eventually became a paradise for recreational boaters, canoeists and kayakers. Large cruisers from Canada and the United States are able to travel easily and safely, thanks to Colonel By's insisting that this canal be deeper and wider than had been the first suggestions. Toward the end of the 1900s, hotels along the waterway and guided fishing trips became popular with tourists. Soon many wanted more permanence and built their own cottages. On Memorial Day weekend in 2015, the large parking lot at Newboro Lock near Upper Rideau Lake held more U.S. plates—New York, Michigan, Pennsylvania—than Canadian.

Locals, not surprisingly, are fiercely proud of their canal system. One is the adventurer and author Max Finkelstein, who still cherishes the calm Rideau.

"I grew up fishing with my dad on the Rideau," he says. "We would head out after he came home from work . . . to Mosquito Creek, to Long Island Locks, sometimes as far as Kars, where there was a swing bridge with piers that we could fish from. We were after pickerel but accepted large black crappies (which you could catch after dark with a piece of twisted foil from the cigarette packages that my dad always had with him). As a kid, I enjoyed returning to the same place night after night, watching the mink families go about their business, watching the muskrats swimming across the water (and occasionally being eaten by big muskies!), the families of ducks growing up, the chorus of bullfrogs as spring turned into summer."

Finkelstein's first canoe trips were along the Rideau system. His son Isaac is on the river virtually every day as he trains with the Rideau Canoe Club. Max often dresses as a *coureur de bois* and guides paddlers along the Rideau in one of the club's two voyageur canoes. "So many of my childhood core memories were created there," he says, "and now I see my son's memories being created on the Rideau. So, yeah, it means a lot to me."

"I grew up on the system," says Mike Dier, who is in his fourth summer working the Narrows Lock. "It's the place where we came to fish and swim, stay cool in the summer, have an ice cream cone. It's always been a staple of my community."

Upkeep has always been an issue with the system. In 2016, federal environment minister Catherine McKenna announced $57 million worth of infrastructure spending along the length of the canal that will see locks and bridges repaired and include the addition of accessible canoe-friendly docks.

With such extensive use of the waterway, the Rideau Valley Conservation Authority becomes an important factor in its maintenance. With a stated mission of "clean drinking water, natural shorelines, and sustainable land use throughout the Rideau Valley watershed," the challenge for the RVCA is to use its $10-million-a-year budget and sixty-five employees as a worthy watchdog.

The key, says Michael Yee, a staff biologist with the Authority, is the management of people far more so than of the system. "We want to see a lighter touch and a smaller footprint around the shorelines," says Yee. "The past couple of decades people around the lakes have set up cottage associations and they're more engaged—they've taken ownership."

"The water quality is better now than it was," he adds. "But you can't get complacent. We do a lot of monitoring of the river and its tributaries. The watershed is changing. Things aren't as they used to be. You've got climate change. You've got invasive species. So you absolutely cannot be complacent. The Rideau is in fairly good shape—but we can always do better."

What amazes Yee is how little has changed in the canal system since it was completed 184 years ago and how remarkably well Colonel John By's vision has stood up. "Colonel By should have been knighted for what he did," says Yee. "Even with today's technologies, could we do what he did? I doubt it."

It is a remarkable legacy: a waterway designed for defence yet never used for defence, a military project that became a political scandal, a good man denounced and disgraced only to today be honoured with a statue, his work considered one of the greatest engineering feats of a century.

Mixing politics and water, however, has a long tradition in Canada.

CHAPTER THIRTEEN

RIVER OF POLITICS: THE COLUMBIA

WOODY GUTHRIE A *SELLOUT*?

It is hard to imagine, three-quarters of a century on, America's most famous folksinger-activist—a man who admired communism and boldly taped a sign onto his guitar saying "This Machine Kills Fascists"—working for a big power company, but it happened.

It was 1941 and Guthrie, out of work in California and with a wife and three young children to support, agreed to a month-long contract with Bonneville Power Administration in the Pacific Northwest. For a sum of $266.66, he would travel about the Columbia and write songs about the great river that begins in Canada's Rocky Mountains and empties into the Pacific Ocean at the Washington-Oregon border.

That Woody Guthrie would take on such a contract is a stark illustration of how perspectives can change over time. There was no environmental movement in those days. In 1941, hydroelectricity was seen as natural, clean and cheap enough that it would improve the lives of farmers and the poor. Guthrie approached his assignment with great enthusiasm, writing twenty-six songs that extolled the power agency and development. The best known of those songs, "Roll On, Columbia," includes a chorus that repeats, *"Roll on, Columbia, roll on. / Your power is turning our darkness to dawn, / Roll on, Columbia, roll on."* He sang about ports being built for "shiploads of plenty." He called the Grand Coulee Dam "The mightiest thing ever built by man," a magnificent project that would "run these great factories and water the land."

The dam was built to provide irrigation for 2,400 square kilometres of mostly farmland. President Franklin Roosevelt signed the bill to build it in 1933 and it was still under construction when the Second World War began. Irrigation suddenly seemed less pressing than the need for a secure hydroelectricity supply. Once completed, Grand Coulee Dam was 1.6 kilometres across and created a lake with nearly 1,000 kilometres of shoreline. Roosevelt declared that the electricity produced here would bring new opportunities to those who had seen none during the years of the Great Depression.

Guthrie, not surprisingly, thought that an admirable goal—unaware that soon the Americans would join the war and the power drawn from the Columbia River would be used for other purposes. It would be sent to aluminum factories for the manufacture of airplanes. It would be used to help produce the plutonium for the atomic bombs that would be dropped on Hiroshima and Nagasaki.

The Hanford nuclear site, at one point with nine reactors and related facilities, would eventually be dumping fifty thousand curies of radioactive material a day into the Columbia River—a fact kept secret for decades. From 1944 to 1971, pumps drew cooling water from the river, used it in the reactors and returned the now radioactive water to the river again. Though the reactors were decommissioned toward the end of the Cold War, Hanford remains the most contaminated nuclear site in America.

But none of this, of course, was known in 1941.

Woody Guthrie's "Roll On, Columbia" became such a hit that it was covered by dozens of performers, from Harry Belafonte to the Canadian folksinging group the Travellers. As his friend Pete Seeger would say many years later in a short documentary on Guthrie's Columbia River ballads, "People aren't quite so enthusiastic about building dams."

Canada's most charming statue stands in a small park in the small Columbia Valley town of Invermere in eastern B.C. It is a tribute to exploration but also to marriage: David Thompson, the Great Mapmaker, and Charlotte Small, the half-Cree woman he married when he was twenty-eight and she only thirteen. They stayed together fifty-eight years, Charlotte and several of their thirteen children often accompanying the explorer on his journeys. When he died in 1857, penniless and forgotten, the family buried him in Montreal's Mount Royal Cemetery, where it is said Charlotte lay weeping throughout the night on the fresh grave. Three months later, she was buried beside him.

This magnificent bronze statue, which depicts Thompson and Charlotte staring off toward the nearest range, is the creation of Rich Roenisch of Longview, Alberta. Roenisch insisted that Charlotte be included, and though there was some local grumbling about the propriety of paying tribute to a marriage that involved a thirteen-year-old child, there is nothing but pride to be found today in Invermere. Thompson, for that matter, could today be called a "child labourer," as he was only fourteen when he signed on with the Hudson's Bay Company and set off on the ship that took him to Churchill Factory, on the Hudson Bay shore of present-day Manitoba, where he began his seven-year apprenticeship learning the fur-trading business.

A few years ago, Spring Hawes, then a town councillor in Invermere, told me that it is "a strange commentary on our society that the female companion is so rarely recognized that we find it noteworthy when she is." A fair point, as Hawes added: "There is no doubt that behind the much-recognized men who helped establish our country and its society, there were—and are—equally strong, adventurous and brave women."

"The man who measured Canada," reads the engraving on the statue plinth. Thompson is also the first European to descend the length of the Columbia River. Its gaping mouth had been crossed in 1792 by American sea captain Robert Gray, who named the river after his ship, the *Columbia Rediviva*. Gray was on a fur-trading expedition financed by Boston merchants and did not travel far upstream. He spent several days around the mouth trading with Natives, and this was enough for the United States to claim "discovery" when the ownership of the Oregon Country was being disputed with other countries, including Great Britain and Russia. At one point, the U.S. and Britain shared rights to the territory for a decade, and it seemed likely that the Lower Columbia would become the border between the United States and British North America. However, the 1840s saw such a mass migration of American settlers into the territory that the Indigenous population was crushed and pushed aside and any British claim to the land effectively dashed. The Oregon Treaty of 1846 set the American boundary at the 49th parallel, much farther north than had been expected. The river instead became the natural border between two U.S. states, Oregon achieving that status in 1859 and Washington thirty years later.

An early British map had shown the river Gray briefly sailed into connecting to the Missouri River. The map was eventually proven wrong, but in the meantime competing fur traders became convinced that if they could find the source of this river it would open up the Pacific Coast to great new trade possibilities. Thompson, then working for the North West Company, was assigned the task of finding where the Columbia had its beginning, then determining whether the river provided a navigable means to reach the Pacific Ocean. It took him several years—he lost a full year by mistaking the Kootenay River for the Columbia, and he was once turned back by unfriendly Peigans—but he eventually reached the mouth of the Columbia River on July 15, 1811.

The waterway Thompson had travelled follows a twisting, difficult route that covers two thousand kilometres from Columbia Lake near Invermere to the Pacific Ocean. It actually flows north at first, turning slowly westward, and then, as it passes by the Selkirk mountain range, turns abruptly south, passing through Revelstoke, the Arrow Lakes, Castlegar and Trail. Joined now by the Kootenay River, which also flows west out of the Rockies south of Invermere, it enters Washington State and joins with the Spokane River, the Okanogan River and the Wenatchee River before forming nearly five hundred kilometres of interstate border.

When the Grand Coulee Dam was completed in central Washington during the Second World War, it was the largest hydroelectric dam in the world and remains the largest such facility in the United States. Today there are fourteen hydro dams on the Columbia's main stem and roughly four hundred dams on the entire watershed for hydro production, irrigation and flood control. The river's power is legendary: one flood in early summer 1948 wiped out the town of Vanport, Oregon, leaving forty-one people dead.

So dammed, in fact, is today's Columbia River that it has lost its original seasonal patterns. A century ago, three-quarters of the flow occurred from April through September. By the end of the twentieth century, the flow was roughly equal between April–September and October–March.

"This river may have been shaped by God, or glaciers, or the remnants of the inland sea, or gravity or a combination of all, but the Army Corps of Engineers controls it now," Timothy Egan wrote in his 1990 book, *The Good Rain: Across Time and Terrain in the Pacific Northwest*. "The Columbia rises and falls, not by the dictates of tide or rainfall, but by a computer-activated, legally arbitrated, federally allocated schedule that changes only when significant litigation is concluded, or a United States Senator nears election time. In that sense, it is reliable."

By the 1970s, twenty-eight dams along the system were producing hydroelectricity. Nearly half of all hydroelectric power used in the entire United States of America comes from the Columbia River, the north-and-south dispersion of that power controlled by the Columbia River Treaty, which was signed between Canada and the United States in 1964. The treaty was also important for flood control, with Canada agreeing to build dams and provide reservoir storage of the water and the U.S. agreeing to deliver to Canada one-half of the increase in downstream power benefits.

That pivotal treaty is now up for renewal.

Woody Guthrie was certainly enthusiastic about the possibilities that cheap electricity would open up for poor families. His songs in praise of development along the Columbia River were public. His growing concerns, however, he kept to his private correspondence.

From Portland, he wrote to his old friend Millard Lampell, a fellow musician who, along with Pete Seeger, was a member of the Almanac Singers, a group that sometimes included Guthrie. "Some of the factories are dumping refuse and chemical garbage into the nation's greatest salmon powerstream, the Columbia River," Guthrie said in his letter. "Millions of fish are destroyed and the Indians are plenty sore. The dried salmon means grub for the hard winter. A disposal plant was offered the company for a few thousand dollars but the company refused. All running water is public property under federal law—why this poisoning of the river?"

With the war effort, this poisoning of the river got worse, much worse. And following the war, development along the length of the Columbia brought even more pollutants. Slag from the lead-zinc mines around Trail, B.C., has covered the river bottom for great distances. Pulp mills have been blamed for mercury poisoning. At Hanford, Washington, a town turned over during the Second World War to the production of uranium and plutonium, it was estimated in 2008 that one million U.S. gallons of radioactive waste is slowly working its way through the groundwater. One estimate warned that if it is not completely cleaned up, the waste could reach the river by 2020.

Such abuse seems improbable for a watershed that contains or touches on Yoho National Park, Glacier National Park, Mount Revelstoke National Park and Kootenay National Park in Canada, and Yellowstone National Park, Mount Rainier National Park, North Cascades National Park, Glacier National Park and Grand Teton National Park in the United States. It is also the traditional home to dozens of North American Indigenous groups—all of whom relied on the river's bountiful salmon as a major source of food.

"Rivers spin our turbines, powering industry and lighting the cities," my *Globe and Mail* colleague Mark Hume wrote in his 1992 book *The Run of the River*. "They carry away our industrial and residential waste. But they do not wash away our sins. Long before the environmental stress on a river becomes obvious to most of us, it shows up in the fish. They are canaries in the mine—but canaries that cannot sing. We must pay attention to what the fish are telling us, and to the whispering voices of our rivers, for they are speaking about our future."

High upstream in British Columbia, at Revelstoke, where a massive dam was constructed in 1979, the estimates of fishery losses have been pegged at 4,000 Dolly Varden, 1,000 rainbow trout and 500,000 salmon a year. Hume says scientists have estimated that "Over a 50-year period then, roughly 550 million salmon were eradicated from the system."

Scientists believe that, prior to the damming of the Columbia, annual salmon runs in the system would run as high as 16 million fish. With the dams in place, the biggest run in recent times was in 1986, when 3.2 million salmon entered the Columbia. But they don't get as far upstream as they used to. Near Bridgeport, Washington, Chief Joseph Dam, ironically named after a Nez Perce chief, has no fish ladders, thereby completely blocking any salmon migration into the Upper Columbia River system and Canada.

Bonneville Power Administration spends many millions a year on restoring salmon runs south of the border, with limited success because of the dams. There is even a program that carries young salmon past dams by barge and truck. North of the border, in Canada, salmon remain but are landlocked and rarely grow to the same proportions as their American cousins.

Robert Sandford, the EPCOR Chair for Water and Climate Security at the United Nations University Institute for Water, Environment and Health, has written extensively on the Columbia and other rivers in the Rockies. The blocking of the salmon runs, he believes, was an assault on the culture of the region. "Wherever we find salmon," the resident of Canmore, Alberta, has written, "we also find Indigenous peoples whose cultural heritage has lined them directly to the ecological energy of the Columbia River for hundreds of generations. . . . We realize now that we turned off our biodiversity-based planetary life support system function so that we could turn on our lights in the Pacific Northwest."

Elizabeth Hendriks, vice-president of freshwater conservation at WWF-Canada, sharpens the concern: "B.C.'s environment is already under pressure with droughts and industrial developments that can affect water flow, which in turn will have a domino effect on the ecosystems and wildlife and communities that depend on them."

Where WWF-Canada found some hope is in the watershed's ability to cleanse itself. Water flow remains good, even with the dams, and researchers on the Upper Columbia found no serious decline in the native fish. Columbia Lake near Invermere, B.C., for example, flashes orange each fall with salmon that live out their entire lives near the source.

It speaks to both the fragility and resilience of rivers. It says there can be hope if there will be help.

The notion behind the Columbia River Treaty was simple. If Canada agreed to control the flow of the Upper Columbia to maximize the hydroelectric dams, then the United States, to be fair, would share some of the power generated downstream in the American portion of the river.

While next to nothing has been said in Canada about the renegotiation of this important treaty, the same cannot be said for the Pacific Northwest. Ever since the treaty came up for review upon its fiftieth anniversary in 2014, state politicians have been pleading for State Department officials in Washington, D.C., to get on with it. United States senators and representatives from four states in the area wrote to former secretary of state John Kerry in 2016 requesting that the talks begin and that Kerry's people prod Canada to appoint a chief negotiator.

In early November 2016 the U.S. State Department finalized its Circular 175, which outlines and authorizes the talks with Canada.

Canada had refused to begin discussions until the parameters of the new talks were clarified. Hydro-power generation and flood control are priorities, obviously, but these talks will also take into consideration ecosystem functions and various community concerns, including those of Indigenous groups. All this was undertaken, of course, before the dramatic U.S. election. With Donald Trump as president and a new secretary of state in former oil executive Rex Tillerson, it was unclear early in 2017 which direction such talks might take—or even if they would begin.

Canada receives about $250 million a year from the "Canadian Entitlement" in the treaty, its exchange for the flood protection it has developed upstream. Some U.S. officials consider that money "excessive." American utility providers claim electricity prices are high because of this Canadian payoff. Others say that the flood protection Canada provides is worth much more than any annual entitlement the Americans send north.

Indigenous groups on both sides of the border are keen for this renegotiation, seeing a chance to push for the return of the salmon runs largely cut off by the dams. In June of 2016, a handmade cedar canoe journeyed south along the river from Arrow Lake, B.C., to Kettle Falls, Washington, where it joined with nine other canoes that had made the paddle upstream. There, the Upper Columbia United Tribes (UCUT), a coalition of American tribes and Canadian First Nations, held a salmon ceremony to raise awareness of the need for fish passage around the Chief Joseph and Grand Coulee dams. Along with the Columbia River Inter-Tribal Fish Commission (CRITFC), active in the lower reaches of the watershed, UCUT is determined to see ocean salmon return to the far reaches of the Columbia.

Indigenous voices were not a consideration back in 1964 when the treaty was signed, says Brett VandenHeuvel, an environmental attorney who serves as the executive director of the twelve-thousand-member Columbia Riverkeeper, based in Hood River, Oregon. "The treaty," he says, "was essentially about power and flood control."

As Robert Sandford wrote in a recent United Nations University paper on the situation, "The Indigenous peoples of the Columbia Basin are not going to let the injustice to which they were subjected to in 1964 happen to them again. . . . As U.S. Yakama tribal elder Gerald Lewis pointed out at a conference on the Columbia River Treaty in Ellensburg, Washington, in 2012, we have to keep in mind that we are not reconsidering the Columbia River Treaty just to satisfy ourselves. We are doing this for future generations."

In light of the damage done to the fishery over the past half-century, the area has become far more politicized. Not only are Indigenous interests well organized, but there are environmental groups active today that did not exist in the early 1960s. In fall 2016, Columbia Riverkeeper, for example, celebrated victory following a twelve-year battle to stop the building of new LNG (liquefied natural gas) terminals. As VandenHeuvel wrote in the group's publication, "In the end, LNG's fate was decided locally when the rallying cry of a coastal town reached a New York City board room: We value our river more than a $6 billion fossil fuel export project. The victory prevents the export of 1.2 billion cubic feet per day of fracked natural gas. That's twice as much gas as the entire state of Oregon uses each day."

VandenHeuvel says that the area is particularly attractive to those who would export resources, with talk of new coal and oil terminals needed for the growing Asian markets. Dredging to allow the big ships to dock, however, would have seriously affected the salmon fishery. "It's one of the most threatened rivers in North America," he says.

The head of Columbia Riverkeeper is not without optimism, however. "We can manage the system in such a way as to help the salmon, in ways that aren't just about producing the most power all the time," says VandenHeuvel. "I'm hopeful that we will have a more modern treaty that incorporates clean water, adequate flow, surviving salmon, instead of just having it be this antiquated idea of 'We'll hold back water, you produce power—and give us the money.'"

"A more modern treaty will consider the ecosystem," he says, but cautions that "many of the same powerful forces that created the original treaty are still very powerful—the hydro system is still a major player and a major factor. And it's still a great tug-of-war between the profits from dams and energy and salmon and some of the ecosystem functions that are harmed by dams." But in the complicated game of power and (flood) control leading up to negotiation of the treaty, those like VandenHeuvel who hold the Columbia dear see an opportunity for great and positive change: "It's a whole new ball game, one that will test the notion of integrated watershed governance in the twenty-first century. It also has the potential to set an example for the rest of the world on enlightened management of issues associated with international water treaties in a changing climate."

Sandford, who has studied the treaty for years, says it "is almost dizzying in some ways." Consideration will need to be given to the power, agriculture and industrial sectors, but also to such pressing factors as fish protection, water quality, climate change and, of course, the Indigenous concerns that were ignored a half-century back.

"I think you're going to see Aboriginal peoples on both sides of the border linking together as never before in ways they have never done before," he says.

Sandford has no fears that the Canadian Entitlement will be lost, as the Canadian flood control is much more valuable than the electricity sent north. "The Canadian hand here is quite good if they handle it properly," he says, though he stressed that a change in government in Washington will have an unknown effect on negotiations.

"There's tremendous pressure to get this one right—and if we don't, then there's going to be huge consequences."

It is considered an unpardonable sin in journalism to end a story with "Only time will tell." A far greater sin would be if time says nothing.

CHAPTER FOURTEEN

"WATER IS LIFE": THE NORTH SASKATCHEWAN

IT IS BARELY PAST THANKSGIVING, and already the RCMP are advising drivers to stay off the roads. An early and largely unexpected blizzard has struck Saskatchewan, and Highway 2 heading north from Saskatoon to Prince Albert appears to have as many vehicles in the ditches as there are 4x4s bouncing nervously through the icy ruts.

The North Saskatchewan River, running black as the ravens that swoop over the Diefenbaker Bridge, will not freeze up for weeks yet, but already Prince Albert city manager Jim Toye is thinking about spring breakup—and worrying. "It can get very tumultuous," he says of the river that passes through this city.

When the ice does break up, it will gouge the sandbars and rake the shallow river bottom. When the runoff from the Rockies passes through in late spring/early summer, the powerful currents will stir things up again, all the way east to Lake Winnipeg.

"They say it will be years before it all gets down," says Toye.

"It" is the up to 225,000 litres of oil that leaked out of a Husky Energy pipeline on July 21, 2016, sending roughly 40 percent of the total spill into the North Saskatchewan near Maidstone, a three-hour drive west in better road conditions than exist on this mid-October day.

This has all taken place at a time when proposed energy pipelines are being hotly debated east and west of Saskatchewan, as well as to the south. Within weeks of my visit, there will be federal and provincial approval of the proposed expansion of Kinder Morgan's Trans Mountain Pipeline from Alberta to Burnaby, B.C. The coming winter will see continuing debate over the Energy East project that, if built, will carry 1.1 million barrels of oil a day to refineries and a marine terminal in New Brunswick. And there is the ongoing battle over the Dakota Access oil pipeline, which has faced heated protests by the Standing Rock Sioux over concerns the pipeline will threaten their water and that building it will harm sacred sites.

Given how Saskatchewan is encircled by such concerns, you might expect that an alarm would be sounded the instant any source of water in the province became contaminated. None was heard in Prince Albert, a city of 45,000 that takes all of its drinking water from the North Saskatchewan and provides potable water to another 1,600 residences beyond—mostly acreages, farms and the Muskoday First Nation.

"We heard about it on the news," says Toye.

Much controversy followed over the amount of time that passed between the beginning of the oil spill and notification of provincial authorities. An initial report said it was fourteen hours, leading one expert, Ricardo Segovia of E-Tech International, based in Santa Fe, New Mexico, to claim that if the delay had been only an hour, the spill could have been contained quickly and communities such as North Battleford and Prince Albert could have avoided shutting down their water-treatment plants.

"It made the problem much, much worse," Segovia said in the report, which was commissioned by groups representing various affected people, including the Assembly of Manitoba Chiefs, the Council of Canadians and the Idle No More movement. "The delayed action by Husky was a lost opportunity to capture oil on the surface and has now become a much more complicated problem of recovering oil below the surface."

Husky, however, quickly pointed out that the first report, even if it came from the oil company, was incorrect. In fact, they said, subsequent internal investigations found that the province was informed within thirty minutes of the discovery of the leak. In a November 17, 2016, report to the province, Husky said the spill was caused by ground movement following a heavy rainfall, and that cleanup operations had been successful to the point that, four months after the spill, 80 percent of the oil had been recovered or removed.

The controversy raged on. Other timelines had come into play, and many in the province were still upset. Prince Albert officials had been told by the province and Husky that it would take five or six days before the spill became a major concern for the city and affected its water supply.

"That ended up being three days," Toye says.

With typical Prairie resolve, city workers moved quickly into action. They shut down businesses with high water usage and set a fine of $1,000 for anyone who defied the order. None did. They built a temporary dam on the Little Red River, which runs into the North Saskatchewan, and piped its water to the treatment plant, stockpiling it in two huge vessels that supplied the city with enough water to get by in the short term. Desperately seeking a longer-term solution, the small city then rented equipment—at a cost of $2 million a month—to pump water some thirty kilometres from the South Saskatchewan River, which runs from southern Alberta and Saskatchewan through the city of Saskatoon and converges with the North Saskatchewan downriver of Prince Albert.

"We were up and running nine days after the call," says Toye with as much civic pride as he can muster.

The city was proud of its quick response but hardly happy about needing to do it. The costs were enormous. Permission had to be granted by First Nations to run the water lines through their territories. A number of roadways and driveways along the pipeline path had to be cut open to ensure the piping wouldn't be run over and crushed. Once the North Saskatchewan River was clean enough to start supplying water again, new equipment, at a cost of $250,000, was purchased to ensure it would stay that way. Included was a special line installed in the river and an alarm in the water treatment plant to sound if the line detects any hydrocarbons.

It was not until mid-September that the provincial Water Security Agency gave North Battleford and Prince Albert the green light to start once again drawing their drinking water from the river. Compensation was paid by Husky to affected First Nations communities, including the James Smith Cree Nation, which launched a suit against the provincial government in summer 2017. Prince Albert itself received a $5-million payment in mid-August that helped cover expenses as it dealt with the spill.

Husky says that as of September 30 the cost of the spill to the company had reached $90 million. While the payments were helpful, and expected, returning the river to what it was before the July 21 spill will require time and likely still more money, as well as no further accidents. In late November, the province introduced legislation that will bring in new safeguards, including increased inspection and compliance powers for the provincial authorities.

"We say to Husky, 'Do your due diligence,'" says Toye. "It's our water. Without our water, where are we?

"It was a bit of an awakening."

The Saskatchewan River system is vast and complicated. It runs from the Columbia Icefields in the Rocky Mountains to Lake Winnipeg, more than 4,600 kilometres if both the north and south branches are measured. It drains an area larger than France, and some three million people live in the basin.

The North Saskatchewan is very much its own river, beginning in the mountains, passing Rocky Mountain House in Alberta, creating the magnificent valley parkland below the table on which Edmonton sits, and running ever east until it passes Prince Albert and connects with the South Saskatchewan, a smaller river that picks up where the Bow River and Oldman River join up. This branch passes through Medicine Hat and heads northeast to run through Saskatoon and on past Batoche, site of the 1885 Northwest Rebellion.

"Eventually, all things merge into one, and a river runs through it," author Norman Maclean wrote. "The river was cut by the world's great flood and runs over rocks from the basement of time. On some of the rocks are timeless raindrops. Under the rocks are words, and some of the words are theirs." In 2005, when the North Saskatchewan Watershed Alliance made a pitch to have the river designated a heritage waterway—so far, only the part that flows within Banff National Park has the designation—the Alliance titled its submission "The Story of This River Is the Story of the West."

The North Saskatchewan, the Alliance wrote, was "the main transportation and communication route from eastern Canada to the Rocky Mountains, from the middle of the 17th Century to the middle of the 20th Century the river played a significant role in Aboriginal displacement westward, the western expansion of the fur trade, early missionary efforts in the West, major exploration, scientific, survey and military expeditions, as well as in the early European settlement of the West." As the two branches flow entirely in Canada, it provided an east-west route through the Prairies safely above the American border. There is here, all along the twisting tracks of the North and South Saskatchewan rivers, what British politician John Elliot Burns once said of the Thames—"liquid history."

"In one way or another the Saskatchewan is associated with every name which became famous in the Canadian West," Hugh MacLennan wrote. "After Kelsey and the Vérendryes came Samuel Hearne, Peter Pangman, the brothers Frobisher, Alexander Henry, and [Peter] Pond himself; then Mackenzie, David Thompson, William McGillivray, and Simon Fraser. In the nineteenth century it was at Batoche on the South Branch that Louis Riel and Gabriel Dumont stood with the tragic, nomadic race of Métis left behind on the plains by the mating of the voyageurs and their Indian women. It was toward the Saskatchewan that the militia of a united Canada marched to put down the rebellion, and in the Saskatchewan territory that the Royal North-west Mounted Police laid the groundwork of their reputations."

This is the watershed where such giants of history as Poundmaker and Big Bear, Louis Riel and Gabriel Dumont played out their dramatic roles in Canadian history.

It was along the banks of the North Saskatchewan that on November 27, 1885, eight First Nations men were hanged at Fort Battleford, making it the largest mass hanging in Canadian history. After the North-West Rebellion had been put down by the Northwest Mounted Police, and Big Bear and Poundmaker jailed, the eight men were sentenced to hang, six of them for partaking in the Frog Lake Massacre. All were granted ten minutes to speak, only one, Wandering Spirit, declining to do so.

One of the condemned men gave a most remarkable speech, saying "I wish to say Goodbye to you all, officers as well as men. You have been good to me; better than I deserved. What I have done, that was bad. My punishment is no worse than I could expect. . . . I am sorry when it is too late. I only want to thank you, redcoats and the sheriff, for your kindness. I am not afraid to die. I may not be able in the morning, so now I say again to you all—goodbye! How! Aquisanee!"

At precisely 8:00 a.m., the eight men were hanged simultaneously, the entire Indigenous population of the residential Battleford Industrial School marched out to witness the event and have the lesson burned into their young minds.

Along the two Saskatchewan rivers the earliest cautions about finite resources were raised, and sadly ignored. In 1855 Hudson's Bay Company trader Henry Moberly left Rocky Mountain House and headed down the North Saskatchewan River with eight boats containing twenty-five hundred buffalo robes, three hundred cured buffalo tongues and many hundred pelts of various animals, all headed for English markets.

The bounty changed quickly, and dramatically. Historian Billie Milholland relates the decline: "By the winter of 1861, the abundance of meat in the area had come to an end. According to the Edmonton House Journal, the Blackfoot had brought neither fur nor meat to RMH. The people at the fort were in danger of starvation." By the summer of 1866 in Rocky Mountain House, "all hands set snares for rabbits to keep themselves alive."

The 9th Earl of Southesk, a widower, came to the Canadian West in 1859 to restore his health. It apparently worked. Invigorated, the Earl returned to England, married again and fathered eight children. He also wrote about his experiences in the West in a book bearing the unwieldy title *Saskatchewan and the Rocky Mountains: A diary and narrative of travel, sport and adventure during a journey through the Hudson's Bay Company's territories, in 1859 and 1860.* In it, he described one hunt in which he killed more than thirty bighorn sheep, claiming that "a man who travels thousands of miles for such trophies may be excused for taking part in one day's rather reckless slaughter."

Being "excused" for such recklessness in Canada, however, makes it seem as if there were enough bighorns that thirty taken would have no effect. The story of the plains, in many ways, is the story of taking as much as possible, from buffalo to fossil fuels, with consequences known and unknown.

Before the railways, the rivers moved people and supplies about by canoe, barge and steamboat. It was the Saskatchewan river system that allowed First Nations to trade with each other, to fish and, at times, to move with the buffalo, so long as there were still buffalo to hunt. The watershed includes grassland plains, deep valleys and rapids, as well as long stretches of slow-moving water and a vast delta. Across this vast watershed, explorers have unearthed dinosaur bones and potash and, most profitably, enormous reserves of oil and natural gas.

"The North and South Saskatchewan rivers were the highways," agrees Greg Goss, professor of biological science at the University of Alberta. "They opened up the West.

"The values of our river systems has been underestimated."

"My God, Edmonton—*look out!*"

This was, according to Billie Milholland's book *Living in the Shed*, the only warning Edmonton residents had in 1915—a frantic telephone call from Rocky Mountain House, more than two hundred kilometres upstream. In only ten hours, the North Saskatchewan River rose three metres. The mountain waters came through in crushing waves, leaving thirty-five city blocks under water and two thousand people homeless.

This annual threat—today dramatically reduced by dam controls— enters the city by way of the Alberta capital's most beautiful feature, the magnificent river valley that now includes 7,400 hectares of parkland and 100 kilometres of hiking and biking trails.

Not so before the big flood. When Frederick Todd, an American urban planner, came to the city in the winter of 1906–07, he found the valley "a beehive, populated with dozens of coal mines, brickyards, lumber operations and even a couple of gold mining operations and boat builders." Todd filed a report pressing the city to create more parkland. "A crowded population," he wrote, "if they are to live in health and happiness, must have space for the enjoyment of that peaceful beauty of nature."

Flood control—particularly following the tragic 2013 flood in southern Alberta—remains a priority in the watershed. In September of 2016, the federal government announced a $77.8-million water project that will be led by Dr. John Pomeroy of the University of Saskatchewan in Saskatoon and will include three Ontario universities: Wilfrid Laurier, the University of Waterloo and McMaster. The University of Saskatchewan will be the main focus of a network that includes nearly four hundred researchers at multiple universities, forty-five research institutes, nineteen federal and provincial agencies and seven First Nations communities.

"We will be developing national level flood, drought, water supply and water quality forecast products," Dr. Pomeroy told the *Calgary Herald*. "These will be based on improved science and improved computer models, instrumented watersheds like the Canadian Rockies Hydrological Observatory and new sensors, such as acoustic snow sensors . . . but also drone-based sensors."

All this is necessary, he believes, because of the increasing number of extreme weather events. "We are experiencing water problems we have never dealt with before," he said, "so we want to become the most advanced in the world at dealing with these water problems and assuring a high quality water supply."

Also of great import, Dr. Pomeroy said in an interview with the *Globe and Mail*, is drinking water, whether affected by oil spills, pollution or drought. "We're going to pay particular attention to source drinking water qualities for First Nations," Pomeroy said, "which is a serious problem in this country."

In early October of 2016, the North Saskatchewan Watershed Alliance held an educational forum at Sherwood Park on the "future of our water supply." They heard from scientists and government experts. They talked about climate change and other changes—the high usage of water in fracking to extract oil and natural gas deposits, for example—and came to the conclusion that the river was actually in pretty good shape, the recent oil spill notwithstanding.

The demands on the watershed are large: 1.4 million people living along the two Saskatchewan rivers and their many tributaries, supported by flood control and hydroelectric dams while working in the chemical sector, agriculture, forestry, oil and gas recovery. With less than 4 percent of the flow used for water-treatment facilities, however, at least one expert has concluded, "We have room to grow." Because of the lower volume in the South Saskatchewan system and the threat of drought in the southern areas of Alberta and Saskatchewan, there is some talk of creating a "water bank" in the south to better ensure supply.

Surprisingly little use is made of the recreation potential in the watershed. Don and Marcia Harris, schoolteachers from Raymore, Saskatchewan, regularly take classes to paddle sections of the river. Like all who use the North Saskatchewan for recreation, the Harrises were deeply upset when they heard news of the oil spill. The Harrises treasure their time on both the Saskatchewan rivers. "You can put in anywhere," says Don. "It's particularly easy wherever there is a ferry crossing.

"Its appeal is access. It's a huge, wide river, sometimes up to a kilometre wide, and it's easy access. It's lovely to be on the water. You're very close to civilization but you don't see it. You might see the top of a farmhouse or a barn, but not much else. It's not a destination river. It's just a big river running through the prairies—but you don't really see the prairie. You're always down in a valley."

It is indeed a different experience from the other large and significant rivers in the country, the Saint John, the Ottawa, the Mackenzie, the Fraser, the Columbia.

"For along most of the Saskatchewan, whether on the North Branch or the South," novelist Hugh MacLennan wrote in his *Seven Rivers of Canada*, "the world has been reduced to what W.O. Mitchell called the least common denominator of nature, land and sky." MacLennan also called it "the loneliest looking" of all Canada's major rivers. The author, of course, was more used to the busy-ness—rocks, trees, cliffs, white water—of eastern rivers than the placid flow of rivers in the flat and relatively barren Prairies. Yet it is in the soft valleys created by such rivers as the North and South Saskatchewan, the Bow and Oldman and, especially, the Qu'Appelle that a great beauty lies. Rather than "lonely," I would say "content." These rivers seem to know they matter.

"We're lucky," says the University of Alberta's Goss. "The North Saskatchewan is at least a 'managed' river, and it's been managed a fairly long time." Managed in the sense that it's mostly been one of the country's cleaner big rivers. "If you go to eastern Canada or the eastern U.S., they've had fifty or seventy years of industrial revolution, in some cases a hundred years, of relatively unregulated pollution." Canada's regulatory oversights aren't perfect, he argues, citing *E. coli* levels in the Saskatchewan rivers in the 1950s, when raw sewage was dumped directly into the water. But that doesn't stop him from taking pride in how far we've come. "You go around the world and you still see open sewers, you still see industries with low levels of pollution control and high levels of input into those rivers. Those issues are ones that Canada can solve. Clean up the big problems and solve the minor problems."

Goss, now in his mid-fifties, became fascinated with river pollutants in a unique manner. He grew up in Kenora, where his father was warden of the area prison in the early 1970s, when mercury poisoning from area pulp mills became a national issue. He was an impressionable youngster when a fishing ban went into effect along the Wabigoon and English River system and led to the economic collapse of Grassy Narrows First Nation (now Asubpeeschoseewagong First Nation), where a successful commercial fishery had operated for decades. While both the paper and chemical companies that had been polluting the waters closed down in 1976, the mercury remained in the water for decades. "That was reflected in my father's jail," remembers Goss. "It was filling up with people's social ills."

Ever since then, he has dedicated his research to finding a workable balance between a sustainable environment and a sustainable economy. "We can find that," he says. We have to. "Most people don't think about [the watershed] because they can turn on the tap and get water.

"We essentially don't appreciate water until it's gone."

Months after the Husky oil spill, months after the communities that draw their drinking water from the river were again drinking that water, there remained an anger that something like that could happen.

The spill begat a new advocacy group, the Kisiskatchewan Water Alliance Network (KWAN), which grew out of a week-long hunger strike by Emil Bell, a seventy-five-year-old elder from the Canoe Lake Cree First Nation, "Water is life," Bell told *Saskatoon StarPhoenix* reporter Alex MacPherson back in August. "No water, no life—it's that simple. I don't want my children, grandchildren, great-grandchildren, future generations to have to be involved in the cleanup of the mess that people make because of their greed."

Bell spent his week of protest in a tepee erected on the Duck Lake property of Okiysikaw Tyrone Tootoosis, a Cree activist who claimed news of the spill was nothing short of a "shock" to the people. "I didn't know anything about the oil and gas industry," Tootoosis told me. "I had no idea there were lines so close to the river. The vast majority of people around here had no clue."

Tootoosis called the spill and public reaction to it a "wake-up call," words echoed by Prince Albert city manager Jim Toye. Others have heard it loud and clear. There is now even a provincial art competition—"As Long as the River Flows"—being organized by the Chapel Gallery in North Battleford and the Mann Art Gallery in Prince Albert.

"I just thought, 'Why aren't we talking about this?'" says Leah Garven, the curator of the North Battleford gallery. "We were passively sitting by a situation that we weren't in control of. We hear of these things happening elsewhere, but not in our pristine world."

"We have so few people and two beautiful rivers. We have to have something to say about what happened. I hope this gets people asking, 'What does the river mean to us?'

"Our river is sick. Let's talk about this. We don't think about things like this.

"It's like breathing. You don't notice it until it's restricted."

In the summer of 2015, the North Saskatchewan River was certainly noticed. The oil spill, while a preventable disaster, also had the effect of reminding those who live along the river what a treasure they have in the North Saskatchewan—a sentiment expressed time and time again by Tyrone Tootoosis. Ill with cancer, he fought to the very end for the river, passing away in early February of 2017, his loved ones posting on Facebook that "Tyrone left us early this morning, riding a comet during the full snow moon. We will miss him dearly."

He left behind not only a family that dearly loved him but also the new Kisiskatchewan Water Alliance Network. "Kisiskatchewan" is what the Plains Cree call the North Saskatchewan, and KWAN has brought together a number of organizations, including the Idle No More movement, to lobby for environmental protection.

"It's a wake-up call," Tootoosis said at the founding of the Alliance. "But not many have woken up. What if there's another oil leak that makes this one look like a birthday party. We have a right to ask the government 'What are you going to do about it?'"

THE NORTH SASKATCHEWAN RIVER

CHAPTER FIFTEEN

COTTAGE COUNTRY BEAUTY AND BATTLES: THE MUSKOKA

WE PADDLE OFTEN TO A LOVELY, lightly splashing waterfall at the end of Flossie Lake, a small pipe-shaped body of water that is named only on the most local of maps and which pokes its stem into the western boundary of Algonquin Park.

The clear, clean water that fills Flossie Lake drains from the Algonquin Highlands and tumbles from an unnamed creek down a long ladder of glacier-planed granite to this tiny lake, where the only summer residents to be found above the water surface are two loons and, in a lucky year, their two babies.

Here the water is so clean that humans who pass their summers on the next body of water over, Camp Lake, drank it straight from the lake for decades and still could if they so wished. I know this for a fact, as my wife Ellen's family has had a cabin on Camp Lake since the late 1960s.

The water flows by a campsite where someone with time and a chainsaw on his hands has carved a giant penis from a dead, but still erect, pine. It is a source of endless fascination, smirks and giggles among the young of Camp Lake, our several grandchildren included.

The water passes into Camp Lake through a short channel where a dilapidated hunt camp—known as "The Tiltin' Hilton" to the few area cottagers—stands guard. The water works its way through Camp Lake and over a flood-control dam into Tasso Lake. At the end of Tasso it falls over another flood-control dam into the East River. Still rolling down from the Algonquin Highlands, it eventually comes to a strange stone monument in the middle of the bush where, high above the manicured grounds and gardens, lie the ashes of Clifton and Betsy Dyer, a wealthy, childless couple from Detroit who first camped here in 1916, during their honeymoon.

Clifton G. Dyer was a very successful lawyer in Detroit. He and Betsy returned in 1936 for a second honeymoon and decided to purchase some property near the river and build their own small cabin. According to the few locals who knew them, it was a charming marriage, warm and admired, the couple's only regret being that they had no children to share in their love of Muskoka.

When Betsy died in 1956, weeks short of their fortieth anniversary, a despondent Clifton formulated his remarkable plan. He would build a monument in the woods the likes of which had never been seen. It would be constructed of quartz-and-mica-flecked granite and stand fourteen metres high, with wide concrete steps leading to this unexpected "altar" at the height of land above the river. He would place her ashes at the top of the monument and he would landscape the grounds with flower beds and ponds. Money would be placed in trust to keep the exquisite little park in perpetuity.

Clifton himself died shortly after the monument was finished in 1956, and his ashes were then placed with Betsy's. A bronze plaque at the bottom, rather out of sync with today, states: "An Affectionate, Loyal and Understanding Wife Is Life's Greatest Gift."

The East River, here known as the Big East River, continues on through Arrowhead Provincial Park, past a sandy area where high spring waters have been known to flood the nearby trailers and homes, and twists and turns its way to the southwest, where it flows quietly into Lake Vernon.

The water that tumbles down the little falls at Flossie Lake next flows through a narrows and an open bay and splits the charming small town of Huntsville, my hometown, where, for the first time, it is known as the Muskoka River. Through Fairy Lake and down past another dam and locks to Port Sidney, it forms the North Branch of the Muskoka, and then on to the town of Bracebridge, where it roars over three impressive falls and past the town's hydroelectric generating stations.

Shortly after, the river doubles its volume with water entering from the South Branch of the Muskoka, which also has its source in Algonquin Park. This water has come down the Oxtongue River, where Tom Thomson and the Group of Seven once painted, and over various rapids and two glorious undammed falls, Ragged and Marsh's, before spilling into Lake of Bays. On the southeast side of this large and popular lake, the flowing water becomes the South Branch of the Muskoka River as it journeys past Grist Mill Park in Baysville. It is here where in 2010 the G8 Legacy Fund provided $274,000 to put up public toilets and a $38,500 plaque to thank the people of Muskoka for holding the completely uneventful summit that, the following week, blew up in Toronto as the G20.

The South Branch flows over another dam and on through a twisted route to Muskoka Falls and four more generating stations. In 1894, Bracebridge was the first town in the country to supply its very own electricity. It is also the town where nurse Rene Caisse claimed to have found an old Ojibwe recipe capable of curing cancer. Sheep sorrel and burdock root and other ingredients are mixed together to create a tea.

Caisse called the concoction "Essiac" (her name reversed), and for a decade during the 1930s, the town became a mecca for desperately ill people from around the world. But that, of course, is a whole other story.

The Muskoka River is whole, finally, as it pushes through the town and on past Santa's Village, Bracebridge being on the 45th parallel and, therefore, "halfway to the North Pole." Santa's Village is where an exhausted Santa Claus is said to spend his summers. The tourist attraction was once owned by a provincial premier, Frank Miller. On a hot August day, a grown person heading out onto Lake Muskoka on a giant swan can sing along with the recorded music: *"walkin' in a winter wonderland . . ."*

Moving ever west, the Muskoka waters pass by $10-million monster summer homes—known as "hockey player cottages" among the locals—and nears where a future lieutenant-governor of Ontario grew up in abject poverty on the edge of a waste dump.

At Bala, two more falls have become a tourist attraction to rival Bracebridge's Santa, after which the flow splits into the Moon and Musquash rivers and eventually pours quietly into Georgian Bay and the Great Lakes.

From the moment that handful of clear water was dropped at the end of Flossie Lake, the "Muskoka River," in all its various permutations, will have fallen four hundred metres and passed through forty-two dams, most to do with water-level control. Approximately a dozen dams are for the production of hydroelectricity.

Plans in Bala are to add one more hydro dam with a new project that would divert most of the water that tourists photograph and play in and reroute it into a generating station that would, among other things, mean an end to Purk's Place, a boat livery and bait shop that has sat on land between Bala's falls for more than a century.

Bill Purkis, who took over the little bait shop from his father, says he will fight this idea to the end, if necessary.

"They can scrape me off the rocks," growls the senior citizen, "and take me to the dump."

Never, ever refer to this area of Canada as "The Muskokas." The phrase, which is commonly used in the big cities and in the national media, causes the locals to cringe. Even more grating is the fortunately rare tag "Hamptons of the North."

The correct usage is plain "Muskoka." One only. The word is believed to have been derived from an Ojibwe chief, Mesqua Ukie, who once lived in the area. "Cottage Country" is also permissible, though the vast majority of locals do not live in cottages, the cottage adjective "Muskoka" having driven prices beyond the station of most locals.

The area's rivers and lakes were never quite as bucolic as portrayed today. The Great Mapmaker David Thompson paddled up the Muskoka River in 1837 in search of a safe military route between Ottawa and Lake Huron and was largely unimpressed by what he saw—though, in his defence, he was sixty-seven, blind in one eye and, because of a broken leg that had never set and healed properly, had trouble getting around. When he paddled into the large, bay-and-island-filled body of water that is famous today as Lake Muskoka, he named it "Swamp Ground Lake." He found the "musketoes" horrible and the rocks "rude."

Not everyone agreed. John Campbell and James Bain, Jr., count as the first summer visitors to Muskoka, leaving Toronto's Union Station aboard the northbound Simcoe and Muskoka Junction Railway on August 5, 1861. They were accompanied by another man they called "Crombie" and Crombie's dog, whose name was not recorded. At Barrie, the end of the line, the group transferred to the steamer *Emily May* and made their way up Lake Simcoe to Orillia. They crossed Lake Couchiching by rowboat and reached Washago in the fading light of the day. They overnighted at Severn Bridge and, first thing in the morning, began walking north again up the rough trail toward Lake Muskoka.

Their equipment was barebones: packs with food, straw hats for the sun, guns and powder in case of bears or wolves, and brandy for the evenings. When they dropped in at McCabe's very rudimentary tavern where Gravenhurst stands today, they were officially in Muskoka and celebrated with McCabe's specialty, the "Stirabout," which was a stiff mixture of water, molasses and moonshine.

The very few locals of that time had no idea what to make of them. They weren't surveyors. They weren't preachers. All they did was walk to Muskoka Bay, where McCabe had told them there was a scow they could use. Rowing with one oar and bailing mightily, as the old boat leaked, they made it out to an island where they gathered flora specimens, took a nap on the rocks and paddled back to shore, still bailing.

Returning to McCabe's Tavern, they supped and talked about their wonderful day, the tranquility of the water and the marvellous finds of plants and wildflowers that so excited them. Those who had mistaken them for surveyors and preachers now must have seen them as insane, for no one there had ever headed out in a boat except to fish or hunt or get somewhere else on the lake; besides, the settlers saw their task as ridding the land of such unwanted wild plants, not carefully packing them away so they could carry them back to the city.

It would not be the first time a year-round resident of Muskoka would fail to comprehend the mind of the summer visitor.

When they got back to Toronto, Bain and Campbell raved about their adventure and the beauty of the landscape. The two young men were peer role models—Bain would become chief librarian for the city, Campbell a brilliant theology professor in Montreal—and soon their friends began planning their own summer adventures in the north. By 1864 they were calling themselves "The Muskoka Club."

For the nominal fee of one dollar per year, the Muskoka Club would organize and "provide an annual expedition" for its exclusive and limited membership. Bain and Campbell remained the leaders, Bain preferring to be called "Finn the Fisherman" on the sojourns and the eclectic Campbell serving as both curate and botanist to the vacationing groups. They took great pride in "roughing it." As D.H.C. Mason, a relative of James Campbell, later put it, "They came to the wilds to leave the city, not to bring it with them. Luxury would have seemed to them as much out of place as oriental rugs, and spring beds in a tent."

If they seemed somewhat precious long before young city visitors to Muskoka were expected to put on summer airs, it was all fairly harmless play-acting. Peter Robinson, who served as unofficial "recording secretary" of the club for many years, told of a climb the group took one summer in search of a spectacular view of the lake, a climb apparently so exhausting that the young men reached the top no longer able to speak English and fell to speaking Greek for the remainder of the trek.

They had soon explored all of Lake Muskoka and pushed on into the adjacent lakes, exploring Lake Rosseau in different summers and one year determining to push through the north channels into Lake Joseph. The area Natives had always claimed Joseph was the most beautiful lake in the district and contained, instead of the tea-like water of Lake Muskoka, water so crystal clear they said you could watch trout swim along the bottom.

When the Muskoka Club members finally reached their destination, they understood what the Natives had been saying. Lake Joseph, recorded Robinson, was "last, loneliest, loveliest, exquisite, apart." So taken were the adventurers with their new discovery that they established a permanent camp on Chaplain's Island near the Joseph River, which flows out of Lake Joe. They also began spreading their social net, bringing more and more people up from the city on their annual forays into the wild. As the young men married they began coming up with their wives—the first female tourists to come to Muskoka.

In 1815, the government had purchased hunting grounds under the control of Chief Yellowhead, an Ojibwe, intending to leave the area from Lake Simcoe far into the north as a reserve. But only three years later, another exchange of land for goods shifted the vague, never-designated reserve, and once more in 1836, when Natives living around present-day Orillia sold their choice land between lakes Simcoe and Couchiching. They sold cheaply and moved to where the village of Port Carling now sits on Lake Muskoka. On January 31, 1862, the "Muskoka" band met with surveyor John Stoughton Dennis in the village they called "Obajewanung" and had Dennis draft a petition that they asked to be sent off to Viscount Monck, the governor general.

"Father," the band stated, after offering condolences to Queen Victoria on the death of her consort, Prince Albert, "we are in trouble and we come to you to help us out. We believe that your ears are always open to listen to the complaints of your Red Children and that your hand is always ready to lead them in the right path." The Muskoka band believed they had been led down the wrong path, partly by government negotiators, partly by their own leadership. According to a treaty signed in Sault Ste. Marie, they were to go to an island near where, today, the town of Parry Sound stands on the shores of Georgian Bay. "Father," the little group pleaded from the shores of Lake Muskoka, "Our feelings have changed. This place is beautiful in our eyes, and we found we could not leave it."

The plea from the little Muskoka band fell on deaf ears. They were soon moved to the designated reserve on Parry Island, where today they are Wasauksing First Nation. By the early 1870s, all the Natives had left Muskoka, a vast boreal territory where they had camped and trapped and lived long before the first Europeans reached North American shores.

Their land was assigned to settlers, and much of that land, especially that found around the shores of the several lakes, would one day pass on to those who, at best, manage to be there only a few choice weeks a year. Doing as little as possible.

Many of the new European settlers, most coming from the British Isles, would find their free land grants a bitter disappointment. Apart from rare pockets, farming was impossible in the rugged Canadian Shield. Poet Al Purdy had good cause to call it "the country of defeat."

In an 1871 letter to the editor that appeared in the *Stratford Beacon*, Albert Sydney-Smith wrote: "Many settlers, after passing through the rocky country between Washago and Bracebridge and still finding rocks staring them in the face, get discouraged or homesick; and, without going into the country to see what it is like, pick up their traps and leave by the first steamer."

There were, however, alternatives to farming. First was lumbering, the Muskoka River watershed being ideal for spring log runs. The new sawmills became centres of small and growing communities. Before the railway and passable roads made the Near North accessible, rail carried supplies as far north as Gravenhurst, where steamboats collected them to finish the journey. Soon they also were transporting early cottagers and then guests of the dozens of lodges and resorts that soon dotted the picturesque lakes.

The lakes and rivers ran thick with fish, as the forests did with game. In this wild but not too distant place, travel by rail and steamer felt almost luxurious. "Muskoka," Canadian author W.E. Hamilton wrote in 1878, "is a virgin field for the great army of tourists."

Muskoka proved most attractive to Americans, especially wealthy families anxious to escape the oppressive summer heat in northern industrial cities. A stretch of Lake Muskoka known as "Millionaires' Row" was first nicknamed "Little Pittsburgh." (Today, it must be pointed out, a mere "millionaire" could never afford a place on the "Row.") One late-nineteenth-century writer described the steel city at night as "Hell with the lid taken off"; by comparison, the Muskoka evening breeze was air-conditioning.

Urbanites well north of Pittsburgh knew what they were missing at home, too. "To appreciate the north country," reported the *Bracebridge Gazette* on July 26, 1906, "one must leave Toronto on a stifling July morning when the pavements, where pavements exist, are a torture to weary feet, and when the lake is the only prospect that pleases."

It was not just the smog-bound who found it easier to breathe in the new country. Allergy sufferers were also quick to note that the fresh air and cool nights of the Ontario bush offered unexpected relief. "The Muskoka air," a brochure for the Grand Trunk Railway read, "is one of the best alleviations known for that very persistent and annoying ailment, Hay Fever . . . there is entire immunity from the disease here. . . . Owing to the high altitude and pureness of the dry atmospheric conditions, perfect immunity from malaria is also assured." It was not exactly true. Hay fever sufferers might sneeze a little less. But it worked.

In 1880 the Beaumaris Hotel opened. It was large enough to serve two hundred guests and offered cricket and lawn tennis as well as fishing and boating, with concerts and dancing in the evening. The daily rate, meals included, was $1.50 to $2.00. Over the years as many as 150 resorts operated in the area, among the more famous being Windermere House, Cleveland's House, Elgin Lodge, Lake Rosseau

Resort, Pratt's Hotel, Prospect House and the Royal Muskoka Hotel, where Prime Minister Sir Robert Borden was frequently a guest. But Beaumaris set the style, even to having its own travelling cricket team that at one point boasted William Lyon Mackenzie King, who would succeed Borden as prime minister, as a player.

Come each summer, the lodges would fill with men in white ducks and flannel suits, women in light muslin summer dresses and fancy hats. Big bands played at Dunn's Pavilion in Bala and Bigwin Inn on Lake of Bays. Count Basie, Duke Ellington, Louis Armstrong and the Dorsey brothers, Tommy and Jimmy, were familiar entertainers. Clark Gable and Carole Lombard were guests. The royal family came from the Netherlands, the Rockefellers from America.

The grand lodge of Beaumaris hosted many of them, surviving even when others died in the 1920s and 1930s, and was still a going concern when it burned down on July 21, 1945. A nineteen-year-old arsonist described in reports at the time as a "borderline case mentally" was sentenced to two years in prison for destroying the grand hotel.

The wealth of these summer visitors was mind-boggling to the poverty-stricken settlers, who were finding it more profitable to work the lakes than the land. The enterprising locals realized early on that whatever could make summer living even more genteel would be rewarded handsomely, and soon there were supply boats working the large family-compound docks so that the vacationers would not even have to think about sending their own help to the local markets.

The king of the Muskoka waters was A.P. Cockburn, whose Muskoka Lakes Navigation Company would eventually have a fleet of 140 boats of various sizes working Lakes Muskoka, Rosseau and Joseph, as well as another fifty working the waters around Huntsville and Lake of Bays. Cockburn would eventually own "the largest and most successful inland steamship navigation company in Canada."

The cottagers killed the steamboats. Following the Second World War, the growing middle class began building and buying simple cottages, and new roads began to rim the lakes. Ground transportation put the boats out of business.

Cottagers and locals soon began a symbiotic relationship: the well-off cottagers had needs the needy locals could fill. Cottagers needed refrigeration in the summer; the locals cut the ice in winter, stored it under sawdust in cottagers' icehouses and would send the bill off to Toronto or Pittsburgh. The first wave of middle-class cottages created such a boom in the building industry that, for a while, seventeen sawmills were operating along Gravenhurst Bay alone. The effect was to produce Canada's first purely tourist-based industry.

There is no record of the first tourist trap, but it may well have been the phony Indian village set up in Port Carling to be part of the Muskoka Lakes Navigation Company's 100-Mile Cruise. Two "Indian Chiefs"— Chief War Eagle and Chief American Horse—were hired and brought in from upstate New York. With their wives, they set up an "Indian" encampment with about twenty other Natives, put up tepees, made and sold handiwork and birchbark souvenirs and even put on "Indian" costumes and danced when the cruise ships docked. No one ever noted that the "Indian Village" had been erected on the very ground where, in 1862, the Muskoka band had met with the government representative and petitioned in vain for the governor general to let them remain.

The vast wealth of the summer visitors created other businesses. Craftsmen began building the exquisite mahogany watercraft that the rich cottagers preferred. As early as the 1890s Muskoka was considered the custom-boat capital of world. Names of local builders— W.J. Johnston, Bert Minett, Henry Ditchburn, C.J. Duke, Thomas and Ernie Greavette—became famous for the boats that are, today, prized possessions, as are the "dippies," lesser yachts built by the Disappearing Propeller Boat Company at Port Carling.

Though there is always a certain undercurrent of resentment in places wholly dependent on tourism—the rich vacationers often condescending in their treatment of locals, the locals often sneering at the vacationers' naïveté in the woods—they make it work in Muskoka and have for more than a century.

Fanny Cox Potts, who wrote under the pen name "Ann Hathaway," wrote a slim novel in 1904 she entitled *Muskoka Memories*. "For the past few years," she wrote, "the population of Muskoka has been gradually dividing itself into two classes—tourists and settlers, otherwise capital and labour, pleasure and toil, butterflies and bees . . . and between the two there is a great gulf fixed . . . one thing is sure, each class would be badly off without the other." It became, in effect, a sort of twentieth-century colonialism.

A century after Ann Hathaway's novel appeared, Muskoka had become a playground for the famous as well as the rich. The rich—Eatons, Labatts, Seagrams, the Mellons of Pittsburgh—had long been discreet, if sumptuous, cottagers, usually owning their own private islands. Once singers, actors and athletes became the very wealthy, they discovered Muskoka. Rich hockey players such as Eric Lindros, Paul Coffey and Steve Yzerman built enormous cottages and boathouses. Comedian Martin Short now summers on the old Lady Eaton estate on Lake Rosseau and often hosts famous actors from Hollywood. Near to Short, actors Goldie Hawn and Kurt Russell bought a place for their family but moved elsewhere when they tired of "incredibly rude" people coming up to their docks with camera in one hand, map in the other.

In 2014, Christie's, the international real-estate powerhouse, said there had been a 66 percent increase in top-end waterfront purchases. Property sales in excess of $2 million set a new record in 2014 after several years of sagging transactions. Perfectly good summer cottages are often razed to the ground and replaced with garish all-season structures.

Bill Purkis is standing at the foot of Bala's gorgeous north falls. He is breaking the law and couldn't care less. He is leaning out over the boiling, roaring water and has a powerful right hand wrapped around a red caution sign as if he were about to throttle it.

"Notice," the sign, one of many along this spot, says, "Public use of this land is prohibited pursuant to Section 28 of the Public Lands Act."

Purkis and others were warned in 2015 that they could be charged with trespassing, but, more than a year after the warning, no one has been. The signs are on Crown land but it is presently leased to Swift River Energy, the company that was approved back in 2006 to construct and manage the new dam that is still in the planning stages. Locals fear that the much-photographed falls, a lovely spot with falling water on both sides and a small park between, will be transformed to a point where it will no longer attract visitors.

Not so, says Swift River. It would remain accessible and, in the company's opinion, picturesque. Spokesperson Karen McGhee, an engineer, points out, "The project is actually located at a site where two existing dams are located. These dams were erected over a hundred years ago." The north dam can be used to control water flow, particularly during the spring freshet. Bala also produced hydroelectricity until the 1950s—it still has one small generator operating mostly out of sight—so Swift River argues that its project is hardly a departure. "Back to the Future" is their motto. "Building on Bala's Legacy" is another. The locals don't always see it that way. So many are against the project that, as of the winter of 2016–17, it was years behind schedule.

The company has tried to assure the village that it would be a good neighbour, producing clean energy and creating local jobs during the sixteen- to eighteen-month construction period. It says it would spend $10.8 million locally during this time and would be good for businesses. But with a growing list of local businesses such as the Bala General Store up for sale or closing down, these promises strike residents as naïve at best.

"Save the Bala Falls" declare signs around the area, or "Stop the Hydro Plant." Among the many signs is a massive one right in front of the old bait shop. "The Muskoka River has been almost totally dammed," says Purkis. "We're doing everything we can to keep this from happening."

Purkis and others hand out brochures saying the new dam project is "too big, too ugly, too dangerous and bad for the area's economy." They argue the new station would reduce the spectacular north and south falls to trickles and destroy the village's only constant tourist draw. Instead, locals say, the falls should be left just as they were when Lucy Maud Montgomery and her family came to the village in the summer of 1922. "When I lie in bed at night," the author of *Anne of Green Gables* wrote in her journal, "it sounds exactly like the old surge roar of the Atlantic on some windy, dark-gray night on the old north shore."

Defenders of the Muskoka watershed and Bala Falls found an ally in someone other than cottagers and the descendants of the early Muskoka loggers and settlers: the nearby Wahta Mohawks First Nation. The Wahta are actually Iroquois from around Oka in Quebec, site of the seventy-eight-day standoff in 1990 between Mohawks and the military. An earlier standoff, dating back to the 1870s, had pitted Protestant Natives against Roman Catholic Natives, and both Native groups against French Canadians. Property was destroyed and a Wesleyan Methodist church burned. After Quebec police arrested dozens of Natives for trespassing, an early morning explosion destroyed the Catholic church. Government authorities intervened and a decision was made to move one group of Natives to Gibson Township in the district of Muskoka. They floated themselves and their possessions by barge across Lac des Deux Montagnes, boarded a train for Toronto, took the northern line to Gravenhurst and, on October 31, 1881, arrived at Bala.

The Wahta Mohawks say they were never consulted about the project and that the very portage they used back in 1881 to move onto their assigned land would be destroyed by it. The portage, in fact, was already well established. David Thompson noted in his 1837 journals that the "carrying place" had been clearly marked and much used.

Many in the town are also against the project for this reason. "Portaging is part of the Canadian identity," township mayor Alice Murphy told the *Globe and Mail* in 2014. "You have the right to portage, because you have the right of navigation."

Bill Purkis smiles as he lists the various opponents of the project. "I was a hippie," he says, "so I'm used to going up against authority."

There are, of course, local supporters and the project has now been the most contentious issue in council and Bala elections. A July 2015 meeting of the Township of Muskoka Lakes council was so disruptive that the provincial police showed up. Locals were furious that they had been forced to cancel their annual Canada Day festivities when they were informed that they could be charged with trespassing if they assembled, as they have done for years, on the disputed site. When the first officer arrived at the council chambers, more than fifty locals, mostly elderly, stood and sang *O Canada*.

Every day, says Purkis, a few more names are added to the petition that his group hopes will stop the project permanently.

One of the most recent signatories was James Bartleman, who served as lieutenant-governor of Ontario between 2002 and 2007. He was raised in a Métis family living at the site of the Port Carling dump and went on—thanks to the largesse of a wealthy cottager from Pittsburgh—to graduate from university and pursue a distinguished career in the foreign service.

He was happy to sign, he says. "Once it's gone, it's gone forever."

CHAPTER SIXTEEN

WHITEWATER ESCAPE ON THE DUMOINE

THE MAN WHO ALMOST DROWNED Pierre Trudeau is standing on the banks of the wild Dumoine River in western Quebec, water tumbling down rapids to his left, water swirling in a vast eddy to his right, water falling from above in a cold, annoying, late spring rain.

The man who saved Pierre Trudeau's life—more on that later—knows there is still snow in the bush, but that is a mere technicality: the season has begun.

Wally Schaber—given that the former prime minister is no longer with us, lost to age rather than drowning, and given that canoeing legend Bill Mason is also long gone—stands today as Canada's best-known paddler in a world where reputations are big but hardly wide. At sixty-seven, the Ottawa-born Schaber is the founder of Black Feather wilderness adventures and, with partner Chris Harris, Trailhead out-fitters. For nearly half a century he has guided on the iconic wilderness rivers of the country: the Nahanni, the Hood, the Coppermine, the Mackenzie, the Mountain, the Keele, the Milk, to name but a few. But it is here he loves best: the Dumoine, a river five hours north from his eastern Quebec home that can be reached only by float plane or by hammering a 4x4 over ill-tended logging roads. It was on the Dumoine River that Schaber took his very first whitewater run in 1969. In 2015, he published a book on the Dumoine, *The Last of the Wild Rivers*, which is part history, part love letter, part plea for preservation of the river that has meant so much to him.

There is something about wild, untouched rivers that speak to the soul of Canada. The mighty St. Lawrence is a river of travel and commerce, the Ottawa River one of discovery, the Niagara and the Fraser of pure power. There is no commerce on the Dumoine apart from tourism, now that the fur trade has vanished and logging is a fading memory. There are no dams along the Dumoine, making it unique among the nine major tributaries flowing from western and northern Quebec into the larger Ottawa River. Its power is spiritual rather than electrical.

There are canoes and kayaks on the Dumoine but none of the cabin cruisers and high-powered fishing boats that pass by the mouth of the Dumoine as it reaches the Ottawa River. A waterfall known as "Ryan's Chute" serves, as one paddler put it, "as a sentinel guarding the river upstream from motorboat access."

This makes the Dumoine watershed a precious commodity in that it is so relatively accessible and offers such immediate reward to those who just wish to "get away from it all"—at least for a short while. It also makes it very Canadian. More than a half-century back, renowned historian W.L. Morton noted that the "alternative penetration of the wilderness and return to civilization is the basic rhythm of Canadian life." This still holds true today for a great many Canadians. Call it "basic rhythm," "cabin fever," whatever. It is an important ritual, one that agrees with U.S. nature writer John A. Murray's contention that "Every so often a disappearance is in order. A vanishing. A checking out. An indeterminate period of unavailability. Each person, each sane person, maintains a refuge, or series of refuges, for this purpose. A place, or places, where they can, figuratively if not literally, suspend their membership in the human race."

There is no cellphone reception along the Dumoine River, no Internet access. Not even one of those increasingly rare newspaper boxes. There are no sounds from a distant highway, no marina, no stores, very often no one else.

In the cold of this particular morning on the Dumoine, with the last of the spring flush churning through the rapids and the water black as ink as it calms and heads downstream, the river may not seem that inviting, but Schaber is already thinking of trips to come in a year that, for him and fellow paddlers, is now only just beginning. "A river has a personality for each season," he says. "You pick different times for your trip and meet a different 'person' each time you go."

He stares out over the water, smiling past the rain. "The great beauty of a river trip," he says, "is you don't have to navigate—you just follow the water."

The Dumoine River is not a long river, only 130 kilometres, but it drains a vast watershed and has many tributaries, guaranteeing a fast current. From Lac Dumoine to the Ottawa River, it tumbles through thirty-nine falls and rapids, seven of which are mandatory portages, too dangerous to risk. Canadian singer Gordon Lightfoot is said to have tagged the Dumoine detours as "the worst goddam portages" he had encountered in a lifetime of paddling.

The largest falls of all, Grand Chute, thunders through rock cliffs beneath a substantial bridge, the waters still foaming white as the river bends out of view in the distance. On the day Wally Schaber came to check the early spring conditions, another group watched helplessly as the small dog accompanying them ventured into the river for a drink and was swept down the chute and lost.

The Dumoine is well known by canoeists for its challenges and is revered for its scenery: looming white pines, tall cliffs, spectacular vistas and superb campsites. Quebec Hydro would love to be able to dam the river and harness its power. It would be a terrible shame if this ever came to pass. The many rapids on the Dumoine River carry names like "Big Steel," "Snake," "Sleeper," "Red Pine" and "Canoe Eater"—one I know personally from both on and below the rushing water.

In the summer of 2010, I joined the Crash-Test Dummies on a trip down the Dumoine. Not to be confused with the pop group out of Winnipeg that had a hit record back in 1991 with "Superman's Song," these "Dummies" are an ever-evolving group of paddlers that are led, somewhat haphazardly, by brothers Lorne and Phil Chester, who have more than a century of hard paddling between them. Respected canoe historian James Raffan, writing in the *Globe and Mail* in 2015, said: "If Bob and Doug McKenzie, of *SCTV* infamy, were canoeists, then the Chester brothers would be their reincarnation, stars of a Mel Brooks-ish tale (think *Blazing Paddles*), parsed with humour and impeccable timing, that navigates the brink between too corny for words and deeply instructive in their zeal for Canada, canoes and all, that melds the two into passion in a country of rivers."

Lorne, an Ontario court judge, and Phil, a retired high-school English teacher, were joined on this particular trip down the Dumoine by three police officers—Scott Duffy, Harry Hughes and Lorne's daughter Kelly—Paul Burns, a printer who has paddled, and won, the gruelling one-day North Bay–to-Mattawa paddle over one of the country's best-known fur trade routes; Terry Smith, a meditating librarian; and an interloping journalist.

All the paddling Dummies live for white water. Lorne Chester, cautious by profession, conservative in politics (he has even run provincially for the Conservative Party), throws caution to the wind and waters when in a canoe: an apparition in gardening knee pads and helmet, the paddler the others call "Riverhawk" will stand straight up in his canoe while approaching rapids, arbitrarily pick a course and plunge into it with a shout. His brother Phil, flamboyant and philosophical in real life, is cautious and wary as a cat on the water, carefully scouting out each rapid, meticulously choosing his routes and ensuring there is, on the shore, help available if help required.

Needless to say, the brothers, who do not paddle together, have been known to have their own churning and swirling discussions on such trips.

Where they stand as one, however, is in a deep and abiding love for white water. Whitewater paddlers and kayakers seek out that frisson of danger, and it is impossible to ignore this basic animal instinct when discussing their passion. A snippet of dialogue from 1951's *The African Queen*, starring Humphrey Bogart (as Charlie Allnut, a Canadian) and Katharine Hepburn, speaks to this instinct:

> CHARLIE: *How'd you like it?*
> ROSE: *Like it?*
> CHARLIE: *Whitewater rapids!*
> ROSE: *I never dreamed.*
> CHARLIE: *I don't blame you for being scared—not one bit. Nobody with good sense ain't scared of white water.*
> ROSE: *I never dreamed any mere physical experience could be so stimulating.*

For as long as there have been canoes and paddlers, that stimulating thrill has been a major attraction. W.F. Butler, a nineteenth-century English officer and explorer, said, "It is difficult to find in life any event which so effectually condenses intense nervous sensation into the shortest possible space of time as does the work of shooting, or running, an immense rapid. There is no toil, no heartbreaking labour about it, but as much coolness, dexterity, and skill as man can throw into the work of hand, eye, and head; knowledge of when to strike and how to do it; knowledge of water and of rocks, and of the one hundred combinations which rock and water can assume."

Some people find in canoeing—particularly when it involves shooting rapids—a sense of adventure that is missing from the rest of their lives, even for those whose lives hold more adventure than most others would wish. Craig Oliver was for decades the main political correspondent for CTV News. He reported on wars, natural disasters, assassinations, murders and political intrigue—but still needed canoeing to give him something his professional life lacked.

Oliver has an ocular condition that eventually put an end to his adventurous canoeing, but not before he had explored many of the most northern and more dangerous rivers in the country. Oliver and a core group of eight paddlers—expanding at various times to include a total of fifteen—called themselves the "Rideau Canal and Arctic Canoe Club" and, beginning in 1973, began annual, and expensive, treks into the Far North. Oliver took up paddling when, as a reporter, he was sent to join an expedition along the Yukon River to Dawson in honour of the seventy-fifth anniversary of the gold rush's "Trail of '98." He was hooked, and he soon hooked others, including the likes of television executives Tim Kotcheff and Dennis Harvey, renowned art historian David Silcox, Toronto magazine editor John Macfarlane, and Liberal politicians Allan Rock and John Godfrey.

What kept them together was friendship. What drew them north each summer was the thrill. "There is a hanging moment of suspension at the top of a big chute or rapid," Oliver wrote in his memoir, *Oliver's Twist.*

The lead canoe team makes an irrevocable decision about whether to enter and what line to take, then contends with whatever faces it. The options can never be adequately judged from a far shore or a high point above the obstacle. At a distance, the forces are almost always under-estimated. Modest standing waves become monsters at water level; ledges are deeper and rocks much wider at their base. In that blood-rushing moment of risk and excitement before the rapid, nothing else exists, no past and no future, only that instant of crazed exhilaration.

Phil Chester and I had our "blood-rushing moment" at Canoe Eater rapids on the Dumoine. We had spent a good deal of time scouting this difficult rapid, its name self-explanatory. We were convinced that the water level was such that a quick buck down the right-hand side would work so long as we avoided several large rocks near the bottom, where you could choose to either go left and slip through a narrow gap, or else go right and run fast along the shore where, we were certain, the water was deep enough that we'd get through with minimal scraping and bouncing.

The alternative was an easy portage of two hundred yards, which we were considering as we stood on a jumble of suitcase-size rocks along the shoreline, carefully tracing the line we might follow. It was not, it turned out, the line Riverhawk would take. As we were standing there trying to be sensible, careful, cautious and smart, Lorne and Kelly Chester's red canoe came into view, Lorne standing on the bow like Leonardo DiCaprio in *Titanic*, "Jack" about to spread his arms and shout *"I AM KING OF THE WORLD!"* while "Rose" (Kate Winslet) stands back of him, watching with total admiration.

In truth, Kelly Chester watched her helmeted, aviator-glassed, garden-protector-kneed father with benign amusement, well used to his disdain for scouting and mapping out lines before shooting rapids. The ultimate freelancer, he would make it up as he went.

From his standing vantage point, Lorne chose the far side, quickly kneeling and prying the bow over into a dark tongue that seemed to pull father and daughter like a giant slingshot down into the churning waters. They danced, slammed, slipped, twisted, shot free and bounced through Canoe Eater, deftly turning to the left at the bottom into quieter water, swirls and small, harmless whirlpools.

Phil had watched Lorne making it up as he and Kelly pounded through the white water, Phil's face split between disdain and admiration for the older brother.

"Let's do it," he said.

We walked and hobbled over the rocks to our canoe. We tightened up our life jackets, strapped on our helmets, knelt with our knees spread wide and ferried back to get a direct run at the closest tongue. Phil was sticking to the route he'd so carefully and thoughtfully mapped out, on the side opposite to what his river-gambler brother had chosen.

"*Hard!*" Phil shouted from behind.

I dug in at the bow, pumping hard as we entered the tongue and dipped down into the first roaring white water of this mechanical bull of a rapids. We splashed hard off a haystack, then lurched right. The roar of the water was more like being on a runway than a river and Phil was at full volume, but I was having some trouble sorting out the instructions.

"Keep to the right of that rock!"

"There's a hydraulic straight ahead! Left! Left! LEFT!"

"Careful! Careful! NOW—HARD PADDLE!"

"Right! Right! RIIIGGGHHHTTTTTTT!"

Sometimes I do not know my left from my right. I have had trouble driving in England. I throw right but bat left. I play hockey left-handed but play golf right-handed. Phil maintains I dug in hard left when he was shouting—no, *screaming*—right. I maintain that he was yelling too much, Canoe Eater was roaring too much, and my personal hard drive had reached capacity about halfway through.

No matter, we were over, and as James Raffan says in his hilarious "Maxims for Happy Paddling," "Don't argue in rapids." (He also says, "Duct tape can save a marriage," "WD-40 on a worm attracts fish," "Grey Owl paddled on both sides" and "Change your underwear.")

Looking back, I am astonished at how slowly it all went. We were in very fast water. We were paddling hard. And yet slowly, ever so slowly, the canoe hit the flat rock Phil wanted to avoid, rode up the rock like a stalled car being ramped onto a flatbed, and stopped. Yes, *stopped*. Stopped dead. For just a moment, but very much long enough for the two of us to ponder the nature of the universe and where, in fact, we fit into it. There was no creaking sound, but there should have been. We stopped, we turned as the water cuffed the stern hard and, a moment later, we began this long, slow, fully aware fall from grace, and the canoe.

The shock of the water is a constant. No matter how often you might have dumped a canoe, either deliberately or by accident, in flat water or white water; no matter whether the water is ice-cold from the mountains or bathtub-warm from the August sun; no matter whether it happens in an instant or happens, as it did on Canoe Eater, over what feels like a matter of several decades—it shocks.

I remember hoping my feet would slip out from under the seat. How they did I have no idea, but instantly I realized I was free of the canoe, under water, and the roar was silenced. I could feel the water—cool and very physical—cuffing me about as I fought to gain the surface. I came up to see a jumble of yellow and red dry bags floating past our overturned canoe.

"On your back!" Phil shouted. "Feet first!"

I was already there, floating along like a kid on a carnival ride as I bounced, Slinky-like, down the "stairs" of Canoe Eater and into a wide, swirling pool at the bottom where, so thoughtfully, the centrifugal force of the circling current deposited me, and Phil, and one pack, in a quiet eddy where we could find our footing on the jumble of small rocks below.

The Algonquins named the river "Aginagawasi Sipi," which translates as "Alder River"—a fitting tribute to the coniferous trees that patch whatever open space the pines leave. Some believe the current name comes from Le Moyne, a fur-trading family in New France. One member of the family, Sieur d'Iberville, paddled up the Ottawa River in 1697 with a party of soldiers and his seventeen-year-old younger brother, Jean Baptiste Le Moyne, Sieur de Bienville, who would go on to serve as governor of French Louisiana and found New Orleans. Others, Schaber among them, believe the name comes from "monk" (*moine* in French), after the missionaries who travelled up the river with the aim of converting the area Algonquins to Christianity.

The river was also a difficult, roundabout route that allowed traders— first Indigenous, later European fur traders—to travel from the Ottawa-Mattawa rivers to Trois-Rivières and Quebec City without having to pass through territory further south along the Ottawa and St. Lawrence routes that was controlled by the Iroquois. It was long, mostly upstream, with many portages, but often considered the safer way to go. The Dumoine River runs through non-ceded land and is the traditional territory of the Wolf Lake First Nation. Wolf Lake elders still call the river Aginagawasi Sipi rather than "Dumoine."

The wider area is currently part of a huge land claim that remains far from settled. A legal paper prepared in 2005 by Winnipeg lawyer James Morrison, "Algonquin History in the Ottawa River Watershed," says there are ten Algonquin communities in western Quebec and eastern Ontario, some of which (Kitigan Zibi) have vast reserve lands, some of which—such as Wolf Lake First Nation—have none at all. The Wolf Lake claim to the Dumoine River watershed is traced to the Algonquin legend "Wiskedjak Pursues the Beaver," which was documented in 1913 by government anthropologist Frank Speck. Speck learned the story from Ben McKenzie, a member of the Kiwegoma Anishinabeg (also known as the Dumoine Band and now Wolf Lake First Nation), who had been born in 1847 and learned the story from band elders.

Wiskedjak, also known as Nenabush, is the great cultural hero of the Anishinabeg and is usually personified by the whisky jack, a social bird also known as the Canada jay. When materials were being gathered in 2005 by the Ottawa River Heritage Committee, in an effort to have the Ottawa designated a heritage river, the tale of Wiskedjak was included in the submission. Basically, the story is about Wiskedjak coming to a lake deep in the woods, identified as Dumoine Lake, and finding a mountainous beaver lodge. In order to capture the giant beaver who must live in such a lodge, Wiskedjak decided to drain the lake. Falling asleep as the water was running out, he awoke to find the lake empty and its waters rushing madly down what would eventually be known as the Dumoine River. In attempting to track the course of the giant beaver, Wiskedjak came to Calumet Chutes, which he passed and then began following his own tracks back, thereby establishing the Calumet portage. Not a very bright bird, but he sure created a magnificent river.

Wally Schaber believes it is incumbent upon any paddler, regardless of ancestry, to know and appreciate the history of those First Nations who first paddled the waters and lived off the natural resources of the watershed. "It's difficult—perhaps even impossible—for a WASP like me to try and tell the story of the Rivière du Moine band," Schaber writes in *The Last of the Wild Rivers*. "It is their story, not mine, although the European and Algonquin tales certainly overlap. It should be told orally by an elder of the tribe, as was the tradition of the Algonquin since time began."

In the past, there was often more appreciation of Indigenous heritage than we see today. Members of the Society of Jesus (Jesuits) who travelled the Ottawa-Mattawa-French rivers route to Huronia in the seventeenth century were even handed a "Commandments" of canoe decorum—however politically insensitive—as written down by Father Paul Le Jeune. Whether the commandments suggest a true appreciation of heritage or are more intended as a guide for staying in the good graces of guides it is impossible to say.

1. You must have sincere affection for the Savages. . . .
2. To conciliate the Savages, you must be careful never to make them wait for you in embarking.
3. You must provide yourself with a tinderbox or with a burning mirror, or with both, to furnish them fire in the daytime to light their pipes, and in the evening when they have to encamp; these little services win their hearts.
4. You should try to eat their *sagamite* or *salmagundi* in the way they prepare it, although it may be dirty, half-cooked and very tasteless. As to the other numerous things which may be unpleasant, they must be endured for the love of God, without saying anything or appearing to notice them.
5. It is well at first to take everything they offer, although you may not be able to eat it all; for, when one becomes accustomed to it, there is not too much.
6. You must try to eat at daybreak unless you can take your meal with you in the canoe; for the day is very long, if

you have to pass it without eating. The Barbarians eat only at Sunrise and Sunset, when they are on their journeys.

7. You must be prompt in embarking and disembarking; and tuck up your gowns so that they will not get wet, and so that you will not carry either water or sand into the canoe. To be properly dressed, you must have your feet and legs bare; while crossing the rapids, you can wear your shoes, and, in the long portages, even your leggings.

8. You must so conduct yourself as not to be at all troublesome to even one of these Barbarians.

9. It is not well to ask many questions. Silence is good equipment at such a time.

10. You must bear with their imperfections without saying a word, even without seeming to notice them. . . . In short, you must try to be, and to appear, always cheerful.

11. Each one should be provided with half a gross of awls, two or three dozen little knives called jam-belles, a hundred fishhooks, with some beads of plain or coloured glass with which to buy fish or other articles when the tribes meet each other, so as to feast the Savages. . . .

12. Each one will try, at the portages, to carry some little thing, according to his strength; however little one carries, it greatly pleases the Savages, if it be only a kettle.

13. You must not be ceremonious with the Savages, but accept the comforts they offer you, such as a good place in the cabin. . . .

14. Be careful not to annoy any one in the canoe with your wide brimmed hat; it would be better to take your nightcap. There is no impropriety among the Savages.

15. Do not undertake anything unless you desire to continue it; for example do not begin to paddle unless you are inclined to continue paddling. Take from the start the place in the canoe that you wish to keep . . .

16. Finally, understand that the Savages will retain the same opinion of you in their own country that they will have formed on the way . . .

Today, Wolf Lake First Nation has close to 250 members. Near the mouth of the Dumoine, in the tiny Quebec village of Rapides-des-Joachims—known as "Swisha" to the locals—the Wolf Lake Algonquins have a small outfitting business and a café. Swisha is but a shadow of what it was in the logging days, when it boasted a large hotel, multiple bars and several stores. A large steamwheeler, the *Pontiac*, ran people and supplies in from Pembroke on the Ontario side.

Today, however, with the fur trade and white-pine logging distant memories, there is little action along the Dumoine River apart from paddling groups challenging themselves on the whitewater rapids. Within the watershed there are several weathered log cabins belonging to hunting and fishing clubs on land leased from the local ZEC (*zone d'exploitation contrôlée*). The ZECs—twenty-three involving rivers such as the Dumoine—were set up in 1978 by the provincial government to take over from the many private hunting and fishing clubs and provide for wider access for the general public.

The ZEC Dumoine covers a territory of more than fifteen hundred square kilometres. At the gate entrance near Swisha, a colourful poster describes it as "a territory to discover—an experience to be lived." In English, those lining up to pay for passes and licences are told they will be able to access "more than four hundred crystalline lakes" and several " impetuous rivers."

Of which the Dumoine, of course, is most impetuous of all.

The Dumoine River was, not surprisingly, a favourite of the late Bill Mason, the Winnipeg-born filmmaker whose film *Paddle to the Sea* was nominated for an Oscar in 1968. It may even have been the river that inspired Mason to claim that "First God created a canoe—then he created a country to go with it."

Bill Mason was a critical mentor for Wally Schaber. Mason was a practised adventurer who was more than twenty years older and became both friend and father figure to the younger man. Schaber was only ten years old when his science-teacher father, Art Schaber, died of a heart attack. May Schaber, Wally's mother, returned to work and, in summers, served as resident nurse at a camp on Golden Lake, and Wally got to go along for free. He says his experiences at On-Da-Da-Waks, an eastern Ontario YMCA camp for boys, "altered the course of my life."

He went from camper to counsellor to trip leader. At nineteen, he ventured deep into the Quebec bush to see if a fire ranger cabin that was being abandoned in favour of air patrols might serve the Y as a wilderness outpost for trekking youths. It was here that he discovered the wonders and excitement of the Dumoine River. The camp outpost worked, sort of, for a couple of summers; then the Y abandoned its plans but allowed Schaber to use the camp mailing list for his own endeavour. Forty letters were sent out, eight parents signed up their youngsters, and off they went.

"It seemed just too easy," remembers Schaber. "I decided, 'I'll make a business out of this.'"

Running a camp from the old outpost became his summer job while he studied environmental science at the University of Waterloo. His intention had been to join Parks Canada after he graduated, but the 1970s saw such an increase in outdoor adventure—in part due to demographics, in part thanks to enormous strides in camping equipment, from tents and canoes to clothing—that he decided to stick with the tripping business.

At first, Schaber and close friend Chris Harris—they met while teaching a paddling course at Algonquin College—ran their tripping business, Black Feather, out of May Schaber's basement. May would scrub the pots if there was to be a quick turnaround in trip schedules. They hired guides, including Schaber's future wife, Louise, and trained them on the Dumoine. "There were four of us and we were supposed to run the river so we'd know it well before taking any clients out," recalls Harris. "We showed with all our equipment, ready to go, and Wally had this VW Bug he expected us to fit into. We couldn't even get all our gear into the car, so one of the other guides and I had to hitchhike."

They led trips to Quetico Provincial Park in Northwestern Ontario and along various rivers in eastern Ontario and western Quebec. A naturalist friend, John Theberge, suggested they investigate various recreational issues to do with the growing number of national parks and then approach Parks Canada to see if the government department might want Black Feather to investigate further. "From running little boys' trips to area parks, overnight I went to national parks all over the country whenever I could find a reason for being sent there," says Schaber. "That launched us into the North."

The Nahanni National Park Reserve, which had been established in 1972 by Prime Minister Pierre Trudeau, an avid paddler, was keen to receive tripping groups but was having trouble trying to figure out how to certify them. Schaber and Harris came up with a plan and an exam that made Schaber the first person certified to lead canoe groups along the fabulous river. Soon Black Feather was leading six trips a year into the Northwest Territories to the Nahanni.

With their travel business thriving, the two young entrepreneurs decided to open Trailhead, their outfitting store in Ottawa, and took in two other partners, Wendy Grater and Fred Loosemore. They sold camping equipment, supplies and clothing but specialized in canoes modelled on the famous Chestnut "Prospector." Trailhead changed wilderness travel forever the day Schaber returned from an outdoors show in England with a new idea. He had noticed one display that used blue plastic barrels for holding tent poles. He measured the barrels and found them to be "perfect for fitting between the gun-wales of a canoe." There was also a sealed cap and handles. Today, canoe trippers around the world carry food and equipment in Trailhead's blue barrels. "They took off like crazy," says Schaber.

While Black Feather sent multiple trips into the Far North, the Dumoine remained the favoured river. Over a twenty-five-year period, Schaber calculates the company took five hundred paddlers a year down the river—with the odd moment of lost dignity but never a loss of life. "The first time I paddled the Dumoine it was just emerging from its pioneer era," says Schaber. "I guess it was instrumental in my discovery of myself. I grew up on the river. And I saw the effect the Dumoine had on people who had paddled it. The river is a perfect blend of adventure and the essential Canadian experience in a natural setting."

Most groups take from four to seven days, depending on where they put in, to paddle the Dumoine. Schaber did it once, alone, in less than twenty-four hours, his entire supplies for the trip amounting to six oranges and a six-pack of beer. "I just wanted to see if I could do it," he laughs.

Today, Schaber considers his career "a fluke"—a summer job that became a full-time job that became a life. A few years back, Schaber and Harris sold their Canada-wide adventure businesses and retired, but hardly from the rivers. As Marjorie Kinnan Rawlings, author of *The Yearling*, put it, "I do not understand how anyone can live without some small piece of enchantment to turn to."

For Wally Schaber, such enchantment is found on the Dumoine River in Quebec and on the Nahanni River in the Northwest Territories. A time of "checking out" from everything from email to news. "Every time you come off a long trip the first thing you say to the first person you run into is 'What's the news?'" says Schaber. "One Nahanni trip it was 'Elvis Presley is dead.' Another one it was 'Wayne Gretzky got traded.'"

In the 1980s Schaber and his wife, Louise, moved to Meech Lake in the Gatineau Hills, in part to be closer to the Mason family. Schaber helped Mason with his definitive canoe-technique book *Path of the Paddle*, and the two are said to have "invented" many of the white-water moves that are now standard among paddlers.

On their frequent exploratory trips together, Mason shot film and took photographs and then put together a slide show when they got home. They did the Mountain River together, and the Hood River. Russ McColl, a former professional hockey player who shares lease rights to a log cabin deep in the Dumoine ZEC with Schaber, accompanied Schaber and Mason on a trip to the Noir one summer and recalls marvelling at Schaber's strength: "Wally had a big pack on and Bill had a big pack on and Bill stumbled and fell on the trail. Wally just reached over and grabs Bill's pack and picks the pack and Bill up and sets him back on the trial. Just like that."

In the late 1980s, when Mason was diagnosed with cancer and decided to refuse treatment, Schaber asked his friend if he had a "bucket list" of things he would like to do before the inevitable. When Mason said he'd love to try one last, big river run, Schaber arranged for family and close friends to travel with Bill for one final run down the Nahanni. He was fifty-nine years old when he died in the fall.

Years later, Schaber was involved in another "bucket list" trip—Pierre Trudeau's final run down the Petawawa. Trudeau was seventy-seven years old, ill and increasingly frail, but he had legendary status among canoeists, in no small part because of an essay he had written back in 1944 he titled "Exhaustion and Fulfillment: The Ascetic in a Canoe."

"Travel a thousand miles by train," the future prime minister had written, "and you are a brute; pedal five hundred on a bicycle and you remain basically a bourgeois; paddle a hundred in a canoe and you are already a child of nature."

They would not be travelling a hundred miles on this trip, but it would be a challenge all the same, as the Petawawa has dangerous rapids. One of them, Rollway, is where Blair Fraser, the well-known Ottawa correspondent for *Maclean's* magazine, had drowned in the spring of 1968. Most of the rapids on this trip with the former prime minister, they would portage. There would be several of Trudeau's paddling friends along, but the job of paddling stern in the former prime minister's canoe would fall to the accepted expert, Schaber.

The trip was uneventful, for the most part. One night after some successful paddling, including the shooting of a few safe rapids, Trudeau asked Schaber, who had prepared the meal for the group, if he might help with the dishes. Schaber gratefully accepted, but he could tell that the older man was exhausted from the long day of paddling and carrying. "I may be the only person who ever got to tell the prime minister, 'Go to bed,'" Schaber chuckles.

On the last of the river's serious runs, called Crooked Chute Rapids, Schaber and Trudeau backpaddled and ferried carefully toward a still eddy where they would disembark. Trudeau reached to draw the canoe out from a rock outcropping and the canoe, caught in a cross-current, moved sharply out. Trudeau had not the strength to counteract the shift and the canoe flipped.

"I had my pack in one hand, the prime minister in the other," Schaber recalls of the harrowing incident. "I got him to shore and safe and then had to go chasing after our equipment and paddles. They were down at the bottom of the rapids, and when I got there another group I had outfitted were there and they got quite a laugh out of seeing me, soaked, picking stuff out of the water.

"I felt like a fool—but at least they didn't know I'd just about drowned the prime minister."

There is a mysticism to canoeing that many writers have tried to capture, few so successfully as the young Pierre Trudeau. Another young man, an Alabama writer named Harry Middleton, might have gone on to stand with Sigurd Olson and the few other giants of wilderness writing, had he lived. Middleton was struggling as a writer—he had to take work as a garbage collector to make ends meet—and, in 1993, at only forty-three years of age, died after suffering an aneurysm while swimming with his children. He left behind, however, words that speak to everyone who has ever been captured by the magic of the canoe.

"Many a time," Middleton wrote, "have I merely closed my eyes at the end of yet another troublesome day and soaked my bruised psyche in wild water, rivers remembered and rivers imagined.

> Rivers course through my dreams, rivers cold and fast, rivers well-known and rivers nameless, rivers that seem like ribbons of blue water twisting through wide valleys, narrow rivers folded in layers of darkening shadows, rivers that have eroded down deep into a mountain's belly, sculpted the land, peeled back the planet's history exposing the texture of time itself. Rivers and sunlight, mountains and fish: they are always there, rising up out of exhaustion, a sudden rush of sound and motion, a Wagnerian assault of light and shadow, hissing water, pounding rapids, chilly mountain winds easing inexorably into a requiem of distant rapids, a fish's silent rise, the splash of blue-green water over the backs of wet black stones.

From a completely other world, Japanese writer and philosopher Masaru Emoto has also attempted to put into words the meaning of what flowing water gives a person:

> All life flows with the flow of water. The Buddha, knowing that flow is a fundamental principle of the Universe, said that all things are in flux and nothing is permanent. Water is a good example of this. Water is always flowing with life, purifying what it encounters as it travels. It carried life while also carrying away impurities, giving life to all. . . . The act of living is the act of flowing. . . . When your soul is allowed to flow, you feel a burden lifted from your weary body. . . . Water teaches us how to live, how to forgive, how to believe. If you open your ears to the possibilities in life, you may just be able to hear the sound of the pure water that flows through your body even now. It is the sound of your life—a melody of healing.

Wally Schaber would never be so effusive as Middleton or Emoto—he's a quiet person in the deep woods—but he would certainly agree with their sentiments. "The Dumoine is more than a river to Wally," says Russ McColl. "It's part of his DNA. The river has always been his great escape."

It has also made him something of a custodian. In the summer of 2016, in an attempt to improve the campsites along the river, he and friends began a program to build and place twenty-five "thunderboxes" along the sites in an effort to prevent paddlers from using the nearest bushes as toilets.

He is also taking his book around to every store in the area and giving slideshow talks to anyone who will listen, in an effort to see the Dumoine fully designated as an aquatic park, something the Quebec government began several years back but has yet to formalize. If it becomes law, there will be no logging, hydro, mining or large commercial developments in the ZEC. "It's time now to make the reserve's status official," he argues in *The Last of the Wild Rivers: The Past, Present and Future of the Rivière du Moine Watershed.*

To Wally Schaber, the Dumoine reserve would be something Canada would want to share with the world. "We change," he writes, "the forest and the river evolve, the next generation will want to travel in ways different from ours—ways that we can't predict. But the raw wilderness must not change: clean water, plentiful wildlife, mature, uninterrupted forests, peace and tranquility, and a beautiful, wild, free-flowing river."

THE DUMOINE RIVER

EPILOGUE

"WATER, WATER EVERYWHERE."

The sign at Kitchissippi Point on the Ottawa River seemed particularly apt during the first week of May 2017. The message is part of a permanent display to show how once, more than 10,000 years ago, the Ottawa Valley was completely under water. The thawing of the last Ice Age led to the formation of the massive Champlain Sea, which formed an inlet for the Atlantic Ocean. The brackish water ran as much as 150 metres higher than the current levels of the St. Lawrence and Ottawa rivers. One spring several millennia later, both rivers were rising dramatically—if not to those levels—as snowmelt and runoff combined with rain, rain, rain, rain . . .

The rain had fallen for most of a week. On Monday, May 1, alone, some areas along the Ottawa River had received 55 millimetres of downpour. Records stretching as far back as 1925 had nothing to compare to it. There was flooding throughout the watershed—cottage property sliding into the swollen Madawaska River at Combermere, basements flooded at Golden Lake, roads and streets closed in communities on both sides of the Ottawa River, two schools closed and a seniors' residence evacuated in Maniwaki, far up the Gatineau River, states of emergency called in Saint-André-Avellin and Rigaud, homes flooded on Montreal's West Island, and Île Mercier actually submerged—all with severe weather warnings continuing and another 55 millimetres of rain predicted for the coming weekend. By that point, the military had been called in to help the hardest-hit areas in Quebec. Further east, along the Saint John River Valley, more than 100 millimetres of rain fell over a two-day span. Water, water everywhere indeed.

Monday evening, with the rain still falling, I went to Shirley's Bay, a large, lake-like widening of the Ottawa River some 15 kilometres north of Parliament Hill. The waves were rolling in, slamming into large boulders placed as a semi-breakwater along the boat ramp. With the rainfall and fog, it was impossible to see across the wide bay to the Quebec shore. I felt like I was standing at the edge of an angry sea rather than this usually placid river. The Champlain Sea returned.

It was a choice moment to reflect on the journeys of the past three years: sixteen Canadian rivers studied in detail for their history, people, issues and future, dozens more rivers touched upon in passing, by canoe, vehicle, air or library. A person could do this forever and never finish. Roderick Haig-Brown had it right when he said, "No book could possibly tell the whole story of Canada's rivers." As a journalist interested in seeing as much as possible of the country I cover, and as a passionate canoeist endlessly intrigued by what lies around that next bend, I had to accept that reality: no book can tell the whole story, no person can journey them all. And Kenneth Grahame's character Mole, whom I quoted at the very beginning of this book, was equally right when he thought about how a simple river "bewitched, entranced, fascinated." Mole believed rivers held "the best stories in the world." True in Grahame's England, true in Canada, true throughout the world.

Standing on the shrinking shoreline of Shirley's Bay, I could only think about how much water there has to be in the atmosphere to permit such a prolonged rain, with even more in the forecasts. Hours away, the Toronto Islands were now under threat of flooding. One of the island ferries was at the ready should an evacuation be ordered. Water, water everywhere—and yet it is rapidly becoming a central issue of the twenty-first century.

Not because there is so much, but because there may be too little.

We often hear that water is the new oil. George W. Bush said it as far back as 2001, *The Economist* has written it, even the head of Dow Chemical, Andrew Liveris, has declared that "water is the oil of the 21st Century." It's an easy and catchy thing to say—both are vital to the world economy, both have supply issues—but it's also an unfair comparison. Oil, once used, is gone forever, its molecular structure changed, its debatable traces gone into the atmosphere. Water, on the other hand, returns. It can be cleaned and restored and used again and again and again, whether it be to irrigate, power, drink, wash, flush . . . The water that rinses your filthy vehicle in the car wash one week might be going down your throat the next. That water flushing down your toilet could soon be cooking your neighbour's dinner. Nothing is more recyclable than water.

This matter that sustains us, however, is not infinite. Nor, obviously, is it equally spread throughout this planet. There exists a severe water crisis in parts of Africa and Australia, with some experts predicting that migrants and refugees fleeing political turmoil will one day pale in comparison to the desperate millions trying to escape drought.

Ironically, water has been part of the problem. The world's population soared in no small part because of hygiene and irrigation. More food meant more people, and healthier humans lived longer. At the turn of the century, the world's population stood around six billion. By 2050 it is estimated that number could reach nine billion, a 50 percent increase in barely half a century. According to *The Economist*, increased food production has led to a tripling of water drawn for farming. It has led to a massive disappearance of important wetlands. It has also meant that the proportion of people living in countries that are chronically short of water—8 percent of the world population in 2000—could rise to 45 percent by the middle of the century. Most threatened would be such high-population countries as China and India, which together have less than 10 percent of the world's available fresh water. Canada, on the other hand, stands with the few blessed countries—including Russia, Brazil, Indonesia, Colombia and Congo—that have an abundance of available fresh supplies.

Potable water is a valuable commodity, obviously. But one has to wonder about values when Harrod's of London offers a bottle of Svalbardi water—harvested from 4,000-year-old icebergs off the coast of Norway—at £80 ($141.52 Canadian) a bottle. Bottled water, unknown to previous generations, has today become a huge international industry, worth more than $200 billion (Canadian) a year and recently outstripping sales of soft drinks in North America. Sadly, the vast majority of sales are to people who live with drinking water available for pennies from their taps. Who saw water becoming a fashion accessory?

It can be fairly said that Canadians are waking up to the importance of their freshwater blessings. A 2017 survey by the Royal Bank of Canada found that 45 percent of Canadians now consider water to be the country's most important natural resource. How this natural resource should be used is, increasingly, a national issue. One current example is the Peace River, which flows from British Columbia's mountains through northern Alberta to the Slave River, a tributary of the Mackenzie River. Opposition has steadily mounted against the Site C Dam, a $9-billion hydro project that would flood nearly 100 kilometres of the Peace Valley. In an unprecedented move, Harry Swain, the former federal civil servant who headed up the joint review panel looking into the dam, has gone public with his concerns, saying, "There is no need for Site C." The B.C. government had hoped to sell electricity to the oil companies working in Alberta's oil sands, but Swain says that plan has degenerated into little more than "a Hail Mary play," given the economic realities of oil. The market for hydro, he has said, has been flat for so long that he can see no future for the hydro that the damming would produce, other than selling it to U.S. markets for perhaps one-third the cost of production. In Swain's opinion, the province would never see $7 billion of the $9-billion cost returned. It would be, in his opinion, "a very big mistake."

It's not likely that Canada would ever follow the lead of New Zealand, which in early 2017 took the unusual step of declaring that, from now on, the Whanganui River on the North Island of the country will be treated as a human being in the eyes of the law. A group of Maori known as the Whanganui Iwi had long fought for such recognition, and the bill, which passed in mid-March, gives the river—which the Maori call Te Awa Tupua—the same rights, duties and obligations that a legal person has in New Zealand. Those rights include representation in court.

All the same, in Canada change is coming. There is a national awakening to water underway, and this awakening can be found in every part of the country. In early 2017, the province of Manitoba launched a public awareness campaign called "Spot the Stripes and Stop the Spread" that is intended to encourage the public to take up the fight against zebra mussels and other invasive species. In Ottawa, the member of Parliament for Ottawa South, David McGuinty, rose in the House of Commons to introduce a private member's bill calling for the creation of an Ottawa River Watershed Council. The legislation calls for a major study on how the various levels of government could "take the management of the Ottawa River watershed to the next level," and is modelled on such initiatives as the Fraser Basin Council in British Columbia, as well as the Red River Basin Commission, which includes both Canadian and American members.

Canadians need to "revamp our thinking when it comes to managing the way we do business and the way we relate to something as essential as a watershed," McGuinty told the Commons. "It is an incredible opportunity for Canada, not just in the context of the Ottawa River watershed but right across the country." McGuinty's cross-river colleague Bill Amos, representing the Quebec federal riding of Pontiac, stood immediately to support the bill.

It gratifies me to see the Ottawa River—still not properly designated a heritage river—get such attention. I am prejudiced, I know. I was born in this watershed. The first water I was bathed in came from the Madawaska River, which begins in the Algonquin Park highlands and slowly—and sometimes quite swiftly—winds its way eastward to the town of Arnprior, where it joins the wider Ottawa and eventually flows past Kanata, where my family and I have lived since the mid-1980s.

That makes the Ottawa, in the smallest of ways, my river. But it is far more Canada's river, a river so important I would argue that it served as the aorta for this improbable country that recently turned 150 years old. The Kitchissippi ("Great River") was the waterway that allowed the Algonquins to travel, fish, hunt and trade. It was the river Samuel de Champlain and Étienne Brûlé journeyed up more than four centuries ago to begin the European penetration into a country far more vast than they could possibly have imagined. It was central to the fur trade, the first economy of Canada, as the voyageurs travelled up it to reach the trapping grounds and trading posts and travelled back down with the pelts destined for sale in Great Britain and Europe. It was the most important river of the timber trade, which dramatically changed the economy and brought settlers to the Ottawa Valley and points west. It provided food and drink, transport; it powered grain and saw mills, delivered electricity; it became Queen Victoria's choice for the capital of the colony that would one day become its own country.

Surely it deserves better than what Judith Flynn-Bedard told us when we met her earlier in this book at Montebello, where she keeps her boat, *Pier Pressure II*, and spends her summers cruising the river she loves. She wants the Ottawa River clean enough so that her grandchildren can swim freely in it. She wonders what the politicians plan to do about this river that flows "right out of the nation's capital." Perhaps now they will do something.

At the end of this long journey through so many, as well as so few, of Canada's rivers, I cannot help but think of Judith Flynn-Bedard and all those whom Ellen and I met along the way. I hope Wally Schaber gets his beloved Dumoine River declared a protected park so that it can remain that "beautiful, wild, free-flowing river" he so adores. May Floyd Roland see that "green" economy that will mean the communities along the mighty Mackenzie will thrive into the future. Let us all trust that Canada and the United Stated listen to Bob Sandford, who says that there is a great opportunity to "get this one right" in the renegotiation of the critical Columbia River Treaty. When Lynda Shneekloth of the University of Buffalo talks of the necessity of "rethinking Niagara," it is a philosophy that could be applied to hundreds of rivers in North America that pass through urban and industrial areas.

When Michael Yee, the biologist with the Rideau Valley Conservation Authority, says that "people are more engaged, taking ownership" of their watersheds, he speaks of something needed across the land. Also needed are scientists like Matt Windle of the St. Lawrence River Institute of Environmental Sciences, who is helping the American eel up and down past the dams. And who ever imagined that the brown trout would one day return to the polluted Grand River in such numbers that Rob Heal could run a successful fly-fishing and guiding operation?

When Kevin Van Tighem, once the superintendent of Banff National Park, devotes so much volunteer time to protecting the Bow River watershed, it underscores his belief that "the most important resource in the province, and the rarest, is water." It is a belief shared by people like Arlen Leeming of the Don Valley Conservation Association, who speaks so surely of hope—and finds it in something as small as the return of mink to what was once the most abused and polluted river in Canada.

I think of all these inspirational people—from teens like the de Gaspé Beaubien cousins and their AquaHacking conventions, Robyn Hamlyn and her campaign against bottled water to older Canadians like Bill Purkis of Bala, who says he will fight to the end to prevent another dam from rising on the Muskoka River. As Jacques Courcelles put it as he stood beside the Red River where now five generations of his family have lived, "Sometimes you have to think beyond your lifetime."

I find that I agree with Gilbert Whiteduck, former chief of the Kitigan Zibi First Nation along Quebec's Gatineau River, that we must continue to fight complacency. As another native leader, Sonny McHalsie of the Sto:lo First Nation along the Fraser River, put it, "We are the river and the river is us." And more than anything else, I take from the North Saskatchewan River the lessons of the late Okiysikaw Tyrone Tootoosis and Cree elder Emil Bell. "Water is life," Bell says. "No water, no life—it's that simple."

And what, then, of Hugh MacLennan, who became so bitter about what was happening to his beloved Canadian rivers in the 1960s and 1970s, and who, in the last book the famous Canadian author would write, seemed to hold little hope for the survival of this overconsuming and greedy world?

Even though he had grown so disenchanted with the youth of the day and the politicians of the times, his old Scots heart could not, it seemed, stop from reaching for something, anything, to hold on to.

In MacLennan's *Voices in Time*, his final book, John Wellfleet, the narrator of this alarmingly bleak vision of the planet's future, finds himself sitting outside in what had once been a lovely garden. It is spring again, and he cannot believe that there is, just for an instant, a whiff of lilac in the air.

"He smiled to himself," MacLennan wrote, "as he remembered those experts who had predicted that a time would soon come when there would be no more animals or birds or lilac trees.

"As usual, they had been wrong."

A few weeks after the Great Spring Flood of 2017, I took a drive along the Ottawa River to see what the situation was like now that the waters were receding. The damage was obvious—ruined carpets, furniture and appliances at the side of shoreline roads waiting for pickup, empty and filled sandbags piled to the sides of homes, some still guarding the water's edge, a few small places still jacked up in the hopes the owners could somehow escape the flooding.

And yet it wasn't all damage. The lilacs were out in full bloom, the "whiff" John Wellfleet caught now pouring in the open window as we drove along back roads on a gorgeous and bright spring day. Where the river had backed away from property it had briefly claimed, daffodils and tulips were already up. Along the Deschênes and Remic rapids at the western edge of the city, some early kayakers were already out dancing toward summer. At Chaudière Falls, close to Parliament Hill, you could not only see but you could *feel* the power of this amazing river that, within the span of a few weeks, had managed to bring destruction and then new life to the region.

The ebb and flow of life itself, awesome and beautiful to behold, is something precious to be respected and protected, for such rivers are what made this country possible. We owe it to them to give back what they gave, and still give, to all of us.

ACKNOWLEDGEMENTS

THE AUTHOR IS DEEPLY INDEBTED to Bruce Westwood, agent and friend, who pushed this idea for a decade before I caved and agreed to do it. I am oh so glad he made me, as it turned out to be an experience of a lifetime. Ellen accompanied me on every trip as we travelled the country together and met so many fascinating, dedicated people. The hospitality, the sharing, the concerns, the inspiration—and the fun— will never be forgotten. It was the greatest "assignment" imaginable, and so I am also indebted to *The Globe and Mail* and editor David Walmsley, who saw the importance of looking afresh at what got us here. Senior editors Sinclair Stewart, Chris Wilson-Smith, Dennis Choquette and, especially, Shawna Richer were all supportive of the project, and for that I am grateful.

I also very much appreciated the guidance of Craig Pyette, my editor at Random House Canada, and his colleague Anne Collins, who has been a treasured friend since our childhoods together in the magazine business. Frances Bedford, who handles media and public- ity, has also become a much-loved friend of ours. And it would be remiss of me not to mention designer Andrew Roberts—who also did such wonderful work on *Canoe Country*, my previous book—as well as freelance copy editor Angelika Glover and proofreader Gillian Watts, who saved me every time I fell overboard. What errors remain are mine and mine alone.

ENDNOTES

INTRODUCTION

4   G.D. Garland, *Glimpses of Algonquin: Thirty Personal Impressions from Earliest Times to the Present* (Whitney: Friends of Algonquin Park, 1989), 21.

4–5   Roderick L. Haig-Brown, *A River Never Sleeps* (Machynlleth, Powsy, Wales: Coch-y-Bonddu Books, 2010), iii.

6   Christopher Armstrong, Matthew Evenden and H.V. Nelles, *The River Returns: An Environmental History of the Bow* (Montreal and Kingston: McGill-Queen's University Press, 2009), 9.
Hugh MacLennan, *Rivers of Canada* (Toronto: Macmillan, 1974), 11.

7   Ibid., 7.
Ibid., 11.
Armstrong et al., *The River Returns*, 11.

8   Roy MacGregor, "A Voice out of Time," *Maclean's*, September 22, 1980, 47.

9   Maude Barlow, *Blue Future: Protecting Water for People and the Planet Forever* (Toronto: Anansi Press, 2013), 14.
Maude Barlow, *Boiling Point: Government Neglect, Corporate Abuse, and Canada's Water Crisis* (Toronto: ECW Press, 2016), xiv.

9   Elizabeth Thompson, "Billions of litres of raw sewage, untreated waste water pouring into Canadian waterways," CBC News, December 12, 2016.

9–10 Barlow, *Boiling Point*, 245.

CHAPTER 1

14   *Northrop Frye on Canada*, vol 12, ed. by Jean O'Grady and David
      Staines (Toronto: University of Toronto Press, 2003), xxxii.

15   Susanna Moodie, *Roughing It in the Bush; or Forest Life in Canada*
      (Toronto: MacLear & Co., 1871). Quote found at www.gutenberg.ca/
      ebooks/moodie-roughingit1871/moodie-roughingit1871-00-h-dir/
      moodie-roughingit1871-00-h.html

17–18 Hugh MacLennan, *Two Solitudes* (Toronto: Wm. Collins Sons &
       Co., 1945), 3.

18   MacLennan, *Rivers of Canada*, 60.

19   Rosemary Rutley, *Voices from the Lost Villages* (Ingleside, Ontario:
      Old Crone Publishing & Communications, 1998), 38.

20   Charles Dickens, *American Notes* (London: Chapman and Hall Ltd.,
      1850), 144–45.
      Tim Cook, *The St. Lawrence River* (Milwaukee: Gareth Stevens
      Publishing, 2004), 26–27.
      MacLennan, *Rivers of Canada*, 54.

21   Conrad Black, *Rise to Greatness: The History of Canada from the Vikings
      to the Present* (Toronto: McClelland & Stewart, 2014), 729.

21–22 Lowell J. Thomas, *The Story of the St. Lawrence Seaway* (Buffalo:
       Stewart, 1957), 13.

22   Daniel Macfarlane, *Negotiating a River: Canada, the U.S., and the
      Creation of the St. Lawrence Seaway* (Vancouver/Toronto: UBC Press,
      2014), 168.
      Ibid., xxiii.

23   http://www.glfc.org/sealamp/.

25–26 Dan Egan, *The Death and Life of the Great Lakes* (New York:
       W.W. Norton & Co., 2017), xiii.

26   Ibid., 3–4.

26–27 Michelle McQuigge, "Canadian politicians outraged at Trump
       Great Lakes funding cuts," Canadian Press, March 17, 2017.

27   Michelle Lalonde, "St. Lawrence faces several dangers, mayors
      tell water summit," *Montreal Gazette*, October 7, 2016.

28   Ibid.

CHAPTER 2

32–33   Robert Legget, *Ottawa Waterway: Gateway to a Continent* (Toronto: University of Toronto Press, 1975), 72.

33   MacLennan, *Rivers of Canada*, 77.

34   Hap Wilson, *Rivers of the Upper Ottawa Valley: Myth, Magic and Adventure* (Erin, Ontario: Boston Mills Press, 2004), 12. https://ottawarewind.com/2016/07/06/monsters-of-the-ottawa-river/.

35   Legget, *Ottawa Waterway*, 18.
Barbara Huck, *Exploring the Fur Trade Routes of North America* (Winnipeg: Heartland Publications, 2000), 75.

35–36   Peter C. Newman, *Caesars of the Wilderness* (Toronto: Viking, 1987), 37.

36–37   Legget, *Ottawa Waterway*, 8.

38   Roy MacGregor, "A visionary's epiphany about water," *The Globe and Mail*, October 5, 2009, A2.

41   Roy MacGregor, "Heritage Lost," *Today Magazine*, June 5, 1982, 13.
Legget, *Ottawa Waterway*, 103.

42   MacLennan, *Rivers of Canada*, 82.
Ibid., 83.

43   Ibid., 83.
Legget, *Ottawa Waterway*, 73.
Ibid., 107.

46   Kim Krenz, *Deep Waters: The Ottawa River and Canada's Nuclear Adventure* (Montreal and Kingston: McGill-Queen's University Press, 2004), 21.

47   Randy Boswell, "Ottawa's 'River of Sawdust,'" *Ottawa Citizen*, August 22, 2016, A5.

48   Jamie Benidickson, "Notes on Water Quality and Pollution History of the Ottawa River," 6.

CHAPTER 3

56   Jennifer L. Bonnell, *Reclaiming the Don: An Environmental History of Toronto's Don River Valley* (Toronto: University of Toronto Press, 2014), xv–xvi.

58   Roy MacGregor, *Escape: In Search of the Natural Soul of Canada* (Toronto: McClelland & Stewart, 2002), 201.

60   Ray Ford, "After a decades-long campaign, Canada's most urban river is nursed back to health," *Canadian Geographic*, June 2011, www.canadiangeographic.ca/article/death-and-rebirth-don-river.

61   Bonnell, *Reclaiming the Don*, 115.

62   Ibid., xix–xx.

       Ibid., 87.

63   Ibid., 189.

CHAPTER 4

69   www.troymedia.com/2014/04/20/at-hells-gate-business-has-been-a-little-dead-lately/.

71   MacLennan, *Rivers of Canada*, 250.

72   Richard C. Bocking, *Mighty River: A Portrait of the Fraser* (Vancouver: Douglas & McIntyre, 1997), 4.

72–73   Alister Thomas, *More of Canada's Best Canoe Routes* (Toronto: Boston Mills Press, 2003), 269.

73   Stephen Hume, *Simon Fraser: In Search of Modern British Columbia* (Madeira Park, B.C.: Harbour Publishing, 2008), 219–20.

73   Stephen Hume, "The sea at last (part two)," *Vancouver Sun*, November 17, 2007, D1.

74   Ibid.

77   David A. Smith, "Salmon Populations and the Stó:lō Fishery," in *A Stó:lō–Coast Salish Historical Atlas*, ed. by Keith Thor Carlson (Vancouver: Douglas & McIntyre, 2001), 120–21.

78–79   Barlow, *Boiling Point*, 124–25.

79   Alan Haig-Brown and Rick Blacklaws, *The Fraser River* (Madeira Park, B.C.: Harbour Publishing, 1996), 8–9.

80   Ibid., 98.

80–81   Bocking, *Mighty River*, 20.

81   Keith Thor Carlson, ed., *A Stó:lō–Coast Salish Historical Atlas* (Vancouver: Douglas & McIntyre, 2001), 92–93.

www.thecanadianencyclopedia.ca/en/article/japanese-internment-banished-and-beyond-tears-feature/.

82   Frances Itani, *Requiem* (New York: Atlantic Monthly Press, 2011), 305.

CHAPTER 5

90   Louis L'Amour, quoted in Lisa Meyers McClintick, *The Dakotas: A Guide to Unique Places* (Connecticutt: Globe Pequot, 2015), 171.

91   MacLennan, *Rivers of Canada*, 169.

92   Newman, *Caesars of the Wilderness*, 320.

93–94   Hudson's Bay Company Archives, www.gov.mb.ca/chc/archives/hbca/spotlight/red_river_flood.html.

94   MacLennan, *Rivers of Canada*, 172.
         Ibid.
         Ibid.

95   Huck, *Exploring the Fur Trade Routes*, 198–99.

95–96   Ibid., 177.

98   Barbara Huck, ed., *Crossroads of the Continent: A History of the Forks of the Red and Assiniboine Rivers* (Winnipeg: Heartland Associates, 2003), 72.

98–99   Roy MacGregor, "Little city of Selkirk sits high and dry, not missing a thing," *The Globe and Mail*, April 11, 2006, A2.

99   Ken Dryden and Roy MacGregor, *Home Game: Hockey and Life in Canada* (Toronto: McClelland & Stewart, 1989), 37.
         David Arnason and Mhari Mackintosh, eds., *The Imagined City: A Literary History of Winnipeg* (Winnipeg: Turnstone Press, 2005), 38–39.

CHAPTER 6

107–8   Sherman Zavitz, *It Happened at Niagara* (Niagara Falls: Lundy's Lane Historical Society, 2014), 126.

108   Ibid., 108.
          Ibid., 14.

109   Ibid., 75.

109–10   Michael S. Quinn, Len Broberg, and Wayne Freimund, eds.,
         *Parks, Peace, and Partnership: Global Initiatives in Transboundary
         Conservation* (Calgary: University of Calgary Press, 2012), 480.

111   Kevin Woyce, *Niagara: The Falls and the River* (Suttons Bay,
       Michigan: Delafield Press, 2014), 40, 45, 100.

112   Ibid., 97.

       Ibid., 27.

114   Zavitz, *It Happened at Niagara*, 149.

       Pierre Berton, *Picture Book of Niagara Falls* (Toronto: McClelland &
       Stewart, 1993), 23.

       Zavitz, *It Happened at Niagara*, 21.

115   Berton, *Picture Book of Niagara Falls*, 20.

       Ibid., 65–66.

       Tom Leonard, "The Walk of Death," *Daily Mail*, June 14, 2012, 38.

115–16   Ibid.

116   Ibid.

118   Woyce, *Niagara*, 6–7.

       Ibid., 132.

120   Annie Michaud, "The Niagara River Remedial Action Plan:
       25 Years of Environmental Restoration," Brock University,
       St. Catharines, 2012.

CHAPTER 7

126   Annie Proulx, *Barkskins* (New York: Scribner, 2016), 302–03.

127–28   John Robert Colombo, *Canadian Literary Landmarks*
         (Willowdale, Ontario: Hounslaw Press, 1984), 47.

128   J.W. Bailey, *The St. John River* (Cambridge: Riverside Press, 1894), 1.

       Colombo, *Canadian Literary Landmarks*, 47.

129   Hugh MacLennan, *Seven Rivers of Canada* (Toronto: Macmillan,
       1961), 98.

130   Roger MacGregor, *When the Chestnut Was in Flower: Inside the
       Chestnut Canoe* (Lansdowne, Ontario: Plumtree Press, 1999), 112.

132 Ernest Hemingway, "The Best Rainbow Trout Fishing," in *The River Reader*, ed. by John A. Murray (New York: Lyons Press, 1998), 212. MacGregor, *When the Chestnut*, xi. Ibid., 20.

134 Letters to the editor, *The Daily Gleaner* (Fredericton), August 23, 2016, A6.

136 Alan White, "Mactaquac dam to be kept going until 2068, NB Power says," CBC News, December 20, 2016.

CHAPTER 8

140 MacLennan, *Rivers of Canada*, 204. www.cbc.ca/history/EPISCONTENTSE1EP17CH2PA1LE.html.

141 Ibid.

142 "WWF urges adoption of Joint Review Panel's conservation standards in implementing the Mackenzie Gas," *Marketwire*, December 17, 2010.

144 Alfred P. Aquilina, *The Mackenzie: Yesterday and Beyond* (Vancouver: Hancock House Publishers, 1981), 36.

145 Roy MacGregor, "In a white vestment made of caribou skin, Pope kept a promise to aboriginals," *The Globe and Mail*, April 4, 2005, A2.

146 Bruce W. Hodgins and Gwyneth Hoyle, *Canoeing North into the Unknown* (Toronto: Natural Heritage, 1994), 113.

146–47 Ibid., 130.

147 MacLennan, *Rivers of Canada*, 194.

149 Matthew Hart, *Diamond: A Journey to the Heart of an Obsession* (Toronto: Viking Canada, 2001).

151 René Fumoleau, *As Long as This Land Shall Last: A History of Treaty 8 and Treaty 11, 1870–1939* (Calgary: University of Calgary Press, 2004).

152–53 Alister Thomas, *More of Canada's Best Canoe Routes* (Toronto: Boston Mills Press, 2003), 233.

153 John Donaldson, *One Day at a Time: A Canoe Quest in the Wake of Canada's "Prince of Explorers"* (Kingston: Artful Codger Press: 2006), 245.

155–56   Farley Mowat, *Canada North Now: The Great Betrayal*, (Toronto: McClelland & Stewart, 1976).

CHAPTER 9

161   From a presentation by William Storrie of Gore, Nasmith and Storrie, Consulting Engineers, Toronto, at the First Annual Convention of the Canadian Institute on Sewage and Sanitation, Toronto, October 18, 1934, 82.

163   MacLennan, *Rivers of Canada*, 149.

164   Fred Dahms, *Wellington County* (Erin, Ontario: Boston Mills Press, 2008), 90.

168   Greg Mercer, "A monumental fight to save Puslinch Lake; Residents are dedicated to dredging silt and battling an invasive plant species," *Guelph Mercury*, July 25, 2015, A1.

170   "Make users of water pay their full share, *Toronto Star*, November 6, 2015.

171   "Our Water Our Future presentations," *Fergus-Elora News Express*, November 4, 2015.

172   Keith Leslie, "Nestlé wants to 'partner' with Ontario town on well," *Ottawa Citizen*, December 14, 2016, A4.
       Kelsey Dunbar, "Save Our Water group shares recommendations to protect local water supply with Centre Wellington council and public," *Fergus-Elora News Express*, August 19, 2015.
       Canadian Press, "Nestlé outbids township to buy well for bottled water," *Waterloo Region Record*, September 23, 2016, A1.

176   Margaret Laurence, *The Diviners* (Toronto: McClelland & Stewart, 1974), 3.

CHAPTER 10

180   Armstrong et al., *The River Returns*, 273–74.
       Gerald T. Conaty, Daryl Betenia and Catharine T. Conaty, *The Bow: Living with a River* (Toronto: Key Porter Books, 2004), 46–47.

181   Ibid, 135.

182   Kevin Van Tighem, *Heart Waters: Sources of the Bow River*, photographs by Brian Van Tighem (Calgary: Rocky Mountain Books, 2015), 57.

183   Bruce Masterman, "Famous fishing," *Calgary Herald*, August 11, 1998, A8.

183–84 Armstrong et al., *The River Returns*, 21.

185   Ibid., 28.

185   Ibid., 58.
       Conaty et al., *The Bow*, 118.
       Armstrong et al., *The River Returns*, 5.

186   Ibid., 152.

187   Conaty et al., *The Bow*, 70.
       Ibid., 67.

188   Armstrong et al., *The River Returns*, 119.

190   Van Tighem, *Heart Waters*, 92.

192   Masterman, "Famous fishing," A8.
       Armstrong et al., *The River Returns*, 358.
       Ibid., 281.

193   WWF-Canada's report on the health of the Bow River watershed can be found at watershedsresports.wwf.ca.

194   Conaty et al., *The Bow*, 11.

CHAPTER 11

198   Don Kealey, *Low Municipality: Reflections of the Past* (Kanata: Paugan Falls Publications, 2015), 107–8.

199   *Ottawa Journal* clipping describing the Battle of Brennan's Hill, November 14, 1895. Library and Archives Canada, Microform Reading Room.
       Kealey, *Low Municipality*, 89.

200   Malak (photographs) and Ron Corbett (text), *The Gatineau* (Toronto: Boston Mills Press, 1994), 45.

201–2 Gordon Robertson, *Memoirs of a Very Civil Servant: Mackenzie King to Pierre Trudeau* (Toronto: University of Toronto Press, 2000), 164.

203   Gary Dimmock, "Inside Brazeau's darkest hour; 'I let a lot of people down,' senator says of his suicide attempt," *Ottawa Citizen*, May 14, 2016, A8.

204   "Residents group demands Low mayor's resignation," *The Low Down to Hull and Back News*, May 4–10, 2016, 1–2.

205   "Gatineau River changing face of country." *The Ottawa Evening Journal*, March 24, 1928, 1.

      Brian Doyle, *Mary Ann Alice* (Toronto: Groundwood Books/Douglas & McIntyre, 2002), 175.

206   John W. Hughson and Courtney J.C. Bond, *Hurling Down the Pine* (Chelsea, Quebec: Historical Society of the Gatineau, 1964), 105.

209   Ibid., 4.

210   Stephen McGregor, *Since Time Immemorial: "Our Story"* (Maniwaki: Kitigan Zibi Education Council, 2004), 172.

211   www.vice.com/en_ca/read/first-nations-communities-are-suing-the-federal-government-over-third-world-water-conditions-909.

CHAPTER 12

217   www.mysteriesofcanada.com/ontario/witch-plum-hollow/.

      www.rideau-info.com/canal/index.html.

218   *War of 1812 Magazine* 13, June 2010, www.napoleon-series.org/military/Warof1812/2010/Issue13/c_Jefferson.html.

219   Robert W. Passfield, *Building the Rideau Canal: A Pictorial History* (Toronto: Fitzhenry & Whiteside, 1982), 19.

220   www.rideau-info.com/canal/index.html.

      Passfield, *Building the Rideau Canal*, 24.

221   Malak and Corbett, *The Gatineau*, 85.

      Passfield, *Building the Rideau Canal*, 85.

222   Ibid., 30.

      Mary Beacock Fryer and Adrian G. Ten Cate, *The Rideau: A Pictorial History of the Waterway* (Brockille, Ontario: Besancourt Publishers, 1981), 85.

      Passfield, *Building the Rideau Canal*, 35.

224   *Sights and Surveys: Two Diarists on the Rideau* (Ottawa: Historical Society of Ottawa, 1979) 23.

CHAPTER 13

230   Kevin Wehr, *America's Fight over Water: The Environmental and Political Effects of Large-Scale Water Systems* (New York: Routledge, 2004), 135.

231   www.youtube.com/watch?v=L8gr2EOmlv8.

234   Timothy Egan, *The Good Rain: Across Time and Terrain in the Pacific Northwest* (New York: Knopf, 1990), 17.

234–35   Elizabeth C. Terhaar, "Roll on Columbia Turns 75," *River Currents*, 2016, 5.

235   Mark Hume, *The Run of the River: Portraits of Eleven British Columbia Rivers* (Vancouver: New Star Books, 1992), 2.

236   Ibid., 9.

       Ibid., 11.

       R.W. Sandford, "Visualizing a New Tomorrow: Water, Equity, Justice and Reconciliation in Reconsideration of the Columbia River Treaty," United Nations University Institute for Water, Environment and Health, Hamilton, Ontario, 4.

237   Eric Elliott, "Columbia River watershed in good health but still at risk, report says," Black Press, July 25, 2016.

238   Betsy Kline, "Calling the salmon by canoeing the Columbia River from Castlegar to Kettle Falls," *Castlegar News*, June 24, 2016.

239   Sandford, "Visualizing a New Tomorrow," 11, 13.

       Terhaar, "Roll on Columbia," 4.

240   Robert William Sandford, Deborah Harford and Jon O'Riordan, *The Columbia River Treaty: A Primer* (Victoria: Rocky Mountain Books, 2014), 129.

CHAPTER 14

245   Alex MacPherson, "Delay made spill 'much, much worse': scientist," *The Leader-Post* (Regina), September 3, 2016, A4.

247   Nina Munteanu, *Water Is . . . : The Meaning of Water . . .*
       (Vancouver: Pixl Press, 2016), 145.

247–48   North Saskatchewan Watershed Alliance, "The Story of This
       River Is the Story of the West," 2005, 5.

248   Ibid., 39.
       MacLennan, *Rivers of Canada*, 186.

249   Billie Milholland, *Living in the Shed: Alberta's North Saskatchewan
       River Watershed* (Edmonton: North Saskatchewan Watershed
       Alliance, 2015), 46–47.

249–50   Ibid., 85.

250   Ibid., 204.

251   Ibid., 161–62
       Colette Derworiz, "Southern Alberta flood leads to 'largest
       university-led water project in the world,'" *Calgary Herald* blogs,
       September 7, 2016.

252   Jeff Lewis, "Five questions with hydrologist John Pomeroy,"
       The Globe and Mail, September 9, 2016.

253   MacLennan, *Rivers of Canada*, 180.

254   Alex MacPherson, "Concerned citizens form Kisiskatchewan Water
       Alliance Network after Husky oil spill," *Saskatoon StarPhoenix*,
       August 22, 2016.

CHAPTER 15

260   Roy MacGregor, "Love's labour is (hopefully) not lost: Dyer
       Memorial: Endearing shrine to millionaire and wife is in need of
       work," *National Post*, August 10, 1999, A9.

263   Susan Pigg, "Muskoka now 'Hamptons of the north' for luxury
       cottage living," *Toronto Star*, May 15, 2015.
       Jack Hutton, "Did David Thompson paddle by your point?"
       The Muskoka Sun, August 2, 2007, B1.

264   MacGregor, *Escape*, 201–2.

265   John McQuarrie, *Spirit of the Place: Muskoka Then and Now* (Ottawa:
       Magic Light Publishing, 2010), 19.
       MacGregor, *Escape*, 203.

266   Ibid., 207.

267   Ibid., 208.

268   Ibid., 212.

McQuarrie, *Spirit of the Place*, 33.

269   MacGregor, *Escape*, 219.

Andrew Hind, "The Lost Resorts," *Muskoka Life*, June 2015, 79.

Gary Long, *This River the Muskoka* (Toronto: Boston Mills Press, 1989), 133.

270   MacGregor, *Escape*, 224.

273   Andrew Hind, "Bala's Roselawn Lodge," *Muskoka Life*, July 2015, 94.

273–74 Geraldine Coombe, *Muskoka: Past and Present* (Toronto: McGraw-Hill Ryerson, 1976), 150–51.

274   Renata D'Aliesio, "A very Canadian question," *The Globe and Mail*, July 12, 2014, F5.

CHAPTER 16

278   Will Hibbard, "Small Miracles," *Kanawa*, Spring 2002, 40.

278–79 John A. Murray, ed., *The Quotable Nature Lover* (New York: Lyons Press, 1999), 23.

280   James Raffan, "Review: In *Canoe Country*, Roy MacGregor pays tribute to Canada's 'favourite means for getting around,'" *The Globe and Mail*, September 4, 2015.

281–82 C.E.S. Franks, *The Canoe and White Water* (Toronto: University of Toronto Press, 1977), 44.

282–83 Craig Oliver, *Oliver's Twist: The Life and Times of an Unapologetic Newshound* (Toronto: Viking Canada, 2011), 111.

285   James Raffan, "Raff's Maxims for Happy Paddling," in Thomas, *More of Canada's Best Canoe Routes*, 278–81.

286   Wilson, *Rivers of the Upper Ottawa Valley*, 53.

287   Ottawa River Heritage Designation Committee, 2005, 18–21.

287–88 Wallace A. Schaber, *The Last of the Wild Rivers: The Past, Present, and Future of the Rivière du Moine Watershed* (Burnstown, Ontario: Burnstown Publishing House, 2016).

288–90 Kenneth G. Roberts and Philip Shackleton, *The Canoe: A History of the Craft from Panama to the Arctic* (Toronto: Macmillan of Canada, 1983), 181–82.

293 Murray, *The Quotable Nature Lover*, 19.

296 Harry Middleton, "Midnight's Rivers," in *The River Reader*, ed. by John A. Murray (New York: Lyons Press, 1998), 225.

297 Masaru Emoto, *The Secret Life of Water* (New York: Atria Books, 2005), 178.

EPILOGUE

303 *The Economist*, August 21, 2008.

303–4 *The Economist*, May 20, 2010.

304 "Bottled water: Liquid gold," *The Economist*, March 25, 2017, 75. *The Globe and Mail*, March 20, 2017, A5.

305 Video interview with Harry Swain at https://www.desmog.ca/. http://mashable.com/2017/03/15/new-zealand-river-human/ #lPStOdPW9Oqa.

305–6 Hansard, 42nd Parliament, 1st Session, vol. 148, no. 146, February 3, 2017.

309 Hugh MacLennan, *Voices in Time* (Toronto: Macmillan, 1980), 17.

INDEX

Aberhart, William, 188
Aboriginal Pipeline Group, 142
Acadians, 128–29
Aiken, John, 164–65
Aitken, Max (Lord Beaverbrook), 187
Akwesasne (ON), 17, 23
Alberta, 185–86, 188–89. *See also* Bow
    River; *specific locations*
   railway and, 180, 182, 185–86, 187
Alexander, Shannon, 212
Algonquin peoples, 40, 44, 209–10,
    286–87, 306. *See also specific nations*
Alston, Joseph, 114
American eels, 24–25, 40, 307
America Rivers, 28–29
Amos, Bill, 306
Anderson, David, 94
Anishinabeg, 209, 210. *See also specific*
    nations
AquaHacking summits, 27, 28, 48–49,
    308
Armstrong, Christopher, 183–84
Assembly of Manitoba Chiefs, 245
Assiniboine River, 93
Asubpeeschoseewagong (Grassy
    Narrows) First Nation, 254

Atlantic Salmon Federation, 126
Aylen, Peter, 206

Bailey, J.W., 128
Bain, James, Jr., 263, 264–65
Baker, Jocelyn, 117–18, 121
Baker, John, 129
Bala (ON), 262–63, 269, 272–75
Banff, 179–80, 192–93
Banff National Park, 180, 247
Barlow, Maude, 8–10, 78–79, 171, 172,
    173, 175
Barnes, Elizabeth Jane "Mother", 217
Barnum, P.T., 111
Barrett, Ed, 136
Barrett, Tony, 60
Bartleman, James, 274–75
Bastedo, Jamie, 151–52
Batoche (SK), 248
Baysville (ON), 261
Bedard, Robert, 31–32, 35
Belcourt, Napoléon, 48
Bell, Emil, 11, 254–55, 308
Benidickson, Jamie, 47
Bennett, R.B., 21, 187
Berger, Thomas, 140–41

Biddell, Jack, 38
Big Bear, 248
Big East River, 261
bison, 91, 185, 249
Black, Gord, 53
Blackfoot, 249
Blacklaws, Rick, 79
Blair, Bob, 140
Blake, Linda, 85
Blondin, Charles, 116
Blue Communities, 173–74
boatbuilding, 132–33, 270
boating, 223–25. *See also* canoes and
      canoeing
Bocking, Richard C., 72
Boldt Castle, 16–17
Bolton, Beatrice, 164
Bond, Courtney C.J., 209
Bonnell, Jennifer, 57, 58, 61, 62, 63
Bonneville Power Administration,
      229, 236
Booth, J.R., 41, 44
bootleggers, 100, 130
Borden, Robert, 269
bottled water, 168–73, 175, 304
Bourassa, Robert, 38
Bow River, 179–94
      dams, 183–84, 187–88, 189–90
      falls, 180–81, 187
      fishing, 182–83, 184
      flooding, 189–91, 193–94
      history, 184–88
      improvements, 192, 308
      and irrigation, 185–87, 192
      lumber industry, 187, 189
      pollution, 192–93
      power generation, 187–88
      source, 179–80, 182
Bow River Basin Council, 188–89
Bow River Quality Council, 193
Bozzo, Sam, 173

Bracebridge (ON), 261–62
Bragg Creek (AB), 2, 191
Brant, Joseph Thayendanegea, 163
Brazeau, Patrick, 203–4
Breau, Gerald, 134
Brennan's Hill (QC), 197–200, 204
Brett, George, 180
Breynat, Gabriel, 150, 151
British Columbia, 78–79. *See also*
      specific rivers and locations
   railway and, 80, 82
Brockhouse, Bertram, 46
Brock University, 117–18, 120
Brooks' Bush Gang, 62–63
Brûlé, Étienne, 32, 108, 306
Brunton, Daniel, 49
Buffalo (NY), 118
Burns, Paul, 280
Burr, Theodosia, 114
Burritts Rapids (ON), 221
Burrows, John, 224
Bush, George W., 8, 303
Butler, W.F., 281–82
By, Esther, 222
By, John, 42, 215, 217–18, 219–20,
      221–22
Bytown, 42, 223. *See also* Ottawa

Caisse, Rene, 261–62
Caledonia (ON), 163
Calgary, 186, 188, 190–91, 192, 194
Calgary Power, 187
Campagnolo, Iona, 72–73
Campbell, John, 263, 264–65
Camp Lake, 259–60
Canada (Government of), 49–50, 209
Canadian Beverage Association, 174–75
Canadian Heritage Rivers System,
      45, 166
Canadian Institute on Sewage and
      Sanitation, 161

Canadian Museum of Civilization, 211

Canadian Pacific Railway (CPR)
in Alberta, 180, 182, 185–86, 187
in British Columbia, 80, 82
in Manitoba, 98–99

Canadian Rivers Institute, 136–37

Canadian Union of Public Employees, 173–74

Canadian Water Summit, 65

canals, 163. *See also specific canals*

Canmore (AB), 187, 190

canoes and canoeing, 132–33, 286–90, 296–97. *See also specific rivers*

Canol Pipeline, 152

Cardinal, Douglas, 44

Carlson, Keith Thor, 81

Carson, Gene, 15, 16

Cartier, George-Étienne, 103, 104

Cartier, Jacques, 18

Catton, Jeri-Lynn, 166

Cazon, Alphonsine, 141

Centre Wellington (ON), 171–73

Chalk River (ON), 46–47

Challinor, John, 175

Champlain, Samuel de, 32–33, 43, 127, 205, 306

Champlain Sea, 301

Chant, Don, 59

Chapel Gallery, 255

Chelsea (QC), 204

Chester, Kelly, 280, 283–84

Chester, Lorne, 280–81, 283–84

Chester, Phil, 280, 281, 283, 284–86

Chestnut Canoe Company, 132–33

Chinese Canadians, 80, 82

Churchill, Winston, 99, 112

Clark, Clifford, 201–2

Clark, Greg, 132

climate change, 78, 155, 193–94, 236–37, 251. *See also* drought

and glaciers, 179–80, 182, 189

and water resources, 9–10, 118

Clowes, Samuel, 219

Cockburn, A.P., 269

Cockburn, Marc, 200, 207

Coderre, Denis, 27, 28

Colorado River, 38

Columbia Lake, 237

Columbia River, 229–41
dams, 38, 230, 233–34, 236–37, 238, 240
First Nations and, 235, 236, 238–39, 240
fishing, 235–37, 238, 239
flood control, 233, 234, 238, 240
history, 229–31, 232–35
pollution, 230, 234–35

Columbia River Inter-Tribal Fish Commission, 238

Columbia Riverkeeper, 239–40

Columbia River Treaty (1964), 234, 237–41, 307

Commanda, William "Grandfather", 44, 204

Conant, Bernadette, 49

Conestoga River, 162

Connors, Stompin' Tom, 39

Conservation Council of New Brunswick, 135

Corbett, Ron, 41, 200

Council of Canadians, 173–74, 245. *See also* Barlow, Maude

Courcelles family, 90, 103, 104

Courcelles, Jacques, 89–90, 103–5, 308

Cowichan peoples, 73

Cree peoples, 91, 98

Cronkite, Walter, 26

Crowfoot, 185

Currier, Ann Crosby, 216

Cuyahoga River, 59

dams, 29, 38. *See also specific rivers*
Day, Stockwell, 111–12
De Beers Group of Companies, 149
Decentralised Energy Canada, 157
Decontie, Peter, 40
Deep River, 46–47
de Gaspé Beaubien Foundation, 10, 27, 48–49, 308
Dennis, John Stoughton, 266
Dettah (NT), 149–50
diamond mining, 147–49
Dickens, Charles, 20, 115
Dickinson, Moss Kent, 224
Diefenbaker, John, 96, 140
Dier, Mike, 225–26
Dimmock, Gary, 203
Disappearing Propeller Boat Company, 270
Dollard des Ormeaux, Adam, 35–36
Donaldson, John, 153
Donnelly, Fin, 71–72, 73, 74–76
Donnelly, Harriet, 19
Don River, 55–67
    deterioration, 59–60, 61–63
    First Nations and, 60
    fishing, 59, 60, 67
    flood control, 64, 66
    history, 57–58, 60–63
    improvements, 63, 64–65, 67
    pollution, 55–56, 59–60, 61, 66
    watershed, 60, 64, 66
Don Valley Conservation Association, 308
Douglas, James, 81
Douglas, Tommy, 202
Doyle, Brian, 205
Dream Unlimited, 44
drinking water
    bottled, 168–73, 175, 304
    for First Nations, 40, 150, 211, 252
    as right, 168–73

threats to, 47–48, 118
drought. *See also* climate change
    in Canada, 93, 102, 160, 252
    in 1930s (Dust Bowl), 93, 102, 186
    worldwide, 118, 174, 303
DuBois, Carolyn, 154
Duffy, Scott, 280
Dumoine River, 277–98
    canoeing on, 278, 280–86
    falls, 278, 279
    First Nations and, 286–90
    history, 286–87
    rapids, 280, 283–86
    tourism, 290
    watershed, 279
Dumont, Gabriel, 248
Dyer, Clifton G. and Betsy, 260

East Grand Forks (MN), 100–101, 102
East River, 261
Eau Claire and Bow River Lumber Company, 187
Eddy, Ezra Butler (E.B.), 44
Edison, Thomas, 109
Edmonton, 250–51
Edmunston (NB), 128–29
eels, 24–25, 40, 307
Egan, Dan, 25–26
Egan, Timothy, 234
Eisenhower, Dwight D., 21
Elbow River, 191
Elgin, Thomas Bruce, 7th Earl of, 209, 210
Elliott, Sam, 183
Elora (ON), 162, 170
Emond, Norman, 167
Emory Creek (BC), 80–81, 82
Emoto, Masaru, 297
Empey, Evelyn, 23
endangered species, 24–25, 29. *See also specific species*

Energy East, 134–35, 136, 244
English River, 254
environmental activism, 7, 10–11,
    59–60, 65, 74–76, 239, 254–56.
    See also specific groups
Environment Probe, 175
Essiac, 261–62
Eurasian water milfoil, 168
Evenden, Matthew, 183–84
Ewins, Peter, 153–54

Faille, Albert, 145
Farwell, Joe, 161
Fergus (ON), 164–65
ferries, 53, 133–34
Finkelstein, Isaac, 225
Finkelstein, Max, 45, 46, 50, 152–53, 225
Fipke, Chuck, 148
First Nations, 145, 212–13. *See also
    specific nations and rivers*
    and canoeing, 286–88
    and drinking water, 40, 150, 211, 252
    environmental activism, 254–56
    land claims, 40, 141, 150–51, 210, 211,
        286–87
    mercury pollution and, 59, 254
    on prairies, 91, 93, 185
    RCMP and, 84–86
Fitzroy Harbour (ON), 34
Five Lakes Fishing Club, 201–2
Flatters, Joseph T., 199
Fleming, Sandford, 98–99
Flossie Lake, 259
Flynn-Bedard, Judith, 31–32, 33, 35, 53,
    307
Ford, Rob, 65
Forrest, Francine, 186
Forrester, Edna and Walter, 103
Fort Garry (Upper and Lower), 91, 92,
    93–94, 98
Fortin, Catherine, 53

Fort Simpson (NT), 144–46
Forty Mile Creek, 189–90
Francis, Michael, 200, 203, 208
Fraser, Blair, 295
Fraser, Simon, 69, 73–74
Fraser River, 69–86
    canoeing on, 84–85
    canyon, 69–70, 77–78
    delta/mouth, 72, 78
    First Nations and, 70, 73–74, 77, 81,
        83–84, 85
    fishing, 76–79, 83–84
    mining, 71, 78–81, 82
    pollution, 75, 78–79
    protective measures, 77–78, 84
    threats, 75–76, 78, 79
Fredericton, 136
Friends of the Gatineau River, 207
Friends of the Grand River, 167
Friends of the Rideau, 224
Frye, Northrop, 14
Fumoleau, René, 150–51
fur trade, 34, 35–36, 147, 184–85,
    232–33, 249, 286. *See also specific
    companies and traders*

Gagetown (NB), 133–34
Gannon, Barry "Icon", 69, 70–71
Garven, Leah, 255
Gatineau du Plessis, Nicolas, 204
Gatineau Park, 201–2
Gatineau River, 197–213
    canoeing on, 202, 207–8
    dams, 205
    First Nations and, 208, 209–10
    flooding, 206, 301–2
    lumber industry, 206, 209, 218–19
    water quality, 207
General, Paul, 161, 169
Georgian Bay Ship Canal, 36–37
German Canadians, 164

Gerretsen, Mark, 173

Ghost Lake, 182, 183

Gilmour Lumber Company, 209

glaciers, 179–80, 182, 189

Glen Morris (ON), 159

gobies, 24

Godfrey, Arthur, 16

Godfrey, John, 282

gold rushes, 71, 79–81, 82, 147

Gordon, C. Mason, 198

Gordon, Charles "Chinese", 39

Gordon, Hugh Donald Lockhart, 152

Gordon, James, 160, 167, 176

Gordon Foundation, 154

Goss, Greg, 250, 253–54

Grahame, Kenneth, 7, 302

Grand Forks (ND), 100–103

Grand River, 159–76

    canoeing on, 159–60, 176

    dams, 165–66

    droughts, 160, 170

    First Nations and, 162–63, 169

    fishing, 166–67, 307–8

    flooding, 165–66

    improvements, 166, 167

    pollution, 160–61

    population growth on, 169, 170, 172

    threats, 167–68, 169

    watershed, 162, 166, 169

    wildlife, 161

Grand River Conservation Authority, 166, 168

Grand River Navigation Company, 163

Grassy Narrows (Asubpeeschoseewagong) First Nation, 254

Grater, Wendy, 293

Gravenhurst (ON), 264

Gray, Robert, 232

Great Bear Lake, 147

Great Farini (William Leonard Hunt), 116

Great Lakes, 23–24, 25–27, 118, 119

Great Recycling and Northern Development (GRAND) Canal, 37–38

Great Spirit Canoes (NB), 133

Greene, Stan, 83

Gretzky, Walter, 162

Grey Owl, 132

Grosse Île, 13–14

Group of Seven, 181, 202, 261

Guelph (ON), 164

Guigues, Joseph-Bruno, 210

Gustafsen Lake, 85–86

Guthrie, Woody, 229–30, 231, 234–35

habitat loss, 29, 78, 79. *See also* wetlands

Haida people, 73

Haig-Brown, Alan, 79

Haig-Brown, Roderick, 4–5, 302

Haldimand Tract (ON), 163

Hamilton, W.E., 268

Hamlyn, Robyn, 10, 173–75, 308

Hanford (WA), 230, 235

Harper, Stephen, 1–2

Harris, Chris, 277, 292

Harris, Don, 252–53

Harris, Marcia, 252

Hart, E.J. "Ted", 181–82, 184, 185, 186–87

Hart, Matthew, 149

Harvey, Dennis, 282

Haudenosaunee (Six Nations of the Grand River), 161, 162, 169, 171

Hawes, Spring, 232

Hawn, Goldie, 271

Hayden, Thomas, 197

Heal, Rob, 166–67, 308

Hemingway, Ernest, 132

Hendriks, Elizabeth, 168, 237

Hennepin, Louis, 108

Heron, Francis, 93–94

Heurtel, David, 49
High River (AB), 190
Hill, Brad, 119, 120–21
Hill, Ed, 84–85
Hochelaga, 18
Hodgins, Bruce W., 146–47
Hooker Chemical Company, 119–20
Hope, Kathy, 82
Hoyle, Gwyneth, 146–47
Hudson's Bay Company, 91, 95
Hughes, Harry, 280
Hughson, John W., 209
Hull-Chelsea-Wakefield Railway, 207
Hull (QC), 42
Hume, Mark, 235–36
Hume, Stephen, 73, 74
Hummel, Monte, 59, 60, 67
Huntsville (ON), 261
hurricanes, 64, 165–66
Husky Energy, 243–46
Hutchison, Bruce, 72
hydroelectricity, 229–30, 304–5.
    See also specific rivers
Hydro Ottawa, 44

Iberville, Pierre Le Moyne, Sieur d',
    286
Idle No More, 245, 256
immigrants, 13–15. *See also specific
    groups*
International Fishways, 77–78
International Joint Commission, 21,
    24, 29
International Niagara Committee, 110
Inuvialuit, 141
Inuvialuit Regional Corporation, 156
Inuvik (NT), 141, 154–55, 156
invasive species, 23–26, 168, 305–6
Invermere (BC), 231–32
Irish Canadians, 13–14, 197–200, 220
Iroquois peoples, 18, 111, 163

irrigation, 186, 192, 230
Itani, Frances, 82

Jackson, A.Y., 181, 202
Jacobs, Mike, 101–3
James Smith Cree Nation (SK), 246
Japanese Canadians, 81–82
Jefferson, Thomas, 218
Jesuits, 288–89
John Paul II, Pope, 144, 145
Johnson, E. Pauline (Tekahionwake), 162
Johnston, Frank H., 181
Jones, Carl, 132
Jones, David, 94
Jones, Steven, 132, 133
Jones Falls (ON), 216–17, 221

Kahnawake (QC), 162–63
Kananaskis River, 190–91
Kazabazua (QC), 202
Keefer, Thomas C., 34
Keller, Helen, 107–8
Kelly, Mary, 13–14
Kelvin, William Thomson, 1st Baron,
    109–10
Kierans, Tom, 37–38
Kinder Morgan, 244
King, William Lyon Mackenzie, 21, 81,
    201, 269
Kingston (ON), 218, 222
Kisiskatchewan Water Alliance
    Network, 254, 256
Kitchener (ON), 161, 164, 170
Kitigan Zibi First Nations, 40, 44, 203,
    209–13, 287
Kiwegoma Anishinabeg. *See* Wolf Lake
    First Nations
Klein, Ralph, 192, 193
Kootenay River, 233
Kotcheff, Tim, 282
Kwakwaka'wakw, 73

Labeaume, Régis, 27
LaBine, Gilbert, 147
Lac Capimitchigama, 39
Lac la Cave, 52–53
Lac-Ste-Marie (QC), 206
Lake Agassiz, 93
Lake Erie, 110, 111
Lake Joseph, 265–66
Lake Minnewanka, 190
Lake Muskoka, 263, 264, 265, 268
Lake of Bays, 261, 269
Lake of Two Rivers, 3–4
Lake Ontario Waterkeeper, 66
Lake Timiskaming, 39, 40
L'Amour, Louis, 90
Lampell, Millard, 234
lampreys, 23
Lasser, Jim, 70–71
Laurence, Margaret, 176
La Vérendrye, Pierre Gaultier de
    Varennes, 98
Lee, Philip, 126, 135
Leech, Troy, 70–71
Leeming, Arlen, 63, 64, 65, 67, 308
Le Jeune, Paul, 288–90
Le Moyne de Bienville, Jean Baptiste, 286
Lewis, Gerald, 239
Lightfoot, Gordon, 279
Lincoln, Abraham, 108–9
Lindblad, Deanna, 117–18, 121
Linton, Kelly, 172
Little Red River, 245
Liveris, Andrew, 303
Long Sault (ON), 19, 35–36
Loosemore, Fred, 293
Lorne, Marquess of, 185
Love Canal, 119–20
Low Township (QC), 197–200, 206
Loyalists, 19, 129, 164
lumber industry, 75, 137, 235, 306.
    See also specific rivers

MacDonald, J.E.H., 202
Macdonald, John A., 41, 91–92
Macfarlane, Daniel, 22–23
Macfarlane, John, 282
MacGregor, Ellen, 203, 259
MacGregor, Roger, 132
MacGregor, Roy, 3–4, 5–6, 7–8, 305–7
    on Dumoine River, 280, 283, 284–86
Mackay, Don, 223
Mackenzie, Alexander, 143–44, 147
Mackenzie, William Lyon, 112–13
Mackenzie River, 139–57
    canoeing on, 152–53
    First Nations and, 140, 150
    pipeline proposals, 140–43, 153–54,
        155–56
    pollution, 149–50, 153
    rapids, 146, 152
    threats, 141–42, 153–54
    as transportation route, 146–47,
        154–57
    watershed, 139, 146, 154
Maclean, Norman, 247
MacLennan, Hugh, 5–8, 10, 163, 308–9
    on Fraser River, 71–72
    on Mackenzie River, 140
    on Ottawa River, 41, 42, 43
    on Red River/Manitoba, 91, 95–96
    on Saint John River, 127–28
    on St. Lawrence River, 17–18, 20
    on Saskatchewan River, 248, 253
MacLeod, W.A., 99
MacTaggart, John, 221
Madawaska, Republic of (NB), 128–29
Madawaska River, 3–4, 301, 306
Maine, 129, 130
Malak (Karsh), 200
Maliseet (Wolastoqiyik) people, 127,
    131
Maloney, Pamela, 24
Manhattan Project, 46–47, 147, 230

Manitoba, 90, 91–92, 93–95, 305.
   See also Red River; *specific locations*
   First Nations in, 91, 93
   railway and, 98–99
Mann Art Gallery, 255
Manotick (ON), 216
Mantell, Art, 202–3
Maori people, 305
Mason, Bill, 132, 202, 291, 294
Mason, D.H.C., 265
Mattrick, Aidan and Tatianna, 10, 48
Mazariego, Kylia, 134
McCaw, Donna, 171
McColl, Russ, 294, 297
McCumber, Eric, 129–30, 137
McCumber, Kim, 129
McGhee, Karen, 272
McGill, Hunter, 220
McGoey, Thomas, 206
McGregor, Gordon, 212
McGuinty, David, 305–6
McHalsie, Albert "Sonny", 70, 83, 84, 308
McKenna, Catherine, 226
McKenzie, Ben, 287
McKinley, William, 118
McNab, Archibald, 13th Laird, 39
McSheffrey, Edward, 199
Mennonites, 164
mercury pollution, 59, 235, 254
Merrickville (ON), 221
Mesqua Ukie, 263
Métis, 91, 248–49
Michaud, Annie, 120
Middlebrook Water Company, 169, 170,
   171–72
Middleton, Harry, 296
Milholland, Billie, 249, 250
Miller, David, 193
Miller, Frank, 262
mining, 147–50, 235. *See also* gold rushes
missionaries, 209–10, 288–89

Mitchell, Simon, 125–26, 131, 136
Mohawks, 17, 23, 162, 163
Monck, Charles, 4th Viscount, 266
Monroe, Marilyn, 114, 181
Montferrand, Joseph, 39
Montgomery, Lucy Maud, 273
Montreal, 20, 27, 28
Monts, Sieur de (Pierre Dugua), 127
Moodie, Susanna, 15
Morrell, Van, 131
Morrison, James, 286–87
Morton, W.L., 278
Moulton, Earl, 85–86
Moulton, Maureen, 85
Murphy, Alice, 274
Murphy, Meaghan, 52
Murray, Glen, 49
Murray, John A., 278–79
Muskoka Club, 265–66
Muskoka Lakes Navigation Company,
   269, 270
Muskoka Lakes (ON), 274
Muskoka region
   First Nations in, 266–67, 270
   tourism in, 263–66, 267–71
Muskoka River, 259–75
   canoeing on, 274
   dams, 260, 262, 272–73
   lumber industry, 267
   watershed, 267
Musqueam people, 73

Nahanni National Park Reserve, 292,
   294
Napoleon Bonaparte, 41, 218, 219
National Assessment of First Nations
   Water and Wastewater (2011), 211
National Capital Commission, 44, 201
National Energy Board, 51, 135, 142, 143
National Museum of the American
   Indian, 211

natural gas. *See* oil and gas industry
Nature Trust of New Brunswick, 125
Nelles, H.V., 183–84
Nenabush (Wiskedjak), 287
Nestlé Waters, 168–73, 174–75
Neutrals, 162–63
New Brunswick Power, 135–36
Newman, Peter C., 92
New Zealand, 305
Niagara Falls, 107–9, 111, 113–14,
 115–17
Niagara Movement, 113
Niagara River, 107–22. *See also* Niagara
 Falls
 environmental initiatives, 120–21
 Goat Island, 108, 110, 111
 Grand Island, 111
 industrialization, 109–10, 117,
 118–19, 120
 Navy Island, 110–11, 112–13
 power generation, 109–10, 111, 114,
 118
 threats, 118–21
 waterflow management, 109–10, 111
Nith River, 159, 162
Nixon, Richard, 119
Nlaka'pamux Nation, 73
Noah, Mordecai Manuel, 111
North Dakota, 99–103
Northern Transportation Company
 Limited, 156–57
North Saskatchewan River, 243–56. *See
 also* Saskatchewan River
 flood control, 250, 251
 oil spill (2016), 50–51, 243–46, 255
 recreational use, 252–53
North Saskatchewan Watershed
 Alliance, 247–48
North West Company, 95, 144
North-West Mounted Police, 92, 248
Northwest Rebellion (1885), 248–49

Northwest Territories, 147–50, 154–57.
 See also Mackenzie River; *specific
 locations*
 mining in, 147–49
Norwegian, Baptiste, 150–51
Norwegian, Herb, 153
Nowlan, Alden, 128

Oak Ridges Moraine, 60, 66
Obajewanung (ON), 266
Obama, Barack, 26
Oblate missionaries, 209–10
O'Connor, Morris, 204
Odjick, Maisy, 212
Ogilvie, Ralph, 18–19
oil and gas industry, 147, 239, 254–55.
 See also pipelines
Okanogan River, 233
Oliver, Craig, 282–83
Oliver, R.S. "Bud", 97, 105
Onderdonk, Andrew, 80
Ontario, 49–50, 164. *See also specific
 rivers and locations*
 and water extraction, 170–71, 172
Ontario Beekeeping Association, 61
Ontario Power Generation, 23, 25
Oregon Treaty (1846), 232
Oromocto First Nation, 133
Ottawa, 42–44, 49–50, 216. *See also*
 Bytown
Ottawa River Heritage Committee, 287
Ottawa River Institute, 48
Ottawa Riverkeeper/Sentinelle
 Outaouais, 48, 49, 52
Ottawa River/Rivière Outaouais,
 31–53
 dams, 34, 36, 40, 49
 development, 36, 44
 falls, 34, 43–44, 309
 First Nations and, 40–41, 43
 flooding, 301–2, 309

heritage designation, 45–46
history, 34, 35–38
improvement initiatives, 49–50, 52–53
lumber industry, 36, 41, 42
pollution, 33, 46–52, 53
power generation, 43–44
Quebec and, 45–46, 50
tourism on, 34–35
watershed, 39–40, 305–6
Ottawa Silver Seven, 216
Ouellette, Christine and Eric, 131
Owen, Pat, 104
Oxtongue River, 261–62

Pacific Salmon Commission, 78
Pakinawatik, Antoine, 209–10
Palliser, John, 185
Palmer, Brendan, 182, 183, 184
Pan-American Exposition (1901), 118
Paper, Michael, 149–50
Parks Canada, 187–88, 224, 292. See also
    specific parks
Paul, Gabe, 131
Peace River, 304–5
Pearce, William, 185–86
Pearson, Lester, 201, 202
Pedneaud-Jobin, Maxime, 49
Peigan peoples, 233
Pépin, Jean-Luc, 155–56
Petawawa River, 294–96
Phillips, Don, 98
Picanoc River, 202
Pikwàkanagàn First Nation, 40, 44
pipelines. See also oil and gas industry
    damage potential, 134, 140–42
    effects on First Nations, 153–54, 244
    leaks, 50–51, 243–46
    proposed, 134–35, 140–43, 153–54
plastics, 51–52
pollution, 9, 253–54. See also specific
    rivers

Pollution Probe, 59
Pomeroy, John, 189, 191, 193–94, 251–52
Pond, Peter, 143
population growth, 169, 170, 172, 303–4
Port Carling (ON), 266, 270
Port Radium (NT), 149
Potemkin, Gregory Alexandrovitch, 56
Potts, Fanny Cox ("Anne Hathaway"),
    271
Poundmaker, 248
Powell, Robert, 142
Prince Albert (SK), 243–44, 245–46
Proulx, Annie, 126
Pulling Together Canoe Society, 84–85
pulp and paper industry, 75, 137, 235
Purdy, Al, 267
Purkis, Bill, 262–63, 272, 273, 274, 308
Puslinch Lake, 168

Quebec, 45–46, 50, 202–3, 290. See also
    specific rivers and locations
Quyon (QC), 53

Raffan, James, 280, 285
Ramsar sites, 121
Rannie, Bill, 97, 99
Rapides-des-Joachims (Swisha), 290
Rawlings, Marjorie Kinnan, 293
Red River, 89–105
    floods, 90, 93–94, 96, 97–98, 101–4,
    105
    floodway, 96–97
    Forks (with Assiniboine), 93, 98
    in North Dakota, 99–103
Red River Floods Interpretive Centre,
    103–4
Red River Rebellion (1869–70), 91–92
Rees, William, 28
Revelstoke (BC), 236
Richmond, Charles Lennox, 4th Duke
    of, 218–19

Rideau Canal and River, 215–27
  construction, 215–16, 220–21
  cost, 220, 222
  labour force, 42, 220–21
  locks, 219–20, 223–24
  planning, 218–19
  use, 223–24, 225
  as World Heritage Site, 218, 223
Rideau Canal and Arctic Canoe Club,
  282
Rideau Canoe Club, 225
Rideau Valley Conservation Authority,
  223, 226
Riel, Louis, 91–92, 104, 248
Risteen, Frank, 132
River Desert Reserve. See Kitigan Zibi
  First Nations
rivers, 3, 45–46. See also specific rivers
  as escape, 278–79
  threatened, 9, 28–29
  as transportation corridors, 34, 306
Rivershed Society of British Columbia,
  75
Robertson, Norman, 201
Robinson, Michael P., 194
Robinson, Peter, 265
Roblin, Duff, 96
Robson, Patrick, 112, 115, 116, 122
Rock, Allan, 282
Rocky Mountain House (AB), 249
Roenisch, Rich, 231
Roland, Floyd, 139, 140–43, 154–55, 156,
  157, 307
Roland, John, 139
Roosevelt, Franklin D., 21, 38, 230
Rosenau, Marvin, 76–77, 78, 79
Royal Canadian Mounted Police
  (RCMP), 84–86, 92
Royal Family, 21, 43, 55–56
Russell, Andy, 184

Ste. Agathe (MB), 89–90, 96, 103–5
Sainte-Anne-des-Pays-Bas (NB), 128
St. Denis, Harry, 40
St. George, Scott, 99
Saint John River, 125–37
  dams, 130, 131, 135–36
  ferries, 133–34
  First Nations and, 128, 131
  fishing, 125–26, 131, 136, 137
  improvement initiatives, 136–37
  lumber industry, 130
  pollution, 137
  power generation, 130, 131, 135–36
St. Laurent, Louis, 21
St. Lawrence River, 13–29, 42. See also
  St. Lawrence Seaway
  dams, 19, 29
  First Nations and, 25
  pollution, 27–28
  power generation, 19, 20, 29
  Thousand Islands, 15–17
  threats, 24, 28–29
St. Lawrence River Institute of
  Environmental Sciences, 24
St. Lawrence Seaway, 19–23, 26
  and American eel, 24–25
  construction, 21–22
  lost communities, 19, 21–22, 23
  United States and, 21, 22
St. Regis Mohawk Reservation (NY), 17
salmon
  Columbia River, 234–36, 237, 238,
    239–40
  Don River, 59, 60, 67
  Fraser River, 70, 76, 77–78, 83–84
  Saint John River, 125–26, 131, 136, 137
Sanderson, Barry, 148
Sandford, Robert, 146, 236, 239, 240, 307
Saskatchewan, 248
Saskatchewan River, 249, 250, 252, 253.
  See also North and South branches

Sauriol, Charles, 61
Save Our Water, 171
Schaber family, 291, 292, 294
Schaber, Wally, 277–78, 279–80, 286,
    287–88, 291–96, 297–98, 307
Schneekloth, Lynda, 119, 121–22, 307
Schnobb, Peter, 204
Schwartzel, Ellen, 170
Scott, Eddie, 53
Scott, Thomas, 91, 104
Scottish Canadians, 39, 94–96, 164, 220
sea lampreys, 23
Second World War, 152, 188, 235
    Manhattan Project, 46–47, 147, 230
Seeger, Pete, 231, 234
Segovia, Ricardo, 244–45
Selkirk, Thomas Douglas, 5th Earl of,
    94–96
Selkirk (MB), 97–99
Seneca people, 162
Serageldin, Ismail, 25
Seven Years' War, 128
Sheldon's Corners (ON), 217
Short, Martin, 271
Silcox, David, 282
Simcoe, Elizabeth Posthuma Gwillim,
    57–58, 59–60
Simcoe, John Graves, 57
Simpson, George, 93
Six Nations of the Grand River
    (Haudenosaunee), 161, 162, 169, 171
Small, Charlotte, 231–32
Smith, Goldwin, 43
Smith, Harry, 216
Smith, Terry, 280
Smiths Falls (ON), 221
Sohi, Amarjeet, 65
Southesk, 9th Earl of, 249–50
South Saskatchewan River, 245–46,
    247, 250. See also Saskatchewan
    River

Speck, Frank, 287
Speed River, 162
Spokane River, 233
Standing Rock Sioux, 244
Stanley Cup, 216
Stewart, Judy, 188
Stó:lō Nation, 70, 73, 77, 81, 83–84
sturgeon, 70, 76–77, 83, 84, 137
Sûreté du Québec, 212–13
Swain, Harry, 304–5
Sweeney, Patrick, 217
Swift River Energy, 272–73
Sydney-Smith, Albert, 267

Tamblyn, Ian, 208
Taseko Mines, 78–79
Task Force to Bring Back the Don, 65
Taylor, Annie Edson, 116–17
Tesla, Nikola, 109
Tête Jaune (BC), 80–81
Thapaliya, Rupak, 29
Theberge, John, 292
Thiess International Riverprize, 166
Thomas, Lowell J., 21–22
Thompson, Aaron, 109, 110
Thompson, David, 4, 184, 231–32, 233,
    263, 274
Thompson, Stanley, 188
Thomson, Tom, 132, 261
Thousand Islands, 15–17
Tillerson, Rex, 238
timber industry. See lumber industry
Todd, Frederick, 201, 251
Tootoosis, Okiysikaw Tyrone, 255, 308
Toronto. See Don River
Toronto and Region Conservation
    Authority, 63, 64, 66
Toronto Islands, 63–64, 303
tourism, 107–9, 113–14, 263–66, 267–71.
    See also specific rivers
Toye, Jim, 243, 244, 245–46, 255

TransAlta Corporation, 189–90
TransCanada Corporation, 134–35
Trans Canada Trail, 151–52
Trans Mountain Pipeline, 244
Trans-Northern Pipeline, 51
Treaty of Paris (1783), 128–29
trout
    Bow River, 182–83
    Columbia River, 236
    Grand River, 161, 166–67, 307
    Great Lakes, 23
    Lake Joseph, 265
Trudeau, Justin, 202
Trudeau, Pierre, 119, 132, 202, 277, 292,
    294–96
Truman, Harry S., 21, 113
Trump, Donald, 26, 238
T'Seleie, Frank, 140
Tsilhqot'in First Nation, 79
Ts'Peten First Nation, 85–86
Turner, John, 38, 55
Twain, Mark, 115
Twin Rivers Paper Company, 137

Ullrich, David, 26–27
Underground Railroad, 113
United States, 92, 163. See also War of
    1812
    agreements with, 113, 129, 232, 234,
        237–41, 307
    and Columbia River, 229–30, 232,
        234, 237–41
    and Great Lakes, 26–27
    Loyalists from, 19, 129, 164
    and Niagara River, 110, 121–22
    and St. Lawrence Seaway, 21, 22
Upper Columbia River Tribes, 238
uranium, 147, 211, 235

Van Alstine, Edie, 208
VandenHeuvel, Brett, 238–39

Van Horne, William Cornelius, 180
Van Tighem, Kevin, 189, 190, 308
Vaux family, 179–80, 181–82
Vermaire, Jesse, 52
Vickers, Roy Henry, 84
voyageurs. See fur trade

Wabigoon River, 254
Wahta Mohawks First Nation, 273–74
Wakefield (QC), 201, 207
Walkerton (ON), 175
Wallenda, Delilah, 116
Wallenda, Nik, 115–16
Wandering Spirit, 248
Ward, Jane, 62–63
Ware, Meredith, 59
War of 1812, 112, 113, 218
Wasauksing First Nation, 266–67
Waterloo Wellington Canoe and Kayak
    Club, 166
water milfoil, 168
water resources
    access to, 37–38, 168–73
    climate change and, 9–10, 118
    extraction of, 168–73, 175, 304
    threats to, 9–10, 173, 188–89, 303–4
    value of, 303–6
Watershed Watch Salmon Society, 78
Watson, Jim, 49
Watson, Ken, 217
Webb, Matthew, 115
Webster-Ashburton Treaty (1842), 129
Welland Canal, 23, 119
Wellington, Arthur Wellesley, 1st
    Duke of, 219, 220
Wells, H.G., 114
Wenatchee River, 233
West Hull (QC), 204
wetlands, 121–22, 188, 304
Whanganui River (NZ), 305
Whiteduck, Gilbert, 211–12, 308

Whiteduck, Jean-Guy, 211
Whiteduck, Kirby, 40, 41
Whitelaw, Georgina, 165
Whyte Museum of the Canadian
    Rockies, 179–80, 181–82
Wilde, Oscar, 47, 108
Wilfahrt, Barry, 100
Windle, Matthew, 24–25, 307
Windmill Development Group, 44
Winnipeg, 93, 96, 97, 98, 99. *See also*
    Red River
Winnipeg River, 59
Wiskedjak (Nenabush), 287
Wolf Lake First Nations, 40, 286, 287,
    290
Wolseley, Garnet, 91–92
Woodward, Roger, 117
World Wildlife Federation (WWF)
    Canada, 79, 125, 137, 167–68, 193,
    237

and Mackenzie River, 141–42,
    153–54
Woyce, Kevin, 118
Wright, Hannah, 216
Wright, Philemon, 41–42, 44, 206,
    208–9
Wrong, Hume, 201
Wynn, Graeme, 22–23

Yale (BC), 82
Yee, Michael, 226, 307
Yellowhead, Chief, 266

Zavitz, Sherman, 108–9
zebra mussels, 23, 24
ZECs (*zones d'exploitation contrôlées*),
    290
Zymerman, Art, 168

ROY MacGREGOR is the acclaimed and bestselling author of *The Home Team: Fathers, Sons and Hockey* (shortlisted for the Governor General's Literary Award); *A Life in the Bush* (winner of the US Rutstrum Award for Best Wilderness Book and the CAA Award for Biography); *Canadians: A Portrait of a Country and Its People; Canoe Country: The Making of Canada;* and *Northern Light: The Enduring Mystery of Tom Thomson and the Woman Who Loved Him*; as well as two novels, *Canoe Lake* and *The Last Season*, and the popular Screech Owls mystery series for young readers. MacGregor has been a regular columnist at *The Globe and Mail* since 2002; his journalism has garnered four National Magazine Awards and two National Newspaper Awards. He is an Officer of the Order of Canada, and was described in the citation as one of Canada's "most gifted storytellers." He and his wife, Ellen, live in Kanata.